2nd Workshop on New Frontiers in Summarization (NewSum 2019)

Hong Kong, China
4 November 2019

ISBN: 978-1-7138-0085-9

EMNLP-IJCNLP 2019

The 2nd Workshop on New Frontiers in Summarization (NewSum 2019)

Workshop Proceedings

November 4, 2019
Hong Kong, China

Introduction

Developing intelligent systems which can produce concise, fluent, and accurate summaries has been a long-standing goal in natural language processing. The aim of this workshop is to provide a research forum for cross-fertilization of ideas towards this goal. We seek to bring together researchers from a diverse range of fields (e.g., summarization, visualization, language generation, cognitive and psycholinguistics) for discussions on key issues related to automatic summarization. This includes discussion on novel paradigms/frameworks, shared tasks of interest, information integration and presentation, new evaluation protocols, applied research and applications, and possible future research foci. The workshop aims to pave the way towards building a cohesive research community, accelerating knowledge diffusion, developing new tools, datasets and resources that are in line with the needs of academia, industry, and government.

This is the second edition of the workshop, following our previous workshop at EMNLP 2017. The workshop received 17 long paper submissions, of which 7 were accepted, and 22 short paper submissions, of which 8 were accepted. This resulted in an overall acceptance rate of 38%. We are pleased to have four invited speakers at this year's workshop: Nanyun Peng (USC ISI), Ido Dagan (Bar-Ilan), Wenjie Li (Hong Kong Polytechnic), and Manabu Okumura (Tokyo Institute of Technology). Together, they cover a broad spectrum of work in summarization and adjacent areas. We would like to thank our invited speakers, as well as our programme committee members and workshop participants.

Lu Wang, Giuseppe Carenini, Jackie Chi Kit Cheung, Fei Liu

Organizers:

Lu Wang (Northeastern University, USA)
Giuseppe Carenini (University of British Columbia, Canada)
Jackie Chi Kit Cheung (McGill University, Canada)
Fei Liu (University of Central Florida, USA)

Program Committee:

Abram Handler (UMass Amherst)
Chen Li (Tencent AI lab)
Gabriel Murray (University of the Fraser Valley)
Hardy (The University of Sheffield)
Jessica Ouyang (UT Dallas)
Denis McInerney (Northeastern University)
Jun-Ping Ng (Amazon)
Manabu Okumura (Tokyo Institute of Technology Institute of Innovative Research)
Yashar Mehdad (Facebook)
Yue Dong (McGill University)
Alexander Fabbri (Yale University)
Angela Fan (Facebook AI)
Chris Kedzie (Columbia University)
Enamul Hoque (York University)
Eva Sharma (Northeastern University)
Florian Boudin (University of Nantes)
Horacio Saggion (Universitat Pompeu Fabra)
Hou Pong Chan (The Chinese University of Hong Kong)
Jiacheng Xu (UT Austin)
Jing Li (The Hong Kong Polytechnic University)
Jordon Johnson (UBC)
Kaiqiang Song (University of Central Florida)
Kundan Krishna (CMU)
Linzi Xing (UBC)
Liqiang Xiao (Shanghai Jiao Tong University)
Luyang Huang (Boston University)
Maxime Peyrard (TU Darmstadt)
Michael Elhadad (Ben-Gurion University of the Negev)
Patrick Huber (UBC)
Pengfei Liu (Fudan University)
Ramakanth Pasunuru (UNC Chapel Hill)
Sebastian Gehrmann (Harvard University)
Shashi Narayan (Google)
Tobias Falke (Amazon)
Wei Gao (Victoria University of Wellington)
Wen Xiao (UBC)
Wojciech Kryscinski (KTH Royal Institute of Technology)
Xinyu Hua (Northeastern University)
Yang Liu (The University of Edinburgh)
Yuntian Deng (Harvard University)

Zhe Hu (Baidu)
Alex Bravo Serrano (Universitat Pompeu Fabra)
Ahmed Ghassan Tawfiq AbuRa'ed (Universitat Pompeu Fabra)

Invited Speaker:

Nanyun Peng (USC ISI)
Ido Dagan (Bar-Ilan University)
Wenjie Li (The Hong Kong Polytechnic University)
Manabu Okumura (Tokyo Institute of Technology)

Table of Contents

Workshop Program

07:30–09:00   **Breakfast for all workshops' attendees**

09:00–09:50   **Invited Talk: Nanyun Peng (USC ISI)**

09:50–10:40   **Contributed Talks (12 mins * 4 long papers, 2 mins each for QA)**

Answering Naturally : Factoid to Full length Answer Generation
Vaishali Pal, Manish Shrivastava and Irshad Bhat

Summary Level Training of Sentence Rewriting for Abstractive Summarization
Sanghwan Bae, Taeuk Kim, Jihoon Kim and Sang-goo Lee

Abstractive Timeline Summarization
Julius Steen and Katja Markert

Learning to Create Sentence Semantic Relation Graphs for Multi-Document Summarization
Diego Antognini and Boi Faltings

10:40–11:00   **Break**

11:00–11:50   **Invited Talk: Ido Dagan (Bar-Ilan University)**

11:50–12:30   **Contributed Talks (10 mins * 4 short papers, 2 mins each for QA)**

Unsupervised Aspect-Based Multi-Document Abstractive Summarization
Maximin Coavoux, Hady Elsahar and Matthias Gallé

BillSum: A Corpus for Automatic Summarization of US Legislation
Vladimir Eidelman

An Editorial Network for Enhanced Document Summarization
Edward Moroshko, Guy Feigenblat, Haggai Roitman and David Konopnicki

Towards Annotating and Creating Summary Highlights at Sub-sentence Level
Kristjan Arumae, Parminder Bhatia and Fei Liu

12:30–02:00   **Lunch**

02:00–02:50   **Invited Talk: Wenjie Li (The Hong Kong Polytechnic University)**

02:50–03:30   **Contributed Talks (12 mins * 3 long papers, 2 mins each for QA)**

SAMSum Corpus: A Human-annotated Dialogue Dataset for Abstractive Summarization
Bogdan Gliwa, Iwona Mochol, Maciej Biesek and Aleksander Wawer

A Closer Look at Data Bias in Neural Extractive Summarization Models
Ming Zhong, Danqing Wang, Pengfei Liu, Xipeng Qiu and Xuanjing Huang

Global Voices: Crossing Borders in Automatic News Summarization
Khanh Nguyen and Hal Daumé III

Answering Naturally : Factoid to Full length Answer Generation

Vaishali Pal
LTRC, IIIT-H, Hyderabad
vaishali.pal@research.iiit.ac.in

Irshad Bhat
IMS, University of Stuggart
bhatid@ims.uni-stuttgart.de

Manish Shrivastava
LTRC, IIIT-H, Hyderbad
m.shrivastava@iiit.ac.in

Abstract

In recent years, the task of Question Answering over passages, also pitched as a reading comprehension, has evolved into a very active research area. A reading comprehension system extracts a span of text, comprising of named entities, dates, small phrases, etc., which serve as the answer to a given question. However, these spans of text would result in an unnatural reading experience in a conversational system. Usually, dialogue systems solve this issue by using template-based language generation. These systems, though adequate for a domain specific task, are too restrictive and predefined for a domain independent system. In order to present the user with a more conversational experience, we propose a pointer generator based full-length answer generator which can be used with most QA systems. Our system generates a full-length answer given a question and the extracted factoid/span answer without relying on the passage from where the answer was extracted. We also present a dataset of 315,000 question, factoid answer and full-length answer triples. We have evaluated our system using ROUGE-1,2,L and BLEU and achieved 74.05 BLEU score and 86.25 Rogue-L score.

1 Introduction

Factoid question answering (QA) is the task of extracting answers for a question from a given passage. These answers are usually short spans of text, such as named entities, dates, etc. Modern factoid QA systems which use machine-comprehension datasets, predict the answer span from relevant documents using encoder-decoder architectures with co-attention. Conversely, knowledge-base (KB) oriented QA systems retrieve relevant facts using structured queries or neural representation of the question. Formulating the retrieved factoid answer into a full-length

System Input:
  Question : When were the normans in normandy?
  Factoid Answer : 10th and 11th centuries
System Output :
  During the 10th and 11th centuries , the normans were in normandy.

Table 1: Full-length natural answer generation from the question and the factoid answer

natural sentence is, hence, a natural extension and post-processing step of any QA system.

A simple approach for this task might be to use hand-crafted rules to restructure the question into a declarative statement as described in (Jurafsky and Martin, 2018). However, such rule based approaches fail when the extracted answer span, contains words from the question or when there are multiple independent clauses and the system has to choose words specific to the question to formulate the answer. This leads to unnatural repetition of words in the full-length answer or grammatically incorrect sentence formulation.

On the other hand, neural-network based approaches in modern dialogue systems use end-to-end encoder-decoder architectures to convert an abstract dialogue action into natural language utterances. Such modern task-oriented dialogue systems usually learn to map dialogue histories to system response. Non-task oriented dialogue systems such as generative systems can formulate responses not present in the training data but lacks the capability to incorporate factual information without external knowledge bases.

Unlike conversational chat-bots designed to mimic human conversation without the need to be factually correct, or task-oriented dialogue systems which place the retrieved answer in a predefined template, our system automatically gener-

Proceedings of the 2nd Workshop on New Frontiers in Summarization, pages 1–9
Hong Kong, China, November 4, 2019. ©2019 Association for Computational Linguistics

ates accurate full-length answers, thereby, enhancing the system's usage in these situations. Table 1 shows a sample of our system input and output. Our system can be used in any such task-specific scenarios where natural answers are desired, without being restricted to a limited set of templates.

Our overall research contributions are listed as follows:

- We introduce a system which generates factually correct full-length answers from the questions and the factoid answers. Our system can be used as a post-processing plug-in to any QA system, be it a KB-based system or machine comprehension based system, thereby improving readability of the system output and promoting fluency and variation in the natural answer generation.

- We have also released a dataset comprising of tuples of questions, factoid answers and full-length answers which can be further augmented using any other QA datasets using the techniques we describe in section 3.1.

2   Related Work

There has been a lot of interest recently in QA and task-oriented dialogue systems. End-to-end memory networks (Sukhbaatar et al., 2015) use a language modelling architecture which learns query embeddings in addition to input and output memory representations from source sequences and predicts an answer. Rule based systems such as (Weston et al., 2015) sets up a variety of tasks for inferring and answering the question. (Bordes and Weston, 2016) improves on the memory networks and handles out-of-vocabulary (OOV) words by inserting special words into the vocabulary for each knowledge base entity types. These systems are dependent on templates or special heuristics to reproduce facts. We demonstrate through our baseline model that generating template-like sentences from factual input can be achieved with limited success.

Recent works on KB-based end-to-end QA systems such as (Yin et al., 2015; He et al., 2017a; Liu et al., 2018a) generate full-length answers with neural pointer networks(Gülçehre et al., 2016; Vinyals et al., 2015; He et al., 2017b) after retrieving facts from a knowledge base (KB). Dialogue systems such as (Liu et al., 2018b; Lian et al., 2019) extract information from knowledge bases to formulate a response. Systems such as (Fu and Feng, 2018) uses KB based key-value memory after extracting information from documents or external KBs. However, these systems are restricted to only information modeled by the KB or slot-value memory. Our system, is generic and can be used with any knowledge source, structured such as a knowledge base or free form such as machine-comprehension dataset. Since our system doesn't use any additional relational information as modelled in a KB, it is invariant to the type of dataset. The pointer generator network, introduced in (See et al., 2017), is a generative summarization model that can copy out-of-vocabulary (OOV) words from a source sequence. Our work is inspired from the ability of this network to accurately reproduce information from source.

To the best of our knowledge, there is no existing QA data-set which addresses the task directly. However, Knowledge-based QA dataset such as (Yin et al., 2015) creates a knowledge-base from Chinese websites and extracts question-answer pairs from Chinese communityQA webpage. The system built over this dataset, is able to generate natural answers to simple questions. The recently released CoQA dataset(Reddy et al., 2018) is an abstractive conversational question answering dataset through which the system generates free-form answers from the whole conversational history using the aforementioned pointer-generator network. While the CoQA challenge extracts free-form text from the passages, our system incorporates the structure of the question to give a full-length sentence as answer to the given query.

3   Data

Since there is no available dataset for the task, we used the standard machine comprehension datasets such as SQuAD (Rajpurkar et al., 2016) and HarvestingQA (Du and Cardie, 2018) to create auto-annotated data. This provide us with questions and factoid answers which we use as input to our system. For the ground-truth, we automatically extract full-length answers from the passages of these datasets by applying certain heuristics (explained in section 3.1). We extract $\sim$300,000 samples (question, factoid answer, full-length answer) from SQuAD and HarvestingQA. Additionally, we have manually annotated 15000 samples from SQuAD of which 2500 are used for development, 2500 for testing and we augment the rest

10000 with the auto-annotated data.

3.1 Automatic Data Generation

Creating datasets for any new task is a challenge since modern systems based on neural architectures requires a large amount of data to train. To make the data creation task scalable, most of our training data is automatically generated from SQuAD and HarvestingQA. For each question-answer pair, we automatically extract the target full-length answers from corresponding passages. We iterate over the sentences in the context passage that contain the factoid answer and select the one that has the highest BLEU score with the question, given $BLEU\,score \geq 35\%$. Given the question-answer pair (Q, A) and the passage P, the full-length answer T is the sentence, S, in the passage:

$$T = \underset{S \in P}{\mathrm{argmax}}\, BLEU(Q, S)$$
$$iff\ A \in S\ \&\ BLEU(Q, S) \geq 35\% \tag{1}$$

The target sentences having a low BLEU score(between $35\% - 50\%$) may not be completely aligned with the question but provide sufficient information to train the system to generate full-length sentences containing the factoid answer.[1] As the whole sentence is extracted from the corresponding passage, these samples may also contain additional information from the passage which is not related to the question.

Our method of automatically extracting samples from existing QA datasets is scalable and can be reproduced with any modern QA datasets to generate more samples to augment our auto-generated samples extracted from HarvestingQA and SQuAD. The table 2 shows some auto-generated samples from the dataset. Our auto-generated data samples follow a similar question distribution as SQuaD and is biased towards what" and "who" questions as shown in the trigram distribution of the questions in figure 1.

3.2 Manual Data Generation

The auto-generated samples contain extra information in the ground-truth full-length sentences which are not aligned with the question or factoid answer. To refine our dataset to be more attuned to questions and also to capture the variabil-

---

[1]We found that samples with BLEU score of less than 35 were significantly noisy.

Question : what is the name of the term that is used in the united states ? **Factoid** : great plains **Target** : the term great plains is used in the united states to describe a sub-section of the even more vast interior plains physiographic division
Question : who is the only country among the united nations security council ? **Factoid** : germany **Target** : germany is the only country among the top five arms exporters that is not a permanent member of the united nations security council .
Question : what lake is now connected to the sea ? **Factoid** : lake voulismeni **Target** : lake voulismeni at the coast , at aghios nikolaos , was formerly a sweetwater lake but is now connected to the sea .
Question : what is a bus driving on this route ? **Factoid** : the capacity of the lane will be more and will be more and will increase when the traffic level increases **Target** : when there is a bus driving on this route , the capacity of the lane will be more and will increase when the traffic level increases .

Table 2: Automatically created dataset samples

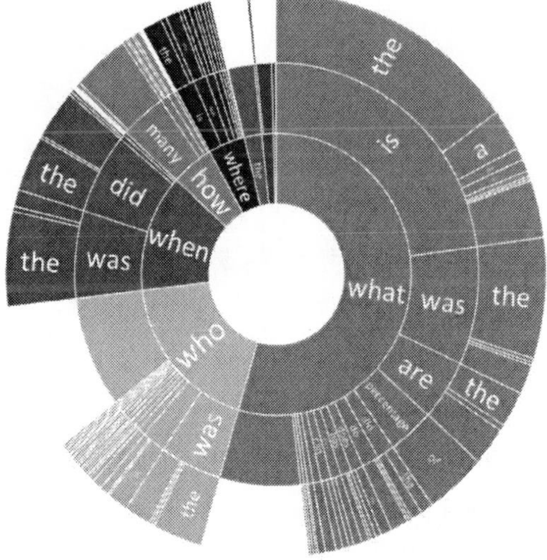

Figure 1: Question trigram distribution of automatically created dataset

ity humans bring when generating new sentences, we manually annotated 15000 QA pairs, from the

SQuAD dataset. We used multiple ways to answer the same question, such as in active and passive voice, to incorporate more variation to the target sentences. Apart from generating samples with the full-length answers well aligned with the question, we have also chosen complex samples from SQuAD which have long phrasal factoid answers to add more complexity to the data samples. These samples have sentential factoid answers containing more than one independent clause which are not present in the ground-truth full-length natural answer. The inclusion of such examples is to aid to the system to learn to only choose words which are required to form a syntactically correct answer and omit other synonymous or superfluous words. The table 3 shows some manual generated samples. The manual samples contains questions more evenly distributed than the auto-generated ones as shown in the figure 2 displaying the trigram distribution of questions.

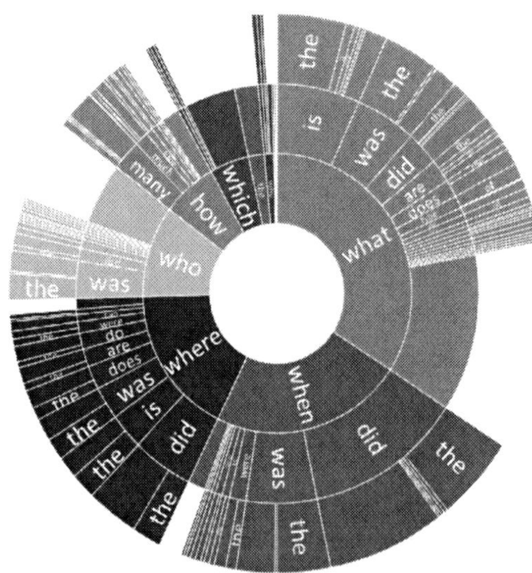

Figure 2: Question trigram distribution of manually created dataset

4 System Architecture

We framed the problem of generating full-length answer from the question and the factoid answer into a Neural Machine Translation (NMT) task using two approaches. We built a model based on the pointer-generator architecture described in (See et al., 2017) except we use two encoders on the source side to encode question and factoid answer separately as shown in Figure 3.

Question : How much more were her earnings that the year before? **Factoid** : more than double her earnings **Target 1** : Her earnings were more than double than that of the year before. **Target 2** : She earned more than double her earnings than that of the year before.
Question : How many digital copies of her fifth album did Beyonc sell in six days? **Factoid 1** : one million **Factoid 2** : one million digital copies **Target** : Beyonc sold one million digital copies of her fifth album in six days.
Question : How well did Kanye do in high school? **Factoid** : A's and B's **Target** : Kanye did well in high school by scoring A's and B's.
Question : What do scholars recognize about the life of the Buddha? **Factoid** : Most accept that he lived, taught and founded a monastic order **Target** : Most scholars recognize and accept that Buddha lived, taught and founded a monastic order.
Question : Where did english and scotch irish descent move to florida from? **Factoid** : English descent and americans of scots-irish descent began moving into northern florida from the backwoods of georgia and south carolina **Target** : English and Scotch Irish descent moved to Florida from the backwoods of Georgia and South Carolina.

Table 3: Manual dataset samples

Let the question be represented by words $Q = \{q_1, q_2, ..., q_n\}$. Let the factoid answer be represented by words $A = \{a_1, a_2, a_3, ..., a_m\}$.

We encode the question and answer sequence using two 3-layered bidirectional LSTMs which share weights. This produces two sequences of hidden states

$$h_Q^t = BILSTM(h_Q^{t-1}, q_t) \qquad (2)$$

$$h_A^t = BILSTM(h_A^{t-1}, a_t) \qquad (3)$$

We choose to encode the source sequences separately, since there is no syntactic connection between the question and the factoid answer. We

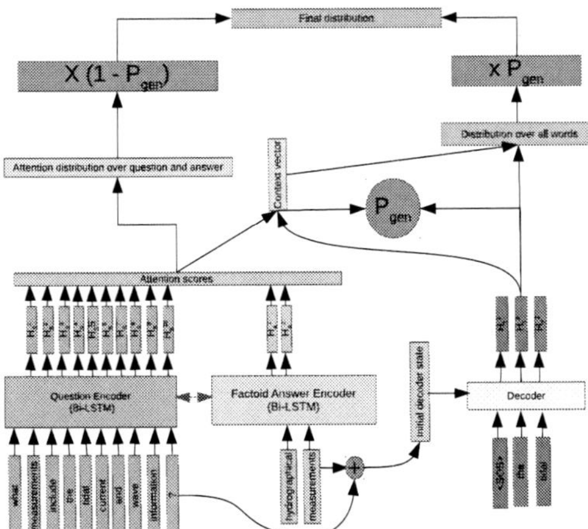

Figure 3: The 2 encoder pointer generator uses the question and factoid answer as input to generate a full-length answer in an end-to-end learning environment.

then stack together the encoded hidden states of the 2 encoders to produce a single list of source hidden states, $h_S = [h_Q; h_A]$. The decoder is initialized with the combined final states of the two encoders as

$$h_T^0 = h_Q^n + h_A^m \qquad (4)$$

Following the global attention mechanism described in (Luong et al., 2015), context vector, C_t, is generated. For each decoder state, h_T^t, at time t, the alignment score, $a(h_T^t, h_S^i)$, with each encoder state, h_S^i, is calculated as follows:

$$a(h_T^t, h_S^i) = softmax(h_T^t W_a h_S^i) \qquad (5)$$

The challenge to correctly reproduce factual information in the full-length answer led us to use copy attention from the pointer generator network as described in (See et al., 2017). The copy distribution, using an extended vocabulary comprising of source words, will capture the probability of replicating words from either the question or answer, whereas the global attention distribution has the ability to generate new words from the vocabulary. The final probability of predicting a word is as follows:

$$P(W_{final}) = p_g P_{gen} + (1 - p_g) P_{copy} \qquad (6)$$

The parameter, p_g, is learned as

$$\sigma(W_c C^t + W_{h_t} h_T^t + W_x X^t) \qquad (7)$$

where C^t is the context vector and X^t is the input to the decoder. We calculate the copy distribution, a distribution over the source words, $w = Q \cup A$:

$$P_{copy}(w) = \sum_{i:w_i=w} a(h_T^t, h_S^i) \qquad (8)$$

The final probability of generating a word is as shown in equation 6. For out-of-vocabulary words which are present only in the source $w \in (Q \cup A)$ and $w \notin V$, only P_{copy} is used predict the word. These words are usually factual information from the question or answer, such as dates and named entities and hence needs to be copied exactly as it appears in the source sequences. Prepositions, conjunctions and other placeholders, such as at, $between$, in, which help in combining the question and answer sequences are usually in-vocab words not present in the source ($w \notin (Q \cup A)$ and $w \in V$), and are predicted with P_{gen}. For in-vocabulary words which are present in the source, $w \in (Q \cup A)$ and $w \in$ V, the final probability of predicting the word uses both the terms of equation 6.

5 Experiments

For all our experiments, we used a 6GB 1060TX Nvidia GPU. We trained the system on batch size of 32, dropout rate of 0.5, RNN size of 512 and decay steps 10000. Since, our dataset is small, we shared the vocabulary between source and target. We used pre-trained GloVe embeddings (300 dimension) to initialize both the encoder and decoder words. Since our manually created samples are less, we oversampled the manually annotated data 3 times to mitigate any bias introduced by the synthetic dataset. We have built our system over the OpenNMT-pytorch code base(Klein et al., 2017). We have tested our models independently on both the manual dataset and auto-created dataset. We have used 2500 samples of the manually annotated SQuAD data set and 3284 samples of the auto-generated dataset to evaluate the models' performance. These samples were selected randomly from the respective datasets. To evaluate the effectiveness of the manual data samples, we have compared the performance of our 2-encoder pointer-generator network trained on the auto-generated data and on the whole augmented dataset, containing both the manual and auto-generated data. For this comparison, training on the whole augmented data instead of only the

Model	Training Dataset	BLEU	ROGUE-1	ROGUE-2	ROGUE-L
Seq2Seq+Attention+Mask	Augmented	62.2	86.23	72.23	79.52
2 Encoder Pointer-Gen	Auto-only	67.5	87.94	77.85	82.77
2 Encoder Pointer-Gen	Augmented	**74.05**	**91.24**	**81.91**	**86.25**
Seq2Seq+Attention+Mask	Augmented	71.10	90.03	81.82	85.09
2 Encoder Pointer-Gen	Auto-only	73.63	91.50	85.02	87.56
2 Encoder Pointer-Gen	Augmented	**73.69**	**91.65**	**84.98**	**87.40**

Table 4: The top section displays BLEU and ROGUE scores for the models tested on the manually created test dataset. The bottom section displays the scores for the models tested on the auto-created test dataset. (All scores are in the range of 0-100)

Model	Training Dataset	BLEU	ROGUE-1	ROGUE-2	ROGUE-L
2 Encoder Pointer-Gen	Auto-only	71.54	92.64	82.31	90.06
2 Encoder Pointer-Gen	Augmented	**73.29**	**95.38**	**87.18**	**93.65**
2 Encoder Pointer-Gen	Auto-only	64.67	91.17	75.58	82.87
2 Encoder Pointer-Gen	Augmented	**75.41**	**93.46**	**82.29**	**87.50**

Table 5: The top section displays the scores for the models tested on the 500 randomly chosen NewsQA dataset. (All scores are in the range of 0-100). The bottom section displays BLEU and ROGUE scores for the models tested 900 randomly chosen Freebase test samples.

manual data is required due to the limited number of samples(15000) of the manual annotated data. We have compared our system with a Seq2Seq model with attention where only the question and full-length answer are considered as source and target to the model respectively. We mask the factoid answer in the target full-length answer with the string *a-n-s-w-e-r*. The mask, which acts as a placeholder to the factoid answer, is replaced with the actual factoid answer in a post-processing step. The masking in the data copes with the named entities and other OOV words in the dataset.

We have also performed cross-dataset evaluation on a knowledge base dataset(Freebase) and a machine comprehension dataset(NewsQA) to test the generalization capability of our system. We randomly selected 900 samples, comprising of question and object-names(factoid answers), from the test samples provided by SimpleQA(Golub and He, 2016) which were extracted from the KB dataset Freebase(Bollacker et al., 2008). We also randomly extract 500 test samples, questions and factoid answers, from the machine comprehension NewsQA(Trischler et al., 2017) dataset. The system predictions were compared with the manually annotated ground-truth full-length answers for these samples.

Model	Training Dataset	Acc
2-Enc Pointer-Gen	Synthetic-only	83.4
2-Enc Pointer-Gen	Augmented	**92.8**

Table 6: Accuracy Scores(in the range of 0-100) for the various models

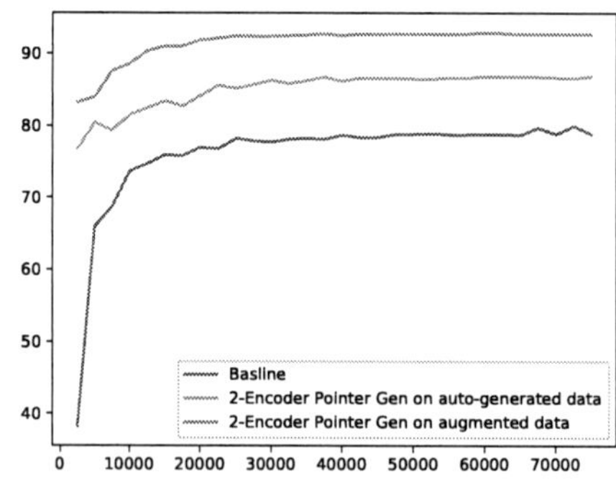

Figure 4: Validation Accuracy

6   Results

As shown in table 4, 5, 6 and 7, augmenting the manually annotated data with the auto-generated data for training leads to significant improvements for the 2-encoder pointer generator network. From our best assumption, this is not only due to cleaner samples in the manually annotated data which

Question : who was the eldest son of alfonso iii and what did he become king of?
Factoid Answer : garca , became king of len
Target : the eldest son of alfonso iii was garca and he become king of len.
Seq2Seq+Attention+Mask: he became king of garca , became king of len.
Modified PointerGen : the eldest son of alfonso iii was garca and he become king of len.
Question : where does the catalan word alfabia come from?
Factoid Answer : of arabic origin
Target : the catalan word alfabia is of arabic origin.
Seq2Seq+Attention+Mask: the catalan word alfabia comes from of arabic origin .
Modified PointerGen : the catalan word alfabia is of arabic origin .
Question : what job does debra byrd do on american idol?
Factoid Answer : vocal coach
Target : debra byrd is a vocal coach on american idol.
Seq2Seq+Attention+Mask: amy byrd has vocal coach on american idol.
Modified PointerGen : debra byrd is the vocal coach on american idol.
Question : when did the yuan dynasty start and end?
Factoid Answer : 1271 to 1368
Target : the yuan dynasty ruled from 1271 to 1368
Seq2Seq+Attention+Mask: the yuan dynasty started and ended in 1271 to 1368
Modified PointerGen : the yuan dynasty started in 1271 to 1368

Table 7: Comparison of predictions of the Seq2Seq+Attention+Mask and Augmented Pointer generator systems. Example 1 depicts non-contiguous factoid answer which have to be interleaved in the full-length answer. Example 2 shows that the pointer generator is able to suppress conflicting preposition Example 3 depicts that masking is unable to handle named entities in the question where they are not masked. Masking is also unable to capture contextual information while formulating the natural sentence as depicted in Example 4

does not contain extra unnecessary information, but also samples with variations in the factoid and full-length groundtruth. The manual data also has

long phrasal factoid answers from which the system has to learn to copy and generate words as needed. Table 7 shows that the pointer-generator system handles tense agreement and generation of new words. The Seq2Seq model suffers to capture contextual information, resolve anaphora, or reproduce factual information and handle out-of-vocabulary words. As shown in table 7, non-contiguous factoid answers are not interleaved in the full-length sentence predictions as expected. The pointer-generator network is able to handle these issues. The *BLEU* and *ROGUE* scores are better on the auto-generated test data as it lacks the variation and complexity in the full-length answers compared to the manually created dataset. The validation accuracy of the 2-encoder pointer generator network as shown in the figure on the development dataset also shows significant improvement from the start of the training, with the augmented dataset providing significant increase in accuracy as shown in figure 4. The performance of our models on a KB dataset such as SimpleQA and a machine comprehension dataset such as NewsQA is shown in the table 5. As observed from the BLEU and ROGUE scores, the augmented dataset improves performance across these datasets and provide better generalization capability to the system. Some of the failure cases of the system can be observed in the table 8.

7 Conclusion

In this work, we have introduced the task of generating full-length natural answers given the question and the factoid answer. We framed the problem into an NMT task using two different approaches. Our approach uses a 2-encoder pointer generator model, where factoid answers along with the questions are inputs to the system and the full-length answers for training and is better than the baseline model for both the *BLEU* and *ROGUE* scores. Additionally, as there were no datasets which directly address this task, we released a new dataset containing tuples of *questions, factoid answers, and full-length answers* of which 300,000 samples were automatically extracted and 15000 samples were manually annotated. Our automatic dataset creation approach is scalable and can be used over any other QA datasets to retrieve more samples. We have provided the additional manually annotated clean samples to introduce complexity and variation in

Question : what kind of metal is on handful of rain?   Factoid Answer : heavy metal   **Target :** on handful of rain is heavy metal .   **Modified PointerGen :** heavy metal is on handful of rain.
Question : Name an actor.   Factoid Answer : Collien Ulmen-Fernandes   **Target :** collien ulmen-fernandes is an actor.   **Modified PointerGen :** collien ulmen-fernandes .
Question : Will the 10 be punished?   Factoid Answer : no one should   **Target :** no one should be punished.   **Modified PointerGen :** the 10 be punished no one should punished.
Question : in which country the construction of the mosque is   Factoid Answer : turkey   **Target :** the construction of the mosque is in turkey .   **Modified PointerGen :** in turkey .

Table 8: Failure Cases. Example 1 is from the Freebase dataset where the system confuses between the subject and the object. Example 2 is from Freebase not present in the training and validation data. Example 3 is from NewsQA dataset where the system fails to understand the semantics. Example 4 id from NewsQA dataset where the system fails to generate the complete full-length answer

the training data. We have performed cross-dataset evaluation by testing on a KB dataset(Freebase) and a machine comprehension dataset(NewsQA) to test the generalization capability of our system.

8 Future Work

For a deep learning model to generalize well with greater accuracy, a larger dataset comprising of a bigger vocabulary and sample size is required. Due to the limited data provided, even though our system handles tense agreement, there are instances where it fails to predict the correct tense for the verb. We plan on adding more variation to the data by annotating additional QA and machine comprehension datasets. Additionally, there is no explicit co-reference resolution module in our model. Further work needs to be done using state of the art architectures which can handle such cases and improve results. Augmenting our full-length natural answer generation system with a question answering module or a knowledge-base will provide insights into how the system performs with noisy and incorrect factoid answers. This needs to be explored further.

References

Kurt Bollacker, Colin Evans, Praveen Paritosh, Tim Sturge, and Jamie Taylor. 2008. Freebase: A collaboratively created graph database for structuring human knowledge. In *Proceedings of the 2008 ACM SIGMOD International Conference on Management of Data*, SIGMOD '08, pages 1247–1250, New York, NY, USA. ACM.

Antoine Bordes and Jason Weston. 2016. Learning end-to-end goal-oriented dialog. *CoRR*, abs/1605.07683.

Xinya Du and Claire Cardie. 2018. Harvesting paragraph-level question-answer pairs from wikipedia. In *Association for Computational Linguistics (ACL)*.

Yao Fu and Yansong Feng. 2018. Natural answer generation with heterogeneous memory. In *Proceedings of the 2018 Conference of the North American Chapter of the Association for Computational Linguistics: Human Language Technologies, Volume 1 (Long Papers)*, pages 185–195, New Orleans, Louisiana. Association for Computational Linguistics.

David Golub and Xiaodong He. 2016. Character-level question answering with attention. *ArXiv*, abs/1604.00727.

Çaglar Gülçehre, Sungjin Ahn, Ramesh Nallapati, Bowen Zhou, and Yoshua Bengio. 2016. Pointing the unknown words. In *ACL (1)*. The Association for Computer Linguistics.

Shizhu He, Cao Liu, Kang Liu, and Jun Zhao. 2017a. Generating natural answers by incorporating copying and retrieving mechanisms in sequence-to-sequence learning. In *Proceedings of the 55th Annual Meeting of the Association for Computational Linguistics, ACL 2017, Vancouver, Canada, July 30 - August 4, Volume 1: Long Papers*, pages 199–208.

Shizhu He, Cao Liu, Kang Liu, and Jun Zhao. 2017b. Generating natural answers by incorporating copying and retrieving mechanisms in sequence-to-sequence learning. In *Proceedings of the 55th Annual Meeting of the Association for Computational Linguistics (Volume 1: Long Papers)*, pages 199–208, Vancouver, Canada. Association for Computational Linguistics.

Daniel Jurafsky and James H. Martin. 2018. *Speech and Language Processing*. Draft, Stanford University.

Guillaume Klein, Yoon Kim, Yuntian Deng, Jean Senellart, and Alexander M. Rush. 2017. OpenNMT: Open-source toolkit for neural machine translation. In *Proc. ACL*.

Rongzhong Lian, Min Xie, Fan Wang, Jinhua Peng, and Hua Wu. 2019. Learning to select knowledge for response generation in dialog systems. *CoRR*, abs/1902.04911.

Cao Liu, Shizhu He, Kang Liu, and Jun Zhao. 2018a. Curriculum learning for natural answer generation. In *IJCAI*, pages 4223–4229. ijcai.org.

Shuman Liu, Hongshen Chen, Zhaochun Ren, Yang Feng, Qun Liu, and Dawei Yin. 2018b. Knowledge diffusion for neural dialogue generation. In *Proceedings of the 56th Annual Meeting of the Association for Computational Linguistics, ACL 2018, Melbourne, Australia, July 15-20, 2018, Volume 1: Long Papers*, pages 1489–1498.

Minh-Thang Luong, Hieu Pham, and Christopher D. Manning. 2015. Effective approaches to attention-based neural machine translation. *CoRR*, abs/1508.04025.

Pranav Rajpurkar, Jian Zhang, Konstantin Lopyrev, and Percy Liang. 2016. Squad: 100,000+ questions for machine comprehension of text. *arXiv preprint arXiv:1606.05250*.

Siva Reddy, Danqi Chen, and Christopher D Manning. 2018. Coqa: A conversational question answering challenge. *arXiv preprint arXiv:1808.07042*.

Abigail See, Peter J. Liu, and Christopher D. Manning. 2017. Get to the point: Summarization with pointer-generator networks. In *Proceedings of the 55th Annual Meeting of the Association for Computational Linguistics (Volume 1: Long Papers)*, pages 1073–1083. Association for Computational Linguistics.

Sainbayar Sukhbaatar, Arthur Szlam, Jason Weston, and Rob Fergus. 2015. End-to-end memory networks. In *Proceedings of the 28th International Conference on Neural Information Processing Systems - Volume 2*, NIPS'15, pages 2440–2448, Cambridge, MA, USA. MIT Press.

Adam Trischler, Tong Wang, Xingdi Yuan, Justin Harris, Alessandro Sordoni, Phillip Bachman, and Kaheer Suleman. 2017. Newsqa: A machine comprehension dataset. In *Rep4NLP@ACL*.

Oriol Vinyals, Meire Fortunato, and Navdeep Jaitly. 2015. Pointer networks. In C. Cortes, N. D. Lawrence, D. D. Lee, M. Sugiyama, and R. Garnett, editors, *Advances in Neural Information Processing Systems 28*, pages 2692–2700. Curran Associates, Inc.

Jason Weston, Antoine Bordes, Sumit Chopra, and Tomas Mikolov. 2015. Towards ai-complete question answering: A set of prerequisite toy tasks. *CoRR*, abs/1502.05698.

Jun Yin, Xin Jiang, Zhengdong Lu, Lifeng Shang, Hang Li, and Xiaoming Li. 2015. Neural generative question answering. *CoRR*, abs/1512.01337.

Summary Level Training of Sentence Rewriting
for Abstractive Summarization

Sanghwan Bae, Taeuk Kim, Jihoon Kim and **Sang-goo Lee**
Department of Computer Science and Engineering
Seoul National University, Seoul, Korea
`{sanghwan,taeuk,kjh255,sglee}@europa.snu.ac.kr`

Abstract

As an attempt to combine extractive and abstractive summarization, *Sentence Rewriting* models adopt the strategy of extracting salient sentences from a document first and then paraphrasing the selected ones to generate a summary. However, the existing models in this framework mostly rely on sentence-level rewards or suboptimal labels, causing a mismatch between a training objective and evaluation metric. In this paper, we present a novel training signal that directly maximizes summary-level ROUGE scores through reinforcement learning. In addition, we incorporate BERT into our model, making good use of its ability on natural language understanding. In extensive experiments, we show that a combination of our proposed model and training procedure obtains new state-of-the-art performance on both CNN/Daily Mail and New York Times datasets. We also demonstrate that it generalizes better on DUC-2002 test set.

1 Introduction

The task of automatic text summarization aims to compress a textual document to a shorter highlight while keeping salient information of the original text. In general, there are two ways to do text summarization: *Extractive* and *Abstractive* (Mani and Maybury, 2001). *Extractive* approaches generate summaries by selecting salient sentences or phrases from a source text, while *abstractive* approaches involve a process of paraphrasing or generating sentences to write a summary.

Recent work (Liu, 2019; Zhang et al., 2019c) demonstrates that it is highly beneficial for extractive summarization models to incorporate pre-trained language models (LMs) such as BERT (Devlin et al., 2019) into their architectures. However, the performance improvement from the pre-trained LMs is known to be relatively small in case

of abstractive summarization (Zhang et al., 2019a; Hoang et al., 2019). This discrepancy may be due to the difference between extractive and abstractive approaches in ways of dealing with the task—the former *classifies* whether each sentence to be included in a summary, while the latter *generates* a whole summary from scratch. In other words, as most of the pre-trained LMs are designed to be of help to the tasks which can be categorized as classification including extractive summarization, they are not guaranteed to be advantageous to abstractive summarization models that should be capable of generating language (Wang and Cho, 2019; Zhang et al., 2019b).

On the other hand, recent studies for abstractive summarization (Chen and Bansal, 2018; Hsu et al., 2018; Gehrmann et al., 2018) have attempted to exploit extractive models. Among these, a notable one is Chen and Bansal (2018), in which a sophisticated model called *Reinforce-Selected Sentence Rewriting* is proposed. The model consists of both an extractor and abstractor, where the extractor picks out salient sentences first from a source article, and then the abstractor rewrites and compresses the extracted sentences into a complete summary. It is further fine-tuned by training the extractor with the rewards derived from sentence-level ROUGE scores of the summary generated from the abstractor.

In this paper, we improve the model of Chen and Bansal (2018), addressing two primary issues. Firstly, we argue there is a bottleneck in the existing extractor on the basis of the observation that its performance as an independent summarization model (i.e., without the abstractor) is no better than solid baselines such as selecting the first 3 sentences. To resolve the problem, we present a novel neural extractor exploiting the pre-trained LMs (BERT in this work) which are expected to perform better according to the recent studies (Liu,

Proceedings of the 2nd Workshop on New Frontiers in Summarization, pages 10–20
Hong Kong, China, November 4, 2019. ©2019 Association for Computational Linguistics

2019; Zhang et al., 2019c). Since the extractor is a sort of sentence classifier, we expect that it can make good use of the ability of pre-trained LMs which is proven to be effective in classification.

Secondly, the other point is that there is a mismatch between the training objective and evaluation metric; the previous work utilizes the *sentence-level* ROUGE scores as a reinforcement learning objective, while the final performance of a summarization model is evaluated by the *summary-level* ROUGE scores. Moreover, as Narayan et al. (2018) pointed out, sentences with the highest individual ROUGE scores do not necessarily lead to an optimal summary, since they may contain overlapping contents, causing verbose and redundant summaries. Therefore, we propose to directly use the summary-level ROUGE scores as an objective instead of the sentence-level scores. A potential problem arising from this apprsoach is the sparsity of training signals, because the summary-level ROUGE scores are calculated only once for each training episode. To alleviate this problem, we use *reward shaping* (Ng et al., 1999) to give an intermediate signal for each action, preserving the optimal policy.

We empirically demonstrate the superiority of our approach by achieving new state-of-the-art abstractive summarization results on CNN/Daily Mail and New York Times datasets (Hermann et al., 2015; Durrett et al., 2016). It is worth noting that our approach shows large improvements especially on ROUGE-L score which is considered a means of assessing fluency (Narayan et al., 2018). In addition, our model performs much better than previous work when testing on DUC-2002 dataset, showing better generalization and robustness of our model.

Our contributions in this work are three-fold: a novel successful application of pre-trained transformers for abstractive summarization; suggesting a training method to globally optimize sentence selection; achieving the state-of-the-art results on the benchmark datasets, CNN/Daily Mail and New York Times.

2 Background

2.1 Sentence Rewriting

In this paper, we focus on single-document multi-sentence summarization and propose a neural abstractive model based on the *Sentence Rewriting* framework (Chen and Bansal, 2018; Xu and Dur-

rett, 2019) which consists of two parts: a neural network for the *extractor* and another network for the *abstractor*. The extractor network is designed to extract salient sentences from a source article. The abstractor network rewrites the extracted sentences into a short summary.

2.2 Learning Sentence Selection

The most common way to train extractor to select informative sentences is building extractive oracles as gold targets, and training with cross-entropy (CE) loss. An oracle consists of a set of sentences with the highest possible ROUGE scores. Building oracles is finding an optimal combination of sentences, where there are 2^n possible combinations for each example. Because of this, the exact optimization for ROUGE scores is intractable. Therefore, alternative methods identify the set of sentences with greedy search (Nallapati et al., 2017), sentence-level search (Hsu et al., 2018; Shi et al., 2019) or collective search using the limited number of sentences (Xu and Durrett, 2019), which construct suboptimal oracles. Even if all the optimal oracles are found, training with CE loss using these labels will cause underfitting as it will only maximize probabilities for sentences in label sets and ignore all other sentences.

Alternatively, reinforcement learning (RL) can give room for exploration in the search space. Chen and Bansal (2018), our baseline work, proposed to apply policy gradient methods to train an extractor. This approach makes an end-to-end trainable stochastic computation graph, encouraging the model to select sentences with high ROUGE scores. However, they define a reward for an action (sentence selection) as a sentence-level ROUGE score between the chosen sentence and a sentence in the ground truth summary for that time step. This leads the extractor agent to a suboptimal policy; the set of sentences matching individually with each sentence in a ground truth summary isn't necessarily optimal in terms of summary-level ROUGE score.

Narayan et al. (2018) proposed policy gradient with rewards from summary-level ROUGE. They defined an action as sampling a summary from candidate summaries that contain the limited number of plausible sentences. After training, a sentence is ranked high for selection if it often occurs in high scoring summaries. However, their approach still has a risk of ranking redundant sen-

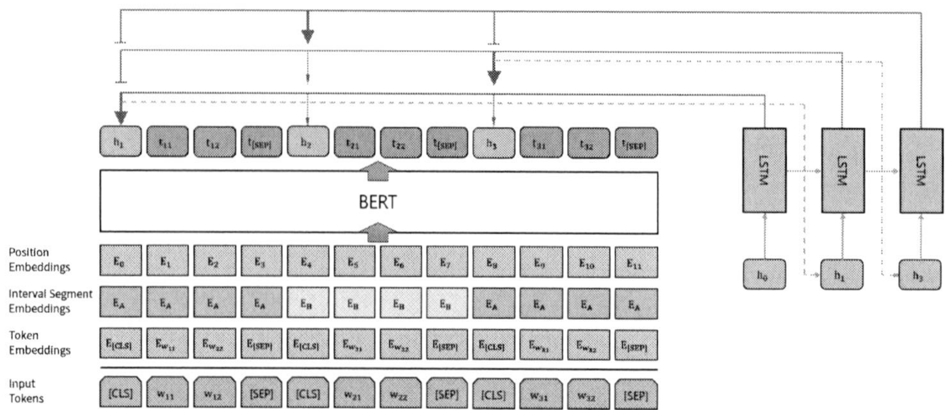

Figure 1: The overview architecture of the extractor netwrok

tences high; if two highly overlapped sentences have salient information, they would be ranked high together, increasing the probability of being sampled in one summary.

To tackle this problem, we propose a training method using reinforcement learning which globally optimizes summary-level ROUGE score and gives intermediate rewards to ease the learning.

2.3 Pre-trained Transformers

Transferring representations from pre-trained transformer language models has been highly successful in the domain of natural language understanding tasks (Radford et al., 2018; Devlin et al., 2019; Radford et al., 2019; Yang et al., 2019). These methods first pre-train highly stacked transformer blocks (Vaswani et al., 2017) on a huge unlabeled corpus, and then fine-tune the models or representations on downstream tasks.

3 Model

Our model consists of two neural network modules, i.e. an extractor and abstractor. The extractor encodes a source document and chooses sentences from the document, and then the abstractor paraphrases the summary candidates. Formally, a single document consists of n sentences $D = \{s_1, s_2, \cdots, s_n\}$. We denote i-th sentence as $s_i = \{w_{i1}, w_{i2}, \cdots, w_{im}\}$ where w_{ij} is the j-th word in s_i. The extractor learns to pick out a subset of D denoted as $\hat{D} = \{\hat{s}_1, \hat{s}_2, \cdots, \hat{s}_k | \hat{s}_i \in D\}$ where k sentences are selected. The abstractor rewrites each of the selected sentences to form a summary $S = \{f(\hat{s}_1), f(\hat{s}_2), \cdots, f(\hat{s}_k)\}$, where f is an abstracting function. And a gold summary consists of l sentences $A = \{a_1, a_2, \cdots, a_l\}$.

3.1 Extractor Network

The extractor is based on the encoder-decoder framework. We adapt BERT for the encoder to exploit contextualized representations from pretrained transformers. BERT as the encoder maps the input sequence D to sentence representation vectors $H = \{h_1, h_2, \cdots, h_n\}$, where h_i is for the i-th sentence in the document. Then, the decoder utilizes H to extract $\hat{D}$ from D.

3.1.1 Leveraging Pre-trained Transformers

Although we require the encoder to output the representation for each sentence, the output vectors from BERT are grounded to tokens instead of sentences. Therefore, we modify the input sequence and embeddings of BERT as Liu (2019) did.

In the original BERT's configure, a [CLS] token is used to get features from one sentence or a pair of sentences. Since we need a symbol for each sentence representation, we insert the [CLS] token before each sentence. And we add a [SEP] token at the end of each sentence, which is used to differentiate multiple sentences. As a result, the vector for the i-th [CLS] symbol from the top BERT layer corresponds to the i-th sentence representation h_i.

In addition, we add interval segment embeddings as input for BERT to distinguish multiple sentences within a document. For s_i we assign a segment embedding E_A or E_B conditioned on i is odd or even. For example, for a consecutive sequence of sentences s_1, s_2, s_3, s_4, s_5, we assign E_A, E_B, E_A, E_B, E_A in order. All the words in each sentence are assigned to the same segment embedding, *i.e.* segment embeddings for $w_{11}, w_{12}, \cdots, w_{1m}$ is $E_A, E_A, \cdots, E_A$. An illustration for this procedure is shown in Figure 1.

3.1.2 Sentence Selection

We use LSTM Pointer Network (Vinyals et al., 2015) as the decoder to select the extracted sentences based on the above sentence representations. The decoder extracts sentences recurrently, producing a distribution over all of the remaining sentence representations excluding those already selected. Since we use the sequential model which selects one sentence at a time step, our decoder can consider the previously selected sentences. This property is needed to avoid selecting sentences that have overlapping information with the sentences extracted already.

As the decoder structure is almost the same with the previous work, we convey the equations of Chen and Bansal (2018) to avoid confusion, with minor modifications to agree with our notations. Formally, the extraction probability is calculated as:

$$u_{t,i} = v_m^\top \tanh(W_e e_t + W_h h_i) \tag{1}$$
$$P(\hat{s}_t | D, \hat{s}_1, \cdots, \hat{s}_{t-1}) = \mathrm{softmax}(u_t) \tag{2}$$

where e_t is the output of the glimpse operation:

$$c_{t,i} = v_g^\top \tanh(W_{g1} h_i + W_{g2} z_t) \tag{3}$$
$$\alpha_t = \mathrm{softmax}(c_t) \tag{4}$$
$$e_t = \sum_i \alpha_t W_{g1} h_i \tag{5}$$

In Equation 3, z_t is the hidden state of the LSTM decoder at time t (shown in green in Figure 1). All the W and v are trainable parameters.

3.2 Abstractor Network

The abstractor network approximates f, which compresses and paraphrases an extracted document sentence to a concise summary sentence. We use the standard attention based sequence-to-sequence (seq2seq) model (Bahdanau et al., 2015; Luong et al., 2015) with the copying mechanism (See et al., 2017) for handling out-of-vocabulary (OOV) words. Our abstractor is practically identical to the one proposed in Chen and Bansal (2018).

4 Training

In our model, an extractor selects a series of sentences, and then an abstractor paraphrases them.

As they work in different ways, we need different training strategies suitable for each of them. Training the abstractor is relatively obvious; maximizing log-likelihood for the next word given the previous ground truth words. However, there are several issues for extractor training. First, the extractor should consider the abstractor's rewriting process when it selects sentences. This causes a *weak supervision* problem (Jehl et al., 2019), since the extractor gets training signals indirectly after paraphrasing processes are finished. In addition, thus this procedure contains sampling or maximum selection, the extractor performs a non-differentiable extraction. Lastly, although our goal is maximizing ROUGE scores, neural models cannot be trained directly by maximum likelihood estimation from them.

To address those issues above, we apply standard policy gradient methods, and we propose a novel training procedure for extractor which guides to the optimal policy in terms of the summary-level ROUGE. As usual in RL for sequence prediction, we pre-train submodules and apply RL to fine-tune the extractor.

4.1 Training Submodules

Extractor Pre-training Starting from a poor random policy makes it difficult to train the extractor agent to converge towards the optimal policy. Thus, we pre-train the network using cross entropy (CE) loss like previous work (Bahdanau et al., 2017; Chen and Bansal, 2018). However, there is no gold label for extractive summarization in most of the summarization datasets. Hence, we employ a greedy approach (Nallapati et al., 2017) to make the extractive oracles, where we add one sentence at a time incrementally to the summary, such that the ROUGE score of the current set of selected sentences is maximized for the entire ground truth summary. This doesn't guarantee optimal, but it is enough to teach the network to select plausible sentences. Formally, the network is trained to minimize the cross-entropy loss as follows:

$$L_{\text{ext}} = -\frac{1}{T} \sum_{t=1}^{T} \log P(s_t^* | D, s_1^*, \cdots, s_{t-1}^*) \tag{6}$$

where s_t^* is the t-th generated oracle sentence.

Abstractor Training For the abstractor training, we should create training pairs for input and target sentences. As the abstractor paraphrases on sentence-level, we take a sentence-level search for each ground-truth summary sentence. We find the most similar document sentence s'_t by:

$$s'_t = \text{argmax}_{s_i} (\text{ROUGE-L}^{\text{sent}}_{F_1}(s_i, a_t)) \quad (7)$$

And then the abstractor is trained as a usual sequence-to-sequence model to minimize the cross-entropy loss:

$$L_{\text{abs}} = -\frac{1}{m} \sum_{j=1}^{m} \log P(w_j^a | w_1^a, \cdots, w_{j-1}^a, \Phi) \quad (8)$$

where w_j^a is the j-th word of the target sentence a_t, and Φ is the encoded representation for s'_t.

4.2 Guiding to the Optimal Policy

To optimize ROUGE metric directly, we assume the extractor as an agent in reinforcement learning paradigm (Sutton et al., 1998). We view the extractor has a stochastic *policy* that generates *actions* (sentence selection) and receives the score of final evaluation metric (summary-level ROUGE in our case) as the *return*

$$R(S) = \text{ROUGE-L}^{\text{summ}}_{F_1}(S, A). \quad (9)$$

While we are ultimately interested in the maximization of the score of a complete summary, simply awarding this score at the last step provides a very sparse training signal. For this reason we define intermediate rewards using *reward shaping* (Ng et al., 1999), which is inspired by Bahdanau et al. (2017)'s attempt for sequence prediction. Namely, we compute summary-level score values for all intermediate summaries:

$$(R(\{\hat{s}_1\}), R(\{\hat{s}_1, \hat{s}_2\}), \cdots, R(\{\hat{s}_1, \hat{s}_2, \cdots, \hat{s}_k\})) \quad (10)$$

The reward for each step r_t is the difference between the consecutive pairs of scores:

$$r_t = R(\{\hat{s}_1, \hat{s}_2, \cdots, \hat{s}_t\}) - R(\{\hat{s}_1, \hat{s}_2, \cdots, \hat{s}_{t-1}\}) \quad (11)$$

This measures an amount of increase or decrease in the summary-level score from selecting $\hat{s}_t$. Using the shaped reward r_t instead of awarding the whole score R at the last step does not change the optimal policy (Ng et al., 1999). We define a discounted future reward for each step as $R_t = \sum_{t=1}^{k} \gamma^t r_{t+1}$, where γ is a discount factor.

Additionally, we add 'stop' action to the action space, by concatenating trainable parameters h_{stop} (the same dimension as h_i) to H. The agent treats it as another candidate to extract. When it selects 'stop', an extracting episode ends and the final return is given. This encourages the model to extract additional sentences only when they are expected to increase the final return.

Following Chen and Bansal (2018), we use the *Advantage Actor Critic* (Mnih et al., 2016) method to train. We add a critic network to estimate a value function $V_t(D, \hat{s}_1, \cdots, \hat{s}_{t-1})$, which then is used to compute advantage of each action (we will omit the current state $(D, \hat{s}_1, \cdots, \hat{s}_{t-1})$ to simplify):

$$A_t(s_i) = Q_t(s_i) - V_t. \quad (12)$$

where $Q_t(s_i)$ is the expected future reward for selecting s_i at the current step t. We maximize this advantage with the policy gradient with the Monte-Carlo sample ($A_t(s_i) \approx R_t - V_t$):

$$\nabla_{\theta_\pi} L_\pi \approx \frac{1}{k} \sum_{t=1}^{k} \nabla_{\theta_\pi} \log P(s_i | D, \hat{s}_1, \cdots, \hat{s}_{t-1}) A_t(s_i) \quad (13)$$

where θ_π is the trainable parameters of the actor network (original extractor). And the critic is trained to minimize the square loss:

$$\nabla_{\theta_\psi} L_\psi = \nabla_{\theta_\psi} (V_t - R_t)^2 \quad (14)$$

where θ_ψ is the trainable parameters of the critic network.

5 Experimental Setup

5.1 Datasets

We evaluate the proposed approach on the CNN/Daily Mail (Hermann et al., 2015) and New York Times (Sandhaus, 2008) dataset, which are both standard corpora for multi-sentence abstractive summarization. Additionally, we test generalization of our model on DUC-2002 test set.

CNN/Daily Mail dataset consists of more than 300K news articles and each of them is paired with several highlights. We used the standard splits of Hermann et al. (2015) for training, validation and testing (90,226/1,220/1,093 documents for CNN and 196,961/12,148/10,397 for Daily Mail). We did not anonymize entities. We followed the preprocessing methods in See et al. (2017) after splitting sentences by Stanford CoreNLP (Manning et al., 2014).

The New York Times dataset also consists of many news articles. We followed the dataset splits of Durrett et al. (2016); 100,834 for training and

Models	ROUGE-1	ROUGE-2	ROUGE-L	R-AVG
Extractive				
lead-3 (See et al., 2017)	40.34	17.70	36.57	31.54
REFRESH (Narayan et al., 2018)	40.00	18.20	36.60	31.60
JECS (Xu and Durrett, 2019)	41.70	18.50	37.90	32.70
HiBERT (Zhang et al., 2019c)	42.37	19.95	38.83	33.71
BERTSUM (Liu, 2019)	**43.25**	**20.24**	39.63	**34.37**
BERT-ext (ours)	42.29	19.38	38.63	33.43
BERT-ext + RL (ours)	42.76	19.87	39.11	33.91
Abstractive				
Pointer Generator (See et al., 2017)	39.53	17.28	36.38	31.06
Inconsistency Loss (Hsu et al., 2018)	40.68	17.97	37.13	31.93
Sentence Rewrite (w/o rerank) (Chen and Bansal, 2018)	40.04	17.61	37.59	31.74
Sentence Rewrite (Chen and Bansal, 2018)	40.88	17.80	38.54	32.41
Bottom-Up (Gehrmann et al., 2018)	41.22	18.68	38.34	32.75
Transformer-LM (Hoang et al., 2019)	38.67	17.47	35.79	30.64
Two-Stage BERT (Zhang et al., 2019a)	41.71	**19.49**	38.79	33.33
BERT-ext + abs (ours)	40.14	17.87	37.83	31.95
BERT-ext + abs + rerank (ours)	40.71	17.92	38.51	32.38
BERT-ext + abs + RL (ours)	41.00	18.81	38.51	32.77
BERT-ext + abs + RL + rerank (ours)	**41.90**	19.08	**39.64**	**33.54**

Table 1: Performance on CNN/Daily Mail test set using the full length ROUGE F_1 score. R-AVG calculates average score of ROUGE-1, ROUGE-2 and ROUGE-L.

9,706 for test examples. And we also followed the filtering procedure of them, removing documents with summaries that are shorter than 50 words. The final test set (NYT50) contains 3,452 examples out of the original 9,706.

The DUC-2002 dataset contains 567 document-summary pairs for single-document summarization. As a single document can have multiple summaries, we made one pair per summary. We used this dataset as a test set for our model trained on CNN/Daily Mail dataset to test generalization.

5.2 Implementation Details

Our extractor is built on $\text{BERT}_{\text{BASE}}$ with fine-tuning, smaller version than $\text{BERT}_{\text{LARGE}}$ due to limitation of time and space. We set LSTM hidden size as 256 for all of our models. To initialize word embeddings for our abstractor, we use word2vec (Mikolov et al., 2013) of 128 dimensions trained on the same corpus. We optimize our model with Adam optimizer (Kingma and Ba, 2015) with $\beta_1 = 0.9$ and $\beta_2 = 0.999$. For extractor pre-training, we use learning rate schedule following (Vaswani et al., 2017) with $warmup = 10000$:

$$lr = 2e^{-3} \cdot \min(steps^{-0.5}, steps \cdot warmup^{-1.5}).$$

Models	R-1	R-2	R-L
lead-3 (See et al., 2017)	40.34	17.70	36.57
rnn-ext (Chen and Bansal, 2018)	40.17	18.11	36.41
JECS-ext (Xu and Durrett, 2019)	40.70	18.00	36.80
BERT-ext (ours)	**42.29**	**19.38**	**38.63**

Table 2: Comparison of extractor networks.

And we set learning rate $1e^{-3}$ for abstractor and $4e^{-6}$ for RL training. We apply gradient clipping using L2 norm with threshold 2.0. For RL training, we use $\gamma = 0.95$ for the discount factor. To ease learning h_{stop}, we set the reward for the stop action to $\lambda \cdot \text{ROUGE-L}_{F_1}^{\text{summ}}(S, A)$, where λ is a stop coefficient set to 0.08. Our critic network shares the encoder with the actor (extractor) and has the same architecture with it except the output layer, estimating scalar for the state value. And the critic is initialized with the parameters of the pre-trained extractor where it has the same architecture.

5.3 Evaluation

We evaluate the performance of our method using different variants of ROUGE metric computed with respect to the gold summaries. On the CNN/Daily Mail and DUC-2002 dataset, we use standard ROUGE-1, ROUGE-2, and ROUGE-

	R-1	R-2	R-L
Sentence-matching	52.09	28.13	49.74
Greedy Search	55.27	29.24	52.64
Combination Search	55.51	29.33	52.89

Table 3: Comparison of different methods building upper bound for full model.

Models	R-1	R-2	R-L
Sentence-level Reward	40.82	18.63	38.41
Combinatorial Reward	40.85	18.77	38.44
Sentence-level Reward + rerank	41.58	18.72	39.31
Combinatorial Reward + rerank	**41.90**	**19.08**	**39.64**

Table 4: Comparison of RL training.

L (Lin, 2004) on full length F_1 with stemming as previous work did (Nallapati et al., 2017; See et al., 2017; Chen and Bansal, 2018). On NYT50 dataset, following Durrett et al. (2016) and Paulus et al. (2018), we used the limited length ROUGE recall metric, truncating the generated summary to the length of the ground truth summary.

6   Results

6.1   CNN/Daily Mail

Table 1 shows the experimental results on CNN/Daily Mail dataset, with extractive models in the top block and abstractive models in the bottom block. For comparison, we list the performance of many recent approaches with ours.

Extractive Summarization   As See et al. (2017) showed, the first 3 sentences (lead-3) in an article form a strong summarization baseline in CNN/Daily Mail dataset. Therefore, the very first objective of extractive models is to outperform the simple method which always returns 3 or 4 sentences at the top. However, as Table 2 shows, ROUGE scores of lead baselines and extractors from previous work in *Sentence Rewrite* framework (Chen and Bansal, 2018; Xu and Durrett, 2019) are almost tie. We can easily conjecture that the limited performances of their full model are due to their extractor networks. Our extractor network with BERT (BERT-ext), as a single model, outperforms those models with large margins. Adding reinforcement learning (BERT-ext + RL) gives higher performance, which is competitive with other extractive approaches using pretrained Transformers (see Table 1). This shows the effectiveness of our learning method.

Abstractive Summarization   Our abstractive approaches combine the extractor with the abstractor. The combined model (BERT-ext + abs) without additional RL training outperforms the Sentence Rewrite model (Chen and Bansal, 2018) without reranking, showing the effectiveness of our extractor network. With the proposed RL training procedure (BERT-ext + abs + RL), our model exceeds the best model of Chen and Bansal (2018). In addition, the result is better than those of all the other abstractive methods exploiting extractive approaches in them (Hsu et al., 2018; Chen and Bansal, 2018; Gehrmann et al., 2018).

Redundancy Control   Although the proposed RL training inherently gives training signals that induce the model to avoid redundancy across sentences, there can be still remaining overlaps between extracted sentences. We found that the additional methods reducing redundancies can improve the summarization quality, especially on CNN/Daily Mail dataset.

We tried Trigram Blocking (Liu, 2019) for extractor and Reranking (Chen and Bansal, 2018) for abstractor, and we empirically found that the reranking only improves the performance. This helps the model to compress the extracted sentences focusing on disjoint information, even if there are some partial overlaps between the sentences. Our best abstractive model (BERT-ext + abs + RL + rerank) achieves the new state-of-the-art performance for abstractive summarization in terms of average ROUGE score, with large margins on ROUGE-L.

However, we empirically found that the reranking method has no effect or has negative effect on NYT50 or DUC-2002 dataset. Hence, we don't apply it for the remaining datasets.

Combinatorial Reward   Before seeing the effects of our summary-level rewards on final results, we check the upper bounds of different training signals for the full model. All the document sentences are paraphrased with our trained abstractor, and then we find the best set for each search method. *Sentence-matching* finds sentences with the highest ROUGE-L score for each sentence in the gold summary. This search method matches with the best reward from Chen and Bansal (2018). *Greedy Search* is the same method explained for extractor pre-training in section 4.1. *Combination Search* selects a set of sentences

Models	Relevance	Readability	Total
Sentence Rewrite (Chen and Bansal, 2018)	56	59	115
BERTSUM (Liu, 2019)	58	60	118
BERT-ext + abs + RL + rerank (ours)	**66**	**61**	**127**

Table 5: Results of human evaluation.

which has the highest summary-level ROUGE-L score, from all the possible combinations of sentences. Due to time constraints, we limited the maximum number of sentences to 5. This method corresponds to our final return in RL training.

Table 3 shows the summary-level ROUGE scores of previously explained methods. We see considerable gaps between Sentence-matching and Greedy Search, while the scores of Greedy Search are close to those of Combination Search. Note that since we limited the number of sentences for Combination Search, the exact scores for it would be higher. The scores can be interpreted to be upper bounds for corresponding training methods. This result supports our training strategy; pretraining with Greedy Search and final optimization with the combinatorial return.

Additionally, we experiment to verify the contribution of our training method. We train the same model with different training signals; Sentence-level reward from Chen and Bansal (2018) and combinatorial reward from ours. The results are shown in Table 4. Both with and without reranking, the models trained with the combinatorial reward consistently outperform those trained with the sentence-level reward.

Human Evaluation We also conduct human evaluation to ensure robustness of our training procedure. We measure relevance and readability of the summaries. Relevance is based on the summary containing important, salient information from the input article, being correct by avoiding contradictory/unrelated information, and avoiding repeated/redundant information. Readability is based on the summarys fluency, grammaticality, and coherence. To evaluate both these criteria, we design a Amazon Mechanical Turk experiment based on ranking method, inspired by Kiritchenko and Mohammad (2017). We randomly select 20 samples from the CNN/Daily Mail test set and ask the human testers (3 for each sample) to rank summaries (for relevance and readability) produced by 3 different models: our final model, that of Chen and Bansal (2018) and that of Liu (2019). 2, 1 and 0 points were given according to the ranking.

Models	R-1	R-2	R-L
Extractive			
First sentences (Durrett et al., 2016)	28.60	17.30	-
First k words (Durrett et al., 2016)	35.70	21.60	-
Full (Durrett et al., 2016)	42.20	24.90	-
BERTSUM (Liu, 2019)	**46.66**	26.35	42.62
Abstractive			
Deep Reinforced (Paulus et al., 2018)	42.94	26.02	-
Two-Stage BERT (Zhang et al., 2019a)	45.33	26.53	-
BERT-ext + abs (ours)	44.41	24.61	41.40
BERT-ext + abs + RL (ours)	46.63	**26.76**	**43.38**

Table 6: Performance on NYT50 test set using the limited length ROUGE recall score.

Models	R-1	R-2	R-L
Pointer Generator (See et al., 2017)	37.22	15.78	33.90
Sentence Rewrite (Chen and Bansal, 2018)	39.46	17.34	36.72
BERT-ext + abs + RL (ours)	**43.39**	**19.38**	**40.14**

Table 7: Performance on DUC-2002 test set using the full length ROUGE F_1 score.

The models were anonymized and randomly shuffled. Following previous work, the input article and ground truth summaries are also shown to the human participants in addition to the three model summaries. From the results shown in Table 5, we can see that our model is better in relevance compared to others. In terms of readability, there was no noticeable difference.

6.2 New York Times corpus

Table 6 gives the results on NYT50 dataset. We see our BERT-ext + abs + RL outperforms all the extractive and abstractive models, except ROUGE-1 from Liu (2019). Comparing with two recent models that adapted BERT on their summarization models (Liu, 2019; Zhang et al., 2019a), we can say that we proposed another method successfully leveraging BERT for summarization. In addition, the experiment proves the effectiveness of our RL training, with about 2 point improvement for each ROUGE metric.

6.3 DUC-2002

We also evaluated the models trained on the CNN/Daily Mail dataset on the out-of-domain DUC-2002 test set as shown in Table 7. BERT-ext + abs + RL outperforms baseline models with large margins on all of the ROUGE scores. This result shows that our model generalizes better.

7 Related Work

There has been a variety of deep neural network models for abstractive document summarization. One of the most dominant structures is the sequence-to-sequence (seq2seq) models with attention mechanism (Rush et al., 2015; Chopra et al., 2016; Nallapati et al., 2016). See et al. (2017) introduced Pointer Generator network that implicitly combines the abstraction with the extraction, using copy mechanism (Gu et al., 2016; Zeng et al., 2016). More recently, there have been several studies that have attempted to improve the performance of the abstractive summarization by explicitly combining them with extractive models. Some notable examples include the use of inconsistency loss (Hsu et al., 2018), key phrase extraction (Li et al., 2018; Gehrmann et al., 2018), and sentence extraction with rewriting (Chen and Bansal, 2018). Our model improves Sentence Rewriting with BERT as an extractor and summary-level rewards to optimize the extractor.

Reinforcement learning has been shown to be effective to directly optimize a non-differentiable objective in language generation including text summarization (Ranzato et al., 2016; Bahdanau et al., 2017; Paulus et al., 2018; Celikyilmaz et al., 2018; Narayan et al., 2018). Bahdanau et al. (2017) use actor-critic methods for language generation, using reward shaping (Ng et al., 1999) to solve the sparsity of training signals. Inspired by this, we generalize it to sentence extraction to give per step reward preserving optimality.

8 Conclusions

We have improved Sentence Rewriting approaches for abstractive summarization, proposing a novel extractor architecture exploiting BERT and a novel training procedure which globally optimizes summary-level ROUGE metric. Our approach achieves the new state-of-the-art on both CNN/Daily Mail and New York Times datasets as well as much better generalization on DUC-2002 test set.

Acknowledgments

We thank anonymous reviewers for their constructive and fruitful comments. This work was supported by the National Research Foundation of Korea (NRF) grant funded by the Korea government (MSIT) (NRF2016M3C4A7952587).

References

Dzmitry Bahdanau, Philemon Brakel, Kelvin Xu, Anirudh Goyal, Ryan Lowe, Joelle Pineau, Aaron C. Courville, and Yoshua Bengio. 2017. An actor-critic algorithm for sequence prediction. In *5th International Conference on Learning Representations, ICLR 2017, Toulon, France, April 24-26, 2017, Conference Track Proceedings*. OpenReview.net.

Dzmitry Bahdanau, Kyunghyun Cho, and Yoshua Bengio. 2015. Neural machine translation by jointly learning to align and translate. In (Bengio and Le-Cun, 2015).

Yoshua Bengio and Yann LeCun, editors. 2015. *3rd International Conference on Learning Representations, ICLR 2015, San Diego, CA, USA, May 7-9, 2015, Conference Track Proceedings*.

Asli Celikyilmaz, Antoine Bosselut, Xiaodong He, and Yejin Choi. 2018. Deep communicating agents for abstractive summarization. In *Proceedings of the 2018 Conference of the North American Chapter of the Association for Computational Linguistics: Human Language Technologies, Volume 1 (Long Papers)*, pages 1662–1675, New Orleans, Louisiana. Association for Computational Linguistics.

Yen-Chun Chen and Mohit Bansal. 2018. Fast abstractive summarization with reinforce-selected sentence rewriting. In *Proceedings of the 56th Annual Meeting of the Association for Computational Linguistics (Volume 1: Long Papers)*, pages 675–686, Melbourne, Australia. Association for Computational Linguistics.

Sumit Chopra, Michael Auli, and Alexander M. Rush. 2016. Abstractive sentence summarization with attentive recurrent neural networks. In *Proceedings of the 2016 Conference of the North American Chapter of the Association for Computational Linguistics: Human Language Technologies*, pages 93–98, San Diego, California. Association for Computational Linguistics.

Jacob Devlin, Ming-Wei Chang, Kenton Lee, and Kristina Toutanova. 2019. BERT: Pre-training of deep bidirectional transformers for language understanding. In *Proceedings of the 2019 Conference of the North American Chapter of the Association for Computational Linguistics: Human Language Technologies, Volume 1 (Long and Short Papers)*, pages 4171–4186, Minneapolis, Minnesota. Association for Computational Linguistics.

Greg Durrett, Taylor Berg-Kirkpatrick, and Dan Klein. 2016. Learning-based single-document summarization with compression and anaphoricity constraints. In *Proceedings of the 54th Annual Meeting of the Association for Computational Linguistics (Volume 1: Long Papers)*, pages 1998–2008, Berlin, Germany. Association for Computational Linguistics.

Sebastian Gehrmann, Yuntian Deng, and Alexander Rush. 2018. Bottom-up abstractive summarization. In *Proceedings of the 2018 Conference on Empirical Methods in Natural Language Processing*, pages 4098–4109, Brussels, Belgium. Association for Computational Linguistics.

Jiatao Gu, Zhengdong Lu, Hang Li, and Victor O.K. Li. 2016. Incorporating copying mechanism in sequence-to-sequence learning. In *Proceedings of the 54th Annual Meeting of the Association for Computational Linguistics (Volume 1: Long Papers)*, pages 1631–1640, Berlin, Germany. Association for Computational Linguistics.

Karl Moritz Hermann, Tomas Kocisky, Edward Grefenstette, Lasse Espeholt, Will Kay, Mustafa Suleyman, and Phil Blunsom. 2015. Teaching machines to read and comprehend. In C. Cortes, N. D. Lawrence, D. D. Lee, M. Sugiyama, and R. Garnett, editors, *Advances in Neural Information Processing Systems 28*, pages 1693–1701. Curran Associates, Inc.

Andrew Hoang, Antoine Bosselut, Asli Celikyilmaz, and Yejin Choi. 2019. Efficient adaptation of pretrained transformers for abstractive summarization. *arXiv preprint arXiv:1906.00138*.

Wan-Ting Hsu, Chieh-Kai Lin, Ming-Ying Lee, Kerui Min, Jing Tang, and Min Sun. 2018. A unified model for extractive and abstractive summarization using inconsistency loss. In *Proceedings of the 56th Annual Meeting of the Association for Computational Linguistics (Volume 1: Long Papers)*, pages 132–141, Melbourne, Australia. Association for Computational Linguistics.

Laura Jehl, Carolin Lawrence, and Stefan Riezler. 2019. Neural sequence-to-sequence models from weak feedback with bipolar ramp loss. *Transactions of the Association for Computational Linguistics*, 7:233–248.

Diederik P. Kingma and Jimmy Ba. 2015. Adam: A method for stochastic optimization. In (Bengio and LeCun, 2015).

Svetlana Kiritchenko and Saif Mohammad. 2017. Best-worst scaling more reliable than rating scales: A case study on sentiment intensity annotation. In *Proceedings of the 55th Annual Meeting of the Association for Computational Linguistics (Volume 2: Short Papers)*, pages 465–470, Vancouver, Canada. Association for Computational Linguistics.

Chenliang Li, Weiran Xu, Si Li, and Sheng Gao. 2018. Guiding generation for abstractive text summarization based on key information guide network. In *Proceedings of the 2018 Conference of the North American Chapter of the Association for Computational Linguistics: Human Language Technologies, Volume 2 (Short Papers)*, pages 55–60, New Orleans, Louisiana. Association for Computational Linguistics.

Chin-Yew Lin. 2004. ROUGE: A package for automatic evaluation of summaries. In *Text Summarization Branches Out*, pages 74–81, Barcelona, Spain. Association for Computational Linguistics.

Yang Liu. 2019. Fine-tune bert for extractive summarization. *arXiv preprint arXiv:1903.10318*.

Thang Luong, Hieu Pham, and Christopher D. Manning. 2015. Effective approaches to attention-based neural machine translation. In *Proceedings of the 2015 Conference on Empirical Methods in Natural Language Processing*, pages 1412–1421, Lisbon, Portugal. Association for Computational Linguistics.

Inderjeet Mani and Mark T Maybury. 2001. Automatic summarization.

Christopher D. Manning, Mihai Surdeanu, John Bauer, Jenny Finkel, Steven J. Bethard, and David McClosky. 2014. The Stanford CoreNLP natural language processing toolkit. In *Association for Computational Linguistics (ACL) System Demonstrations*, pages 55–60.

Tomas Mikolov, Ilya Sutskever, Kai Chen, Greg S Corrado, and Jeff Dean. 2013. Distributed representations of words and phrases and their compositionality. In *Advances in neural information processing systems*, pages 3111–3119.

Volodymyr Mnih, Adria Puigdomenech Badia, Mehdi Mirza, Alex Graves, Timothy Lillicrap, Tim Harley, David Silver, and Koray Kavukcuoglu. 2016. Asynchronous methods for deep reinforcement learning. In *International conference on machine learning*, pages 1928–1937.

Ramesh Nallapati, Feifei Zhai, and Bowen Zhou. 2017. Summarunner: A recurrent neural network based sequence model for extractive summarization of documents. In *Thirty-First AAAI Conference on Artificial Intelligence*.

Ramesh Nallapati, Bowen Zhou, Cicero dos Santos, Çağlar Gulçehre, and Bing Xiang. 2016. Abstractive text summarization using sequence-to-sequence RNNs and beyond. In *Proceedings of The 20th SIGNLL Conference on Computational Natural Language Learning*, pages 280–290, Berlin, Germany. Association for Computational Linguistics.

Shashi Narayan, Shay B. Cohen, and Mirella Lapata. 2018. Ranking sentences for extractive summarization with reinforcement learning. In *Proceedings of the 2018 Conference of the North American Chapter of the Association for Computational Linguistics: Human Language Technologies, Volume 1 (Long Papers)*, pages 1747–1759, New Orleans, Louisiana. Association for Computational Linguistics.

Andrew Y. Ng, Daishi Harada, and Stuart J. Russell. 1999. Policy invariance under reward transformations: Theory and application to reward shaping. In

Proceedings of the Sixteenth International Conference on Machine Learning, ICML '99, pages 278–287, San Francisco, CA, USA. Morgan Kaufmann Publishers Inc.

Romain Paulus, Caiming Xiong, and Richard Socher. 2018. A deep reinforced model for abstractive summarization. In *International Conference on Learning Representations*.

Alec Radford, Karthik Narasimhan, Tim Salimans, and Ilya Sutskever. 2018. Improving language understanding by generative pre-training.

Alec Radford, Jeffrey Wu, Rewon Child, David Luan, Dario Amodei, and Ilya Sutskever. 2019. Language models are unsupervised multitask learners.

Marc'Aurelio Ranzato, Sumit Chopra, Michael Auli, and Wojciech Zaremba. 2016. Sequence level training with recurrent neural networks. In *4th International Conference on Learning Representations, ICLR 2016, San Juan, Puerto Rico, May 2-4, 2016, Conference Track Proceedings*.

Alexander M. Rush, Sumit Chopra, and Jason Weston. 2015. A neural attention model for abstractive sentence summarization. In *Proceedings of the 2015 Conference on Empirical Methods in Natural Language Processing*, pages 379–389, Lisbon, Portugal. Association for Computational Linguistics.

Evan Sandhaus. 2008. The new york times annotated corpus.

Abigail See, Peter J. Liu, and Christopher D. Manning. 2017. Get to the point: Summarization with pointer-generator networks. In *Proceedings of the 55th Annual Meeting of the Association for Computational Linguistics (Volume 1: Long Papers)*, pages 1073–1083, Vancouver, Canada. Association for Computational Linguistics.

Jiaxin Shi, Chen Liang, Lei Hou, Juanzi Li, Zhiyuan Liu, and Hanwang Zhang. 2019. Deepchannel: Salience estimation by contrastive learning for extractive document summarization. In *Proceedings of the AAAI Conference on Artificial Intelligence*, volume 33, pages 6999–7006.

Richard S Sutton, Andrew G Barto, et al. 1998. *Introduction to reinforcement learning*, volume 2. MIT press Cambridge.

Ashish Vaswani, Noam Shazeer, Niki Parmar, Jakob Uszkoreit, Llion Jones, Aidan N Gomez, Łukasz Kaiser, and Illia Polosukhin. 2017. Attention is all you need. In *Advances in neural information processing systems*, pages 5998–6008.

Oriol Vinyals, Meire Fortunato, and Navdeep Jaitly. 2015. Pointer networks. In *Advances in Neural Information Processing Systems*, pages 2692–2700.

Alex Wang and Kyunghyun Cho. 2019. BERT has a mouth, and it must speak: BERT as a Markov random field language model. In *Proceedings of the Workshop on Methods for Optimizing and Evaluating Neural Language Generation*, pages 30–36, Minneapolis, Minnesota. Association for Computational Linguistics.

Jiacheng Xu and Greg Durrett. 2019. Neural extractive text summarization with syntactic compression. *arXiv preprint arXiv:1902.00863*.

Zhilin Yang, Zihang Dai, Yiming Yang, Jaime Carbonell, Ruslan Salakhutdinov, and Quoc V Le. 2019. Xlnet: Generalized autoregressive pretraining for language understanding. *arXiv preprint arXiv:1906.08237*.

Wenyuan Zeng, Wenjie Luo, Sanja Fidler, and Raquel Urtasun. 2016. Efficient summarization with read-again and copy mechanism. *arXiv preprint arXiv:1611.03382*.

Haoyu Zhang, Yeyun Gong, Yu Yan, Nan Duan, Jianjun Xu, Ji Wang, Ming Gong, and Ming Zhou. 2019a. Pretraining-based natural language generation for text summarization. *arXiv preprint arXiv:1902.09243*.

Tianyi Zhang, Varsha Kishore, Felix Wu, Kilian Q Weinberger, and Yoav Artzi. 2019b. Bertscore: Evaluating text generation with bert. *arXiv preprint arXiv:1904.09675*.

Xingxing Zhang, Furu Wei, and Ming Zhou. 2019c. HIBERT: Document level pre-training of hierarchical bidirectional transformers for document summarization. In *Proceedings of the 57th Annual Meeting of the Association for Computational Linguistics*, pages 5059–5069, Florence, Italy. Association for Computational Linguistics.

Abstractive Timeline Summarization

Julius Steen and **Katja Markert**
Department of Computational Linguistics
Heidelberg University
69120 Heidelberg, Germany
`(steen|markert)@cl.uni-heidelberg.de`

Abstract

Timeline summarization (TLS) automatically identifies key dates of major events and provides short descriptions of what happened on these dates. Previous approaches to TLS have focused on extractive methods. In contrast, we suggest an abstractive timeline summarization system. Our system is entirely unsupervised, which makes it especially suited to TLS where there are very few gold summaries available for training of supervised systems. In addition, we present the first abstractive oracle experiments for TLS. Our system outperforms extractive competitors in terms of ROUGE when the number of input documents is high and the output requires strong compression. In these cases, our oracle experiments confirm that our approach also has a higher upper bound for ROUGE scores than extractive methods. A study with human judges shows that our abstractive system also produces output that is easy to read and understand.

1 Introduction

Many newsworthy events are not isolated incidents but part of long-lasting developments. For example, the events of the Syrian civil war in 2019 are intrinsically linked to events that happened during the beginning of that war in 2011. As the amount of reporting grows, it can be difficult to keep track of important events that may have happened a long time ago. Timeline summarization (TLS) alleviates this problem by providing users with automatically generated timelines that identify key dates in a larger development along with short summaries of the events on these dates. Table 1 shows an example of a timeline.

Prior TLS systems are *extractive*, i.e. they identify important sentences in a corpus and copy them directly to the timeline (Nguyen et al., 2014; Chieu and Lee, 2004; Yan et al., 2011b,a; Wang

2011-03-15
First protests after calls on Facebook for a "Day of Dignity."
2011-08-18
US President Barack Obama and his allies urge Assad to quit. Western and Arab states later impose sanctions on his regime.
2011-10-02
Creation of the opposition Syrian National Council SNC.

Table 1: Beginning of an example timeline about the Syrian civil war. (Source: Crisis dataset (Tran et al., 2015))

et al., 2016; Tran et al., 2015, 2013b,a; Martschat and Markert, 2018). However, TLS aggregates information from input corpora that are orders of magnitude larger than for traditional multi-document summarization (MDS) tasks. In addition, documents typically come from many different sources. In this setting, it might be advantageous to generate *abstractive* summaries that combine information from different sentences. While the state of the art in abstractive summarization is achieved by neural networks (Celikyilmaz et al., 2018), these systems require many document/gold summary pairs for training. TLS datasets, on the other hand, have many input documents, but only contain very few gold-standard timelines (between 19 and 22) (Tran et al., 2015, 2013b). Thus, very few input/gold timeline pairs are available for training.

We therefore introduce an *unsupervised abstractive TLS system* that is inspired by the abstractive MDS system in Banerjee et al. (2015). We make the following contributions:

1. We introduce the first abstractive system for TLS and show that it outperforms current ex-

tractive TLS systems such as Martschat and Markert (2018) when the input corpora are large with low compression rate.[1]

2. We show that our system delivers significantly better performance than an abstractive neural model not adapted for TLS.

3. We conduct the first abstractive oracle experiments for TLS. Our abstractive approach improves the ROUGE upper bound on large corpora with low compression rate.

A human evaluation confirms that our system outputs readable sentences. Our system does not need any supervision and only requires lightweight preprocessing. This makes it easy to adapt to other languages. The source code for our system is available online.[2]

2 Task

2.1 Definition

We follow the formalization of TLS of Martschat and Markert (2018). Given a collection of news documents D about the topic for the timeline (such as the *Syrian civil war*), we seek to generate a timeline that summarizes the most important events related to the topic in D. The timeline is a sequence of dates $d_1, \ldots d_n$ and their associated daily summaries $v_1, \ldots v_n$. As in most prior work, we require that $d_1, \ldots d_n$ refer to a specific day.

We constrain the maximum number of dates that may be included in the timeline, the maximum number of sentences or tokens per daily summary, and the time span the timeline is supposed to cover. We discuss how we set these constraints in Section 4.2.

2.2 Differences to MDS

While both TLS and Multi-Document Summarization (MDS) generate summaries from multiple input documents, there are substantial differences between the two tasks. Specifically, Martschat and Markert (2018) cite the following differences:

1. MDS does not have a temporal dimension.

2. Typical MDS datasets do not require systems to summarize multiple events instead focusing on non-event topics or singular events.

---

[1]In summarization, a low compression rate means that a long input must be condensed to a short summary.

[2]`github.com/julmaxi/`
`Abstractive-Timeline-Summarization`

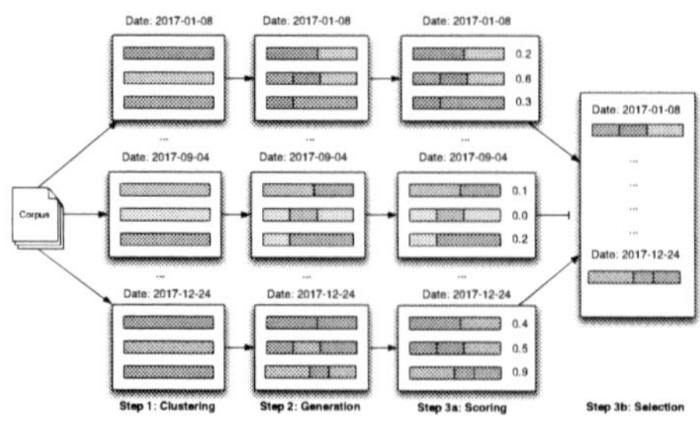

Figure 1: A graphical overview of our system. We can see that not all clusters are included in the timeline.

Even where MDS systems are evaluated on corpora with multiple events, evaluation does not consider the temporal dimension.

3. TLS corpora are larger than MDS corpora with lower compression rates, making content selection and scalability more important.

3 Architecture

We generate timelines in a three step process, outlined in Figure 1. We first cluster sentences that are likely to describe the same event. We then use Multi-Sentence-Compression (MSC) to generate candidate sentences to summarize each cluster. Finally, we score the candidates and select the best ones up to a length limit. Each of our steps is completely unsupervised, which allows us to sidestep the lack of training data in TLS and also makes our system readily adaptable to different datasets.

3.1 Clustering

We need to cluster sentences that describe the same event (such as the formation of the Syrian national council in Table 1) so that the MSC system can generate concise summaries from the resulting clusters. We use Affinity Propagation (AP) clustering (Frey and Dueck, 2007) for this purpose. AP is able to automatically determine the appropriate number of clusters for a dataset. This is advantageous, as different inputs contain different numbers of events. By choosing the number of clusters dynamically, our system can adapt to that without supervision.

AP selects a set of exemplars from the input data points, which can be understood as the centers of the clusters. Non-exemplar points select one of the exemplars to form a cluster with. The algorithm operates over an affinity matrix A, where A_{ij} expresses the appropriateness of item i picking item j as an exemplar. The diagonal of the matrix A, the so-called *preference values*, determines how suitable an item is to become an exemplar and thus regulates the number of exemplars.

We construct A using TF-IDF vector cosine similarity between the input sentences, which has been shown to be a useful similarity metric for TLS (Martschat and Markert, 2018; Chieu and Lee, 2004). However, sentences in the same cluster should not only be similar but also describe the same dates. To determine which date a sentence refers to, we make the following assumptions:

- Every sentence can refer to the document creation time (DCT).

- Sentences with one or more time expressions can refer either to one of the dates in the expressions or to the DCT

- Time expressions that refer to a range of days, such as a month, may refer to any date within that range.

The set of possible references for a sentence s is called $dates(s)$. A date reference d_1 *contains* another reference d_2 if one of the following holds:

1. d_1, d_2 refer to the same exact day.

2. d_1 refers to a range of dates which contains d_2, and d_2 is an exact date.

A sentence s_2 may select a sentence s_1 as an exemplar if there is a $d_1 \in dates(s_1)$ and a $d_2 \in dates(s_2)$ so that d_2 contains d_1. We set $A_{ij} = \cos(\vec{s_i}, \vec{s_j})$, if s_i may select s_j, and $A_{ij} = -\infty$ otherwise. Preference values are the median of incoming similarities (Frey and Dueck, 2007).

This procedure can still form "incorrect" clusters. If an exemplar sentence contains two or more incompatible date references d_1, d_2, the resulting cluster can contain sentences tagged with only d_1 or only d_2. However, this is an infrequent problem as sentences need to be similar to be clustered.

To determine the date of the event a cluster C describes, we let

$$date(C) = \underset{d \in \bigcup_{s \in C}\{dates(s) | d \text{ exact}\}}{\arg\max} cnt(C, d) \quad (1)$$

where $cnt(C, d)$ is the frequency of d being mentioned as a time expression in the sentences in C.

3.2 Sentence Generation

Following Banerjee et al. (2015), we use the unsupervised, low-cost MSC-system by Filippova (2010) to generate summary candidates for each cluster.

Given the sentence cluster C, the algorithm constructs a word-adjacency graph. The nodes are POS-tagged tokens and directed edges indicate adjacency of these tokens in one of the sentences. Occurrences of the same content word in different sentences are mapped to the same node. Given an edge e_{ij}, its weight $w(e_{ij})$ is:

$$w(e_{ij}) = \frac{freq(i) + freq(j)}{freq(i) * freq(j) * \sum_{s \in C} diff(s, i, j)} \quad (2)$$

where $freq(i)$ is the number of tokens that have been mapped to node i and $diff(s, i, j)$ indicates whether the words that were mapped to the nodes i, j in the sentence s appear close together. This is defined in terms of the position $pos(s, i)$ of a token i in the sentence s:

$$diff(s, i, j) = \max(0, (pos(s, j) - pos(s, i))^{-1}) \quad (3)$$

We generate new sentences from this graph by finding paths from the sentence start node to the sentence end node. We use the shortest path algorithm of Yen (1971) as implemented in the networkx-library (Hagberg et al., 2008) to generate up to 2500 candidate summary sentences per cluster. Following Filippova (2010), we filter out sentences that do not contain a verb or are shorter than eight tokens. We also include the original sentences in the selection candidates. Each candidate g is assigned the date of the cluster it was generated from: $date(g) := date(cluster(g))$.

To prevent ungrammatical or spurious sentence merges, we introduce additional filtering based on dependency parses. Specifically, we only accept a path P through the word-adjacency graph if for every node $i \in P$ at least one of the following holds:

1. i is a stopword node

2. At least one token mapped to i is the root node in its dependency tree

3. The head of at least one token mapped to i is contained in the path

Consider the following two input sentences:

An armed attack on a government building was met with international shock .

The people responsible for the attack have yet to be determined.

Without the constraint, it is valid to generate *An armed attack have yet to be determined*. The constraint prevents this as none of the heads of *attack* (i.e. *met* and *for*) are in the path.

3.3 Sentence Scoring and Selection

Given the set of generated sentences, we wish to find sentences that are well-formed and informative about important dates and events. We encode these aspects into multiple scoring functions.

3.3.1 Linguistic Quality

To encourage a readable output, we compute a linguistic quality score for each candidate sentence g by using the average probability of the tokens according to a 3-gram language model (Banerjee et al., 2015). We use the KenLM library (Heafield, 2011) with a pretrained model[3]. We compute the LM-score f_{LM} as follows:

$$f_{LM}(g) = \frac{1}{1 - \sum_{w_i \in g} \log(p(w_i|w_{i-1:i-3}))/|g|} \quad (4)$$

Additionally, we include information from the MSC system by preferring sentences which were generated from shorter paths. We let $f_{path}(g) = (1 + w(g))^{-1}$ where $w(g)$ is the length of the weighted path that generated candidate g.

3.3.2 Date Importance

We determine the importance $dimp(d)$ of a date d by counting how often it is mentioned in the input (Martschat and Markert, 2018). The score f_{date} of a sentence g is $f_{date}(g) = dimp(date(g))$.

3.3.3 Informativeness

We construct a keyword-based scoring function using TextRank (Mihalcea and Tarau, 2004) to efficiently score the importance of our candidates. TextRank scores keywords by constructing an undirected graph of content words where words are connected if they appear near each other. A score is computed for each node similarly to the PageRank algorithm (Page et al., 1999) using the

---

[3] www.keithv.com/software/giga/lm_giga_20k_nvp_3gram.zip

following iterative formula:

$$TR^{(t+1)}(w_i) = (1-\alpha) + \alpha \cdot \sum_{w_j \in adj(w_i)} \frac{TR^{(t)}(w_j)}{|adj(w_j)|} \quad (5)$$

where $adj(w_i)$ is the set of nodes neighbouring w_i and $\alpha = 0.85$ is the dampening factor.

Let D_d be the set of all sentences s in the input corpus D whose cluster $cluster(s)$ was assigned the date d as per Equation 1. We compute one TextRank vector TR_d for each date d by running TextRank over all sentences in D_d. To make scores comparable across different D_d, we rescale the scores in TR_d to a 0 to 1 range. The TextRank-score $f_{TR}(g)$ for a candidate g is then defined as the sum of the scores of its tokens.

We also hypothesize that larger clusters are associated with more important events. We thus use the cluster size as a scoring function: $f_{cluster}(g) = \frac{|cluster(g)|}{\max_{C \in \hat{C}} |C|}$ where $\hat{C}$ is the set of all clusters.

3.3.4 Selection

We determine the final score of each candidate g as the product of the scoring functions:

$$score(g) = \prod_{f \in F} f(g) \quad (6)$$

where F is the set of scoring functions, i.e. $F = \{f_{path}, f_{LM}, f_{TR}, f_{date}, f_{cluster}\}$.

We select sentences greedily starting with the highest scoring ones as long as selecting them does not break any constraints. To reduce redundancy, we select at most one candidate from each cluster (Banerjee et al., 2015) and skip sentences with a cosine similarity of more than 0.5 to a previously selected sentence.

4 Evaluation

4.1 Data

We evaluate on the only two publicly available TLS datasets: Crisis (Tran et al., 2015) and Timeline 17 (TL17) (Tran et al., 2013b). Both contain human written timelines about topics such as civil wars or the BP oil disaster, collected from major news outlets. Each topic also has a set of related news articles scraped from the web (see Table 2).

We also report the median compression rate and the median spread of the datasets. The compression rate is the ratio of sentences in a timeline to the number of input sentences. The spread is the

Corp.	#Tops	#TLs	#Sen/Top.	Comp.	Spr.
TL17	13	19	27,222	0.0019	0.279
Crisis	4	22	150,429	0.0002	0.081

Table 2: Dataset statistics, including number of topics, timelines and the average number of sentences to be summarized for each topic. We also report the median compression and spread of the timelines.

ratio of dates with summaries in the timeline to the number of dates in the timeline span. Low compression rate and spread are typically indicative of a more difficult TLS instance (Martschat and Markert, 2018). We find that the datasets have very different characteristics, with Crisis having lower compression rate and spread.

4.1.1 Corpus Cleaning and Preporcessing

We found that some of the news articles to be summarised in both datasets contained full or partial gold timelines. This might cause TLS systems to inadvertently "cheat" by using the leaked gold timelines. We have manually removed 19 such documents in TL17 and 28 in Crisis.[4]

We preprocess all corpora with Stanford CoreNLP (Manning et al., 2014) and use Heideltime (Strötgen and Gertz, 2013) for resolving time expressions. Unlike several other TLS systems (Martschat and Markert, 2018; Chieu and Lee, 2004), we do not filter sentences with topic-specific keywords (e.g. *war* or *Syria*) to be less dependent on additional human input.[5]

4.2 Experimental Setup and Constraints

Like Martschat and Markert (2018), we generate one timeline per reference. We limit the number of dates to that in the reference, while the number of sentences per summary is set to the average number of sentences per summary in the reference.

As abstractive systems generate new text, they could exploit sentence limits by generating very long sentences. We control for this by limiting the number of tokens instead in one algorithm variation. We estimate the maximum number of tokens in the same way as for the sentence constraint.

4.3 Evaluation Metrics

Summarization is usually evaluated with ROUGE (Lin, 2004). This, however, ignores the temporal

dimension of TLS. We thus use the two TLS measures proposed by Martschat and Markert (2017):

agree Compute ROUGE only between daily summaries which have the same dates.

align Align summaries in the output with those in the reference based on similarity and the distance between their dates, then compute the ROUGE score between aligned summaries. Distant alignments are punished.

We also report ROUGE *concat*, where we concatenate all entries in gold and system timeline and compute ROUGE between the results discarding all date information. While this measure is suboptimal for TLS (Martschat and Markert, 2017), it has been previously used as an evaluation measure (Yan et al., 2011b,a; Wang et al., 2016). We report the F1 score for all ROUGE metrics. To assess how well the systems are at date selection, we compute the F1 score between the dates that have a summary in the gold timeline and in the system timeline. Finally, we report the *copy rate* as the proportion of sentences copied directly from the corpus into the summary. We use an approximate randomization test (Noreen, 1989) to check statistical significance and the Bonferroni correction to correct for comparing on two datasets (Dror et al., 2018).

4.4 Oracle Summaries

One advantage of abstractive summarization is its potential to increase the maximum attainable scores by forming more succinct sentences. We investigate this potential with an oracle to establish an upper bound on summary scores, following similar work for generic summarization (Hirao et al., 2017). As an oracle over all summaries is intractable, we approximate it by replacing the scoring function (Equation 6) with an oracle that predicts the ROUGE-1-agree F1-score of sentences. The rest of our pipeline remains unchanged.

For the extractive oracle, we greedily select from all sentences in the input documents instead. The date of a sentence is the first exact time expression that appears in the sentence, or its DCT if there is none (Chieu and Lee, 2004).

4.5 Comparison Systems

4.5.1 Extractive Systems

We compare our full system with three extractive comparison systems. The first two are from a col-

---

[4] The corresponding document ids can be found at `www.cl.uni-heidelberg.de/~steen/tls/docids.txt`.

[5] However, we do let the competitor systems use filtering.

lection of TLS systems created by Martschat and Markert (2018).[6]

Chieu is a reimplementation of Chieu and Lee (2004), which uses the average cosine similarity of a sentence in a time-window around its date to determine importance and greedy selection. This system is often seen as a baseline for TLS systems (Martschat and Markert, 2018; Tran et al., 2015).

Submod is the state-of-the-art submodular system in Martschat and Markert (2018). Additionally, we have created a version of *Submod* with a token constraint. The same is not possible for *Chieu*, as it always selects one sentence per date.

Extractive is an extractive version of our system. It uses f_{TR} and f_{date} to score sentences. Dates are determined as for the extractive oracle

4.5.2 Neural Baseline

As an abstractive comparison, we use the popular Pointer Generator (See et al., 2017) (*Neural*). It was trained on the CCN/Daily Mail single document summarization corpus (Hermann et al., 2015). We adapt it to TLS as follows:

1. We select the dates for the timeline by ranking them by their frequency $dimp(d)$.

2. For each selected date d, we collect all sentences S_d from the corpus that refer to d.

3. For each collection S_d, we construct a pseudo document for the summarizer. Following Zhang et al. (2018) we use the LexRank score (Erkan and Radev, 2004) to rank the sentences in S_d. We add the top sentences to the document until we reach the maximum input size for the pointer generator (400 tokens).[7]

During our experiments, we found that the self-stopping nature of the pointer generator causes it to generate daily summaries that exceed the token length constraint described in Section 4.2 in 83% of daily summaries. To see if this disadvantages the pointer generator, we tried applying this token constraint to its output. However, this results in lower scores, so we only report results without length constraint.

---

[6]github.com/smartschat/tilse

[7]In an alternative setup, we tried selecting the centroid document for each date and then summarize it. This performs comparably or worse, depending on the corpus.

5 Results

5.1 Oracle Results

While both the extractive and the abstractive oracle perform equally on TL17, the abstractive oracle outperforms the extractive oracle significantly on Crisis. The abstractive copy rate on TL17 is also much higher than on Crisis. (73.7% vs 38.3% for sentence constraints). We hypothesize that this is related to the lower compression rate and greater size of Crisis (see Table 2). Abstractive TLS can only achieve its full potential when a variety of different texts needs to be compressed to short summaries. We investigate this in Section 5.5.

5.2 System Results

5.2.1 Extractive Systems

Our system outperforms *Extractive*, demonstrating the importance of our abstractive components. While *Chieu* performs better than our system in ROUGE-1 concat on Crisis, it is much worse in all date-sensitive measures and on TL17.

When comparing *Submod* and our abstractive system, we see behaviour similar to the oracles. On TL17, *Submod* achieves higher scores, though the differences are mostly not significant. On Crisis, however, we outperform *Submod* across all date-sensitive metrics and almost double the score in ROUGE-2 for agree and align. All improvements are significant except for ROUGE-1 align.

5.2.2 Neural

Neural performs slightly better than our system on the ROUGE-1 concat metric on Crisis, but performs significantly worse than us on almost all other content measures. This underlines the importance of TLS specific approaches.

5.2.3 Effect of Length Constraints

The token constraint has a small positive influence on our system while resulting in lower results for *Submod*. This shows that our system does not unfairly exploit the sentence constraint.

5.3 Example Timeline

Table 4 shows an example timeline generated by our system. Most entries describe events that are directly relevant to the civil war, though only two appear in the corresponding reference timeline. This demonstrates the difficulty of content selection in TLS, where even human timelines on the

	Date	Concat F1		Agree F1		Align F1		Copy
	F1	R1	R2	R1	R2	R1	R2	Rate
Timeline 17								
Chieu	0.195	0.223	0.049	0.024	0.008	0.046	0.012	1.000
Neural	0.518	0.320	0.055	0.061	0.012	0.069	0.013	0.000
Submod (s)	**0.543**[3]	0.364	**0.087**	**0.092**[3]	**0.021**	**0.103**[3]	**0.024**	1.000
Extr. (s)	0.514	0.294	0.063	0.071	0.018	0.081	0.020	1.000
Abstractive (s)	0.512[1]	0.349[12*]	0.081[12*]	0.075[12]	0.020[12]	0.087[12]	0.022[2]	0.446
Extr. Oracle (s)	*0.893***	0.501	0.180	0.317	0.143	0.320	0.144	1.000
Abs. Oracle (s)	0.883	0.504	0.179	0.322	0.142	0.324	0.142	0.729
Submod (t)	0.530	0.353	0.087	0.088	0.020	0.100	0.022	1.000
Extr. (t)	0.514	0.321	0.066	0.071	0.018	0.081	0.020	1.000
Abstractive (t)	0.512[a]	**0.366**[ab*]	0.084[ab*]	0.081[ab]	**0.021**[a]	0.093[ab*]	**0.024**[b]	0.424
Ext. Oracle (t)	0.891	0.511	*0.183*	0.317	0.143	0.320	0.144	1.000
Abs. Oracle (t)	0.885	*0.513*	*0.183*	*0.325***	*0.147*	*0.327***	*0.147*	0.704
Crisis								
Chieu	0.146	**0.348**	0.065	0.026	0.006	0.047	0.010	1.000
Neural	0.279	0.343	0.047	0.049	0.008	0.064	0.010	0.000
Submod (s)	0.288	0.333	**0.071**	0.056	0.012	0.076	0.015	1.000
Extr. (s)	0.273	0.225	0.046	0.037	0.009	0.052	0.011	1.000
Abstractive (s)	**0.297**[1]	0.324*	0.070[2*]	0.066[12*]	0.024[123*]	0.080[1*]	0.026[12*]	0.382
Extr. Oracle (s)	0.934	0.509	0.167	0.359	0.142	0.359	0.142	1.000
Abs. Oracle (s)	*0.936*	*0.530***	*0.190***	*0.396***	*0.168***	*0.397***	*0.168***	0.475
Submod (t)	0.264	0.331	0.065	0.053	0.012	0.072	0.015	1.000
Extr. (t)	0.273	0.229	0.045	0.036	0.009	0.051	0.011	1.000
Abstractive (t)	**0.297**[a]	0.333*	**0.071**[b*]	**0.069**[abc*]	**0.025**[abc*]	**0.082**[ab*]	**0.027**[abc*]	0.331
Ext. Oracle (t)	0.933	0.503	0.164	0.352	0.139	0.353	0.139	1.000
Abs. Oracle (t)	*0.936*	*0.530***	*0.186***	*0.386***	*0.163***	*0.387***	*0.163***	0.472

Table 3: Result of our system, the oracles, and comparison systems. (s) and (t) indicate sentence or token constraint where applicable. * indicates statistically significant difference between abstractive and extractive oracle and our abstractive system and *Extractive* respectively. [123] indicate significant differences between our system with sentence constraint and *Chieu, Neural,* and *Submod* with sentence constraint respectively. [abc] indicate the same for the token constraint ($p < 0.05$). Bold entries indicate best non-oracle results, italic ones best oracle results.

same topic can vary widely (Martschat and Markert, 2018; Tran et al., 2013b).

Most sentences have been edited by the MSC algorithm. We can observe some minor ungrammaticalities resulting from this process, like the phrase "on march" in the first daily summary. The timeline also exhibits some redundancy as the statement about the Red Cross is repeated twice.

5.4 Ablation Experiments

To study the effects of our scoring functions, we conduct an ablation study where we remove one scoring function at a time and rerun our system. The results can be found in Table 5.[8] We find all features contribute to ROUGE scores. Removing f_{TR} and f_{path} has a small negative effect on date F1 but a big effect on ROUGE, while f_{date} mostly affects date F1. It appears that content and date

selection can to some extent be improved independently even with date-sensitive metrics. This might warrant future investigation.

5.5 Utility analysis

Our experiments show that the usefulness of our system is corpus-dependent. We investigate three factors that might explain this difference in performance: The number of input sentences, the compression rate, and the spread (see Section 4.1).

We compute the Spearman-correlation of all three factors with the difference in ROUGE-2-align F1 score between the two oracles as well as between our system and *Submod*. The result can be found in Table 6. For the oracles, we observe a strong negative correlation with compression (plus a weaker one with spread) and a positive one with the number of sentences. With more material the MSC system can generate more new sentences. In the same vein, a lower compression rate makes fusing sentences more useful. The difference be-

---

[8]To preserve space, we focus on the Crisis dataset with sentence constraint. Results are similar on TL17, but removing features there has generally a smaller effect.

2011-03-15
the conflict erupted on march 2011 when protesters inspired by arab world uprisings took to the streets to call for democratic change.
2012-02-04
russia and china vetoed a draft resolution that backed an arab plan to facilitate political transition in syria.
2012-06-13
talk of civil war in syria is not consistent with reality... what is happening in syria is a war against armed groups that choose terrorism, "syrian state news agency sana quoted a foreign ministry statement as saying.
2012-07-15
red cross said sunday it now considers the conflict a civil war, meaning international humanitarian law applies throughout the country.
2012-07-16
the international committee of the red cross declared the conflict a civil war.
2012-07-18
on july blast at the syrian national security building in damascus during a high - level government crisis meeting killed four top regime officials, including the defense minister.

Table 4: Beginning of the timeline generated by our abstractive system with sentence constraint for the timeline in Table 1. Red color indicates sentences that were copied directly from the input corpus. Blue color indicates events which can also be found in the reference timeline.

Feat.	Date	R1	R2
$-f_{date}$	-0.049	-0.007*	-0.002
$-f_{TR}$	+0.004	-0.024*	-0.008
$-f_{path}$	+0.002	-0.028*	-0.015*
$-f_{cluster}$	-0.004	-0.012*	-0.010*

Table 5: Ablation results on Crisis, showing changes of ROUGE align and date selection F1. * indicates significant differences to the full model ($p < 0.05$).

Comparison	♯sents	Compr.	Spread
Abs. Or. - Ext. Or.	0.48	-0.61	-0.31
Abs. - Submod	0.45	-0.41	-0.24

Table 6: Spearman correlation of the score difference between systems and timeline properties.

tween our system and *Submod* exhibits similar, although less extreme behaviour. These results, together with the difference in size and compression rate between the datasets observed in Table 2, explain why our system outperforms the state of the art only on the more compressive Crisis dataset.

6 Readability Analysis

We assess the readability of the summaries generated by our abstractive system, the abstractive oracle (both with sentence constraint) and *Neural*.

We sampled 100 daily summaries for each system and from the gold summaries. We ensured that an approximately equal number of summaries was sampled from each generated timeline. Additionally, we sampled another 100 gold summaries and randomly deleted 25% of their tokens to simulate a compressive system without regard for linguistic quality. We call these summaries *Delete25*. We asked annotators from Amazon Mechanical Turk[9] to rate how well they are able to understand the summaries on a scale from 1 (completely understandable) to 5 (easily understood). The descriptions of the rating scale presented to the workers can be seen in Table 7. Items were grouped in randomly ordered batches, so that each batch had one summary from each system.

Table 8 shows readability results. Unsurprisingly, Gold receives the highest score. Delete25 receives an unexpectedly high score, though notably lower than other systems. We find many sentences remain understandable even after deletions as in the following example: *Saif al-islam has been detained several bodyguards near the town obari by fighters in town of zintan, the justice minister and other officials said. He not wounded.*

Among the systems, ours receives the highest score. The oracle performs slightly worse. We speculate that this is due to the fact that the oracle does not include language model information. In both cases, over 80% of the sentences are easily understood (4 or 5). We also outperform *Neural*. This might be a result of its higher abstractiveness, which allows more errors.

7 Related Work

7.1 TLS

To the best of our knowledge, all systems proposed specifically for TLS have been extractive

---

[9]mturk.com

5	I can understand the text without problems. It does not have any grammaticality or fluency issues.
4	The text has some minor grammaticality or fluency issues but I can still understand it without problems.
3	I can understand the entire text, but it is difficult to do so.
2	I can understand the text only partially.
1	I can not understand the text at all.

Table 7: Rating scale for the readability task.

System	Avg.	#5	#4	#3	#2	#1
Neural	4.02	102	131	41	23	3
Abs. Or.	4.27	142	112	34	10	2
Abs.	4.40	165	103	21	9	2
Delete25	3.43	38	117	90	46	9
Gold	4.52	187	89	17	6	1

Table 8: Results of the readability evaluation. We also report the number of times each category was chosen.

(Nguyen et al., 2014; Chieu and Lee, 2004; Yan et al., 2011b,a; Wang et al., 2016; Tran et al., 2015, 2013b,a; Martschat and Markert, 2018). Several of these evaluate on corpora that are not publicly available (Chieu and Lee, 2004; Yan et al., 2011a,b) so that we cannot compare to their results. Since the advent of TL17 and Crisis, several evaluations have been performed on these datasets (Tran et al., 2015, 2013b,a; Martschat and Markert, 2018; Wang et al., 2016), but only Martschat and Markert (2018) evaluate with appropriate TLS measures. As code and original output are mostly unavailable, it is difficult to compare to them.

7.2 TLS-related Tasks

TLS is related to the TREC real-time summarization task (Lin et al., 2016). Unlike TLS, this task focuses on detecting novel information in a stream of social media posts in real time. TLS, on the other hand, assumes an offline setting and generates timelines for much longer timespans, focusing on the challenges of date selection and dating of information, which are not present in TREC.

There are also several papers that produce timelines by generating a summary for every single date in a given timespan, thus timeline generation without date selection (Wang et al., 2015; Allan et al., 2001). In these cases, the overall compression rate is not as low as for our setting and not comparable to the human timelines in our corpora.

TLS is also related to Task 4 in SEMEVAL 2015 (Minard et al., 2015). In this task, systems need to extract all events a query entity participates in. Unlike TLS the output is not a textual summary but a complete collection of the events in the input. Barros et al. (2019) have proposed narrative abstractive timeline summarization (NATSUM) in which they generate abstractive textual descriptions for the events in the SEMEVAL dataset. However, their work is markedly different from TLS in that "NATSUM [...] aims to generate narrative summaries and not timelines" (Barros et al., 2019, page 15). As a consequence, they do not perform any date selection and do not evaluate with appropriate date-sensitive metrics.

7.3 Generic Summarization

We have already described the differences between TLS and MDS and the limited direct applicability of MDS systems to TLS in Section 2.2. However, our methodology is inspired by the MDS system of Banerjee et al. (2015). We made major adaptations to this system for TLS by (i) using AP clustering to cluster sentences in a date-sensitive way that dynamically adapts to the corpus size and (ii) augmenting sentence scoring and selection to the needs of TLS. Our system is also related to neural abstractive summarization (See et al., 2017; Gehrmann et al., 2018; Cohan et al., 2018; Paulus et al., 2018). However, these methods require large training corpora unavailable for TLS.

8 Conclusion

We have presented a system for abstractive TLS which outperforms the state-of-the-art extractive TLS system when corpora are large and need substantial compression. Our analysis reveals a correlation between the difficulty of a TLS instance (as measured by compression and spread) and the advantage of an abstractive over a purely extractive approach.

Our system requires no supervision, which makes it well suited for TLS where the low number of available timelines makes training supervised systems difficult. We also require only lightweight annotations on the input, which allows for easy adaption to other settings and languages.

References

James Allan, Rahul Gupta, and Vikas Khandelwal. 2001. Temporal summaries of new topics. In *Proceedings of the 24th Annual International ACM SIGIR Conference on Research and Development in Information Retrieval*, SIGIR '01, pages 10–18, New York, NY, USA. ACM.

Siddhartha Banerjee, Prasenjit Mitra, and Kazunari Sugiyama. 2015. Multi-document abstractive summarization using ilp based multi-sentence compression. In *Proceedings of the 24th International Conference on Artificial Intelligence*, IJCAI'15, pages 1208–1214. AAAI Press.

Cristina Barros, Elena Lloret, Estela Saquete, and Borja Navarro-Colorado. 2019. Natsum: Narrative abstractive summarization through cross-document timeline generation. *Information Processing & Management*.

Asli Celikyilmaz, Antoine Bosselut, Xiaodong He, and Yejin Choi. 2018. Deep communicating agents for abstractive summarization. In *Proceedings of the 2018 Conference of the North American Chapter of the Association for Computational Linguistics: Human Language Technologies, Volume 1 (Long Papers)*, pages 1662–1675. Association for Computational Linguistics.

Hai Leong Chieu and Yoong Keok Lee. 2004. Query based event extraction along a timeline. In *Proceedings of the 27th annual international ACM SIGIR conference on Research and development in information retrieval*, pages 425–432. ACM.

Arman Cohan, Franck Dernoncourt, Doo Soon Kim, Trung Bui, Seokhwan Kim, Walter Chang, and Nazli Goharian. 2018. A discourse-aware attention model for abstractive summarization of long documents. In *Proceedings of the 2018 Conference of the North American Chapter of the Association for Computational Linguistics: Human Language Technologies, Volume 2 (Short Papers)*, pages 615–621. Association for Computational Linguistics.

Rotem Dror, Gili Baumer, Segev Shlomov, and Roi Reichart. 2018. The hitchhiker's guide to testing statistical significance in natural language processing. In *Proceedings of the 56th Annual Meeting of the Association for Computational Linguistics (Volume 1: Long Papers)*, pages 1383–1392, Melbourne, Australia. Association for Computational Linguistics.

Günes Erkan and Dragomir R Radev. 2004. Lexrank: Graph-based lexical centrality as salience in text summarization. *Journal of artificial intelligence research*, 22:457–479.

Katja Filippova. 2010. Multi-sentence compression: Finding shortest paths in word graphs. In *Proceedings of the 23rd International Conference on Computational Linguistics*, COLING '10, pages 322–330, Stroudsburg, PA, USA. Association for Computational Linguistics.

Brendan J. Frey and Delbert Dueck. 2007. Clustering by passing messages between data points. *Science*, 315:972–976.

Sebastian Gehrmann, Yuntian Deng, and Alexander Rush. 2018. Bottom-up abstractive summarization. In *Proceedings of the 2018 Conference on Empirical Methods in Natural Language Processing*, pages 4098–4109. Association for Computational Linguistics.

Aric A. Hagberg, Daniel A. Schult, and Pieter J. Swart. 2008. Exploring network structure, dynamics, and function using NetworkX. In *Proceedings of the 7th Python in Science Conference (SciPy2008)*, pages 11–15, Pasadena, CA USA.

Kenneth Heafield. 2011. Kenlm: Faster and smaller language model queries. In *Proceedings of the Sixth Workshop on Statistical Machine Translation*, WMT '11, pages 187–197, Stroudsburg, PA, USA. Association for Computational Linguistics.

Karl Moritz Hermann, Tomáš Kočiský, Edward Grefenstette, Lasse Espeholt, Will Kay, Mustafa Suleyman, and Phil Blunsom. 2015. Teaching machines to read and comprehend. In *Proceedings of the 28th International Conference on Neural Information Processing Systems - Volume 1*, NIPS'15, pages 1693–1701, Cambridge, MA, USA. MIT Press.

Tsutomu Hirao, Masaaki Nishino, and Masaaki Nagata. 2017. Oracle summaries of compressive summarization. In *Proceedings of the 55th Annual Meeting of the Association for Computational Linguistics (Volume 2: Short Papers)*, pages 275–280. Association for Computational Linguistics.

Chin-Yew Lin. 2004. ROUGE: A package for automatic evaluation of summaries. In *Text Summarization Branches Out: Proceedings of the ACL-04 Workshop*, pages 74–81, Barcelona, Spain. Association for Computational Linguistics.

Jimmy Lin, Adam Roegiest, Luchen Tan, Richard McCreadie, Ellen Voorhees, and Fernando Diaz. 2016. Overview of the trec 2016 real-time summarization track. In *Proceedings of the 25th text retrieval conference, TREC*, volume 16.

Christopher Manning, Mihai Surdeanu, John Bauer, Jenny Finkel, Steven Bethard, and David McClosky. 2014. The stanford corenlp natural language processing toolkit. In *Proceedings of 52nd annual meeting of the association for computational linguistics: system demonstrations*, pages 55–60.

Sebastian Martschat and Katja Markert. 2017. Improving rouge for timeline summarization. In *Proceedings of the 15th Conference of the European Chapter of the Association for Computational Linguistics: Volume 2, Short Papers*, volume 2, pages 285–290.

Sebastian Martschat and Katja Markert. 2018. A temporally sensitive submodularity framework for timeline summarization. In *Proceedings of the 22nd Conference on Computational Natural Language Learning*, pages 230–240. Association for Computational Linguistics.

Rada Mihalcea and Paul Tarau. 2004. TextRank: Bringing order into text. In *Proceedings of EMNLP 2004*, pages 404–411, Barcelona, Spain. Association for Computational Linguistics.

Anne-Lyse Minard, Manuela Speranza, Eneko Agirre, Itziar Aldabe, Marieke van Erp, Bernardo Magnini, German Rigau, and Ruben Urizar. 2015. SemEval-2015 task 4: TimeLine: Cross-document event ordering. In *Proceedings of the 9th International Workshop on Semantic Evaluation (SemEval 2015)*, pages 778–786, Denver, Colorado. Association for Computational Linguistics.

Kiem-Hieu Nguyen, Xavier Tannier, and Véronique Moriceau. 2014. Ranking multidocument event descriptions for building thematic timelines. In *Proceedings of COLING 2014, the 25th International Conference on Computational Linguistics: Technical Papers*, pages 1208–1217, Dublin, Ireland. Dublin City University and Association for Computational Linguistics.

Eric W Noreen. 1989. *Computer-intensive methods for testing hypotheses*. Wiley New York.

Lawrence Page, Sergey Brin, Rajeev Motwani, and Terry Winograd. 1999. The pagerank citation ranking bringing order to the web. Technical report, Stanford InfoLab.

Romain Paulus, Caiming Xiong, and Richard Socher. 2018. A deep reinforced model for abstractive summarization. In *International Conference on Learning Representations*.

Abigail See, Peter J. Liu, and Christopher D. Manning. 2017. Get to the point: Summarization with pointer-generator networks. In *Proceedings of the 55th Annual Meeting of the Association for Computational Linguistics (Volume 1: Long Papers)*, pages 1073–1083. Association for Computational Linguistics.

Jannik Strötgen and Michael Gertz. 2013. Multilingual and cross-domain temporal tagging. *Language Resources and Evaluation*, 47(2):269–298.

Giang Tran, Mohammad Alrifai, and Eelco Herder. 2015. Timeline summarization from relevant headlines. In *European Conference on Information Retrieval*, pages 245–256. Springer.

Giang Binh Tran, Mohammad Alrifai, and Dat Quoc Nguyen. 2013a. Predicting relevant news events for timeline summaries. In *Proceedings of the 22nd International Conference on World Wide Web*, pages 91–92. ACM.

Giang Binh Tran, Tuan A Tran, Nam-Khanh Tran, Mohammad Alrifai, and Nattiya Kanhabua. 2013b. Leveraging learning to rank in an optimization framework for timeline summarization. In *SIGIR 2013 Workshop on Time-aware Information Access (TAIA*.

Lu Wang, Claire Cardie, and Galen Marchetti. 2015. Socially-informed timeline generation for complex events. In *Proceedings of the 2015 Conference of the North American Chapter of the Association for Computational Linguistics: Human Language Technologies*, pages 1055–1065, Denver, Colorado. Association for Computational Linguistics.

William Yang Wang, Yashar Mehdad, Dragomir R. Radev, and Amanda Stent. 2016. A low-rank approximation approach to learning joint embeddings of news stories and images for timeline summarization. In *Proceedings of the 2016 Conference of the North American Chapter of the Association for Computational Linguistics: Human Language Technologies*, pages 58–68, San Diego, California. Association for Computational Linguistics.

Rui Yan, Liang Kong, Congrui Huang, Xiaojun Wan, Xiaoming Li, and Yan Zhang. 2011a. Timeline generation through evolutionary trans-temporal summarization. In *Proceedings of the Conference on Empirical Methods in Natural Language Processing*, EMNLP '11, pages 433–443, Stroudsburg, PA, USA. Association for Computational Linguistics.

Rui Yan, Xiaojun Wan, Jahna Otterbacher, Liang Kong, Xiaoming Li, and Yan Zhang. 2011b. Evolutionary timeline summarization: a balanced optimization framework via iterative substitution. In *Proceedings of the 34th international ACM SIGIR conference on Research and development in Information Retrieval*, pages 745–754. ACM.

Jin Y. Yen. 1971. Finding the k shortest loopless paths in a network. *Management Science*, 17(11):712–716.

Jianmin Zhang, Jiwei Tan, and Xiaojun Wan. 2018. Towards a neural network approach to abstractive multi-document summarization. *CoRR*, abs/1804.09010.

Learning to Create Sentence Semantic Relation Graphs for Multi-Document Summarization

Diego Antognini and **Boi Faltings**
Artificial Intelligence Laboratory
École Polytechnique Fédérale de Lausanne
Lausanne, Switzerland
{diego.antognini, boi.faltings}@epfl.ch

Abstract

Linking facts across documents is a challenging task, as the language used to express the same information in a sentence can vary significantly, which complicates the task of multi-document summarization. Consequently, existing approaches heavily rely on hand-crafted features, which are domain-dependent and hard to craft, or additional annotated data, which is costly to gather. To overcome these limitations, we present a novel method, which makes use of two types of sentence embeddings : universal embeddings, which are trained on a large unrelated corpus, and domain-specific embeddings, which are learned during training. To this end, we develop *SemSentSum*, a fully data-driven model able to leverage both types of sentence embeddings by building a sentence semantic relation graph. *SemSentSum* achieves competitive results on two types of summary, consisting of 665 bytes and 100 words. Unlike other state-of-the-art models, neither hand-crafted features nor additional annotated data are necessary, and the method is easily adaptable for other tasks. To our knowledge, we are the first to use multiple sentence embeddings for the task of multi-document summarization.

1 Introduction

Today's increasing flood of information on the web creates a need for automated multi-document summarization systems that produce high quality summaries. However, producing summaries in a multi-document setting is difficult, as the language used to display the same information in a sentence can vary significantly, making it difficult for summarization models to capture. Given the complexity of the task and the lack of datasets, most researchers use extractive summarization, where the final summary is composed of existing sentences in the input documents. More specifically,

extractive summarization systems output summaries in two steps : via sentence ranking, where an importance score is assigned to each sentence, and via the subsequent sentence selection, where the most appropriate sentence is chosen, by considering 1) their importance and 2) their frequency among all documents. Due to data sparcity, models heavily rely on well-designed features at the word level (Hong and Nenkova, 2014; Cao et al., 2015; Christensen et al., 2013; Yasunaga et al., 2017) or take advantage of other large, manually annotated datasets and then apply transfer learning (Cao et al., 2017). Additionally, most of the time, all sentences in the same collection of documents are processed independently and therefore, their relationships are lost.

In realistic scenarios, features are hard to craft, gathering additional annotated data is costly, and the large variety in expressing the same fact cannot be handled by the use of word-based features only, as is often the case. In this paper, we address these obstacles by proposing to simultaneously leverage two types of sentence embeddings, namely embeddings pre-trained on a large corpus that capture a variety of meanings and domain-specific embeddings learned during training. The former is typically trained on an unrelated corpus composed of high quality texts, allowing to cover additional contexts for each encountered word and sentence. Hereby, we build on the assumption that sentence embeddings capture both the syntactic and semantic content of sentences. We hypothesize that using two types of sentence embeddings, general and domain-specific, is beneficial for the task of multi-document summarization, as the former captures the most common semantic structures from a large, general corpus, while the latter captures the aspects related to the domain.

We present *SemSentSum* (Figure 1), a fully data-driven summarization system, which does not depend on hand-crafted features, nor additional data, and is thus domain-independent. It first makes use of general sentence embedding knowledge to build a sentenc semantic relation graph that captures sentence similarities (Section 2.1). In a second step, it trains genre-specific sentence embeddings related to the domains of the collection of documents, by utilizing a sentence encoder (Section 2.2). Both representations are afterwards merged, by using a graph convolutional network (Kipf and Welling, 2017) (Section 2.3). Then, it employs a linear layer to project high-level hidden features for individual sentences to salience scores (Section 2.4). Finally, it greedily produces relevant and non-redundant summaries by using sentence embeddings to detect similarities between candidate sentences and the current summary (Section 2.6).

The main contributions of this work are as follows :

— We aggregate two types of sentences embeddings using a graph representation. They share different properties and are consequently complementary. The first one is trained on a large unrelated corpus to model general semantics among sentences, whereas the second is domain-specific to the dataset and learned during training. Together, they enable a model to be domain-independent as it can be applied easily on other domains. Moreover, it could be used for other tasks including detecting information cascades, query-focused summarization, keyphrase extraction and information retrieval.

— We devise a competitive multi-document summarization system, which does not need hand-crafted features nor additional annotated data. Moreover, the results are competitive for 665-byte and 100-word summaries. Usually, models are compared in one of the two settings but not both and thus lack comparability.

2 Method

Let C denote a collection of related documents composed of a set of documents $\{D_i|i \in [1, N]\}$ where N is the number of documents. Moreover, each document D_i consists of a set of sentences $\{S_{i,j}|j \in [1, M]\}$, M being the number of sentences in D_i. Given a collection of related documents C, our goal is to produce a summary Sum using a subset of these in the input document ordered in some way, such that $Sum = (S_{i_1,j_1}, S_{i_2,j_2}, ..., S_{i_n,j_m})$.

In this section, we describe how *SemSentSum* estimates the salience score of each sentence and how it selects a subset of these to create the final summary. The architecture of *SemSentSum* is depicted in Figure 1.

In order to perform sentence selection, we first build our sentence semantic relation graph, where each vertex is a sentence and edges capture the semantic similarity among them. At the same time, each sentence is fed into a recurrent neural network, as a sentence encoder, to generate sentence embeddings using the last hidden states. A single-layer graph convolutional neural network is then applied on top, where the sentence semantic relation graph is the adjacency matrix and the sentence embeddings are the node features. Afterward, a linear layer is used to project high-level hidden features for individual sentences to salience scores, representing how salient a sentence is with respect to the final summary. Finally, based on this, we devise an innovative greedy method that leverages sentence embeddings to detect redundant sentences and select sentences until reaching the summary length limit.

2.1 Sentence Semantic Relation Graph

We model the semantic relationship among sentences using a graph representation. In this graph, each vertex is a sentence $S_{i,j}$ (j'th sentence of document D_i) from the collection documents C and an undirected edge between S_{i_u,j_u} and S_{i_v,j_v} indicates their degree of similarity. In order to compute the semantic similarity, we use the model of Pagliardini et al. (2018) trained on the English Wikipedia corpus. In this manner, we incorporate general knowledge (i.e. not domain-specific) that will complete the specialized sentence embeddings obtained during training (see Section 2.2). We process sentences by their model and compute the cosine similarity between every sentence pair, resulting in a complete graph. However, having a complete graph alone does not allow the model to leverage the semantic structure across sentences significantly, as every sentence pair is connected, and likewise, a sparse graph does not contain enough information to exploit semantic similarities. Furthermore, all edges have a weight above zero, since it is very unlikely that two sentence embeddings are completely orthogonal. To overcome this

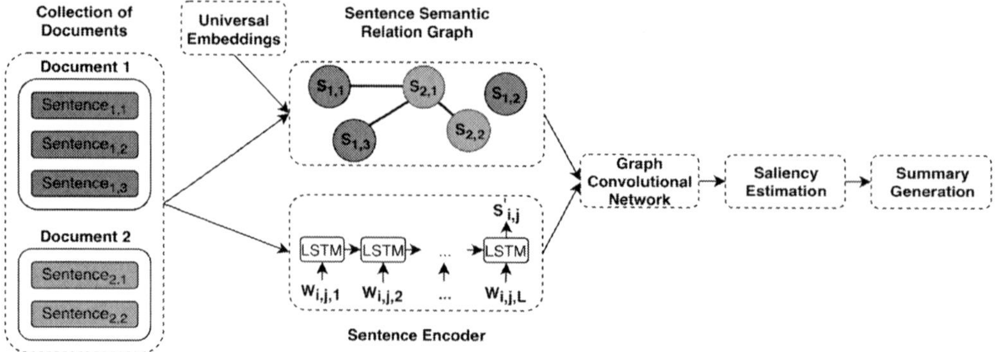

Figure 1: Overview of *SemSentSum*. This illustration includes two documents in the collection, where the first one has three sentences and the second two. A sentence semantic relation graph is firstly built and each sentence node is processed by an encoder network at the same time. Thereafter, a single-layer graph convolutional network is applied on top and produces high-level hidden features for individual sentences. Then, salience scores are estimated using a linear layer and used to produce the final summary.

problem, we introduce an edge-removal-method, where every edge below a certain threshold t^g_{sim} is removed in order to emphasize high sentence similarity. Nonetheless, t^g_{sim} should not be too large, as we otherwise found the model to be prone to overfitting. After removing edges below t^g_{sim}, our sentence semantic relation graph is used as the adjacency matrix A. The impact of t^g_{sim} with different values is shown in Section 3.7.

Based on our aforementioned hypothesis that a combination of general and genre-specific sentence embeddings is beneficial for the task of multi-document summarization, we further incorporate general sentence embeddings, pre-trained on Wikipedia entries, into edges between sentences. Additionally, we compute specialised sentence embeddings, which are related to the domains of the documents (see Section 3.7).

Note that 1) the pre-trained sentence embeddings are only used to compute the weights of the edges and are not used by the summarization model (as others are produced by the sentence encoder) and 2) the edge weights are static and do not change during training.

2.2 Sentence Encoder

Given a list of documents C, we encode each document's sentence $S_{i,j}$, where each has at most L words $(w_{i,j,1}, w_{i,j,2}, ..., w_{i,j,L})$. In our experiments, all words are kept and converted into word embeddings, which are then fed to the sentence encoder in order to compute specialized sentence embeddings $S'_{i,j}$. We employ a single-layer

forward recurrent neural network, using Long Short-Term Memory (LSTM) of (Hochreiter and Schmidhuber, 1997) as sentence encoder, where the sentence embeddings are extracted from the last hidden states. We then concatenate all sentence embeddings into a matrix X which constitutes the input node features that will be used by the graph convolutional network.

2.3 Graph Convolutional Network

After having computed all sentence embeddings and the sentence semantic relation graph, we apply a single-layer Graph Convolutional Network (GCN) from Kipf and Welling (2017), in order to capture high-level hidden features for each sentence, encapsulating sentence information as well as the graph structure.

We believe that our sentence semantic relation graph contains information not present in the data (via universal embeddings) and thus, we leverage this information by running a graph convolution on the first order neighborhood.

The GCN model takes as input the node features matrix X and a squared adjacency matrix A. The former contains all sentence embeddings of the collection of documents, while the latter is our underlying sentence semantic relation graph. It outputs hidden representations for each node that encode both local graph structure and nodes's features. In order to take into account the sentences themselves during the information propagation, we add self-connections (i.e. the identity matrix) to A such that $\tilde{A} = A + I$.

Subsequently, we obtain our sentence hidden features by using Equation 1.

$$S''_{i,j} = \text{ELU}(\tilde{A}\,\text{ELU}(\tilde{A}XW_0 + b_0)W_1 + b_1) \quad (1)$$

where W_i is the weight matrix of the i'th graph convolution layer and b_i the bias vector. We choose the Exponential Linear Unit (ELU) activation function from Clevert et al. (2016) due to its ability to handle the vanishing gradient problem, by pushing the mean unit activations close to zero and consequently facilitating the backpropagation. By using only one hidden layer, as we only have one input-to-hidden layer and one hidden-to-output layer, we limit the information propagation to the first order neighborhood.

2.4 Saliency Estimation

We use a simple linear layer to estimate a salience score for each sentence and then normalize the scores via softmax and obtain our estimated salience score $S^s_{i,j}$.

2.5 Training

Our model *SemSentSum* is trained in an end-to-end manner and minimizes the cross-entropy loss of Equation 2 between the salience score prediction and the ROUGE-1 F_1 score for each sentence.

$$\mathcal{L} = -\sum_C \sum_{D \in C} \sum_{S \in D} F_1(S)\log S^s \quad (2)$$

$F_1(S)$ is computed as the ROUGE-1 F_1 score, unlike the common practice in the area of single and multi-document summarization as recall favors longer sentences whereas F_1 prevents this tendency. The scores are normalized via softmax.

2.6 Summary Generation Process

While our model *SemSentSum* provides estimated saliency scores, we use a greedy strategy to construct an informative and non-redundant summary Sum. We first discard sentences having less than 9 words, as in (Erkan and Radev, 2004), and then sort them in descending order of their estimated salience scores. We iteratively dequeue the sentence having the highest score and append it to the current summary Sum if it is non-redundant with respect to the current content of Sum. We iterate until reaching the summary length limit.

To determine the similarity of a candidate sentence with the current summary, a sentence is considered as dissimilar if and only if the cosine similarity between its sentence embeddings and the embeddings of the current summary is below a certain threshold t^s_{sim}. We use the pre-trained model of Pagliardini et al. (2018) to compute sentence as well as summary embeddings, similarly to the sentence semantic relation graph construction. Our approach is novel, since it focuses on the semantic sentence structures and captures similarity between sentence meanings, instead of focusing on word similarities only, like previous TF-IDF approaches ((Hong and Nenkova, 2014; Cao et al., 2015; Yasunaga et al., 2017; Cao et al., 2017)).

3 Experiments

3.1 Datasets

We conduct experiments on the most commonly used datasets for multi-document summarization from the Document Understanding Conferences (DUC). [1] We use DUC 2001, 2002, 2003 and 2004 as the tasks of generic multi-document summarization, because they have been carried out during these years. We use DUC 2001, 2002, 2003 and 2004 for generic multi-document summarization, where DUC 2001/2002 are used for training, DUC 2003 for validation and finally, DUC 2004 for testing, following the common practice.

3.2 Evaluation Metric

For the evaluation, we use ROUGE (Lin, 2004) with the official parameters of the DUC tasks and also truncate the summaries to 100 words for DUC 2001/2002/2003 and to 665 bytes for DUC 2004. [2] Notably, we take ROUGE-1 and ROUGE-2 recall scores as the main metrics for comparison between produced summaries and golden ones as proposed by (Owczarzak et al., 2012). The goal of the ROUGE-N metric is to compute the ratio of the number of N-grams from the generated summary matching these of the human reference summaries.

3.3 Model Settings

To define the edge weights of our sentence semantic relation graph, we employ the 600-dimensional pre-trained unigram model of Pagliardini et al. (2018), using English Wikipedia as source corpus. We keep only edges having a weight larger than $t^g_{sim} = 0.5$ (tuned on the

---

1. https ://www-nlpir.nist.gov/projects/duc/guidelines.html
2. ROUGE-1.5.5 with options : -n 2 -m -u -c 95 -x -r 1000 -f A -p 0.5 -t 0 and -l 100 if using DUC 2001/2002/2003 otherwise -b 665.

validation set). For word embeddings, the 300-dimensional pre-trained GloVe embeddings (Pennington et al., 2014) are used and fixed during training. The output dimension of the sentence embeddings produced by the sentence encoder is the same as that of the word embeddings, i.e. 300. For the graph convolutional network, the number of hidden units is 128 and the size of the generated hidden feature vectors is also 300. We use a batch size of 1, a learning rate of 0.0075 using Adam optimizer (Kingma and Ba, 2015) with $\beta_1 = 0.9, \beta_2 = 0.999$ and $\epsilon = 10^{-8}$. In order to make *SemSentSum* generalize better, we use dropout (Srivastava et al., 2014) of 0.2, batch normalization (Ioffe and Szegedy, 2015), clip the gradient norm at 1.0 if higher, add L2-norm regularizer with a regularization factor of 10^{-12} and train using early stopping with a patience of 10 iterations. Finally, the similarity threshold t^s_{sim} in the summary generation process is 0.8 (tuned on the validation set).

3.4 Summarization Performance

We train our model *SemSentSum* on DUC 2001/2002, tune it on DUC 2003 and assess the performance on DUC 2004. In order to fairly compare *SemSentSum* with other models available in the literature, experiments are conducted with summaries truncated to 665 bytes (official summary length in the DUC competition), but also with summaries with a length constraint of 100 words. To the best of our knowledge, we are the first to conduct experiments on both summary lengths and compare our model with other systems producing either 100 words or 665 bytes summaries.

3.5 Sentence Semantic Relation Graph Construction

We investigate different methods to build our sentence semantic relation graph and vary the value of t^g_{sim} from 0.0 to 0.75 to study the impact of the threshold cut-off. Among these are :

1. *Cosine* : Using cosine similarity;

2. *Tf-idf* : Considering a node as the query and another as document. The weight corresponds to the cosine similarity between the query and the document;

3. *TextRank* (Mihalcea and Tarau, 2004) : A weighted graph is created where nodes are sentences and edges defined by a similarity measure based on word overlap. Afterward, an algorithm similar to PageRank (Page et al., 1998) is used to compute sentence importance and refined edge weights;

4. *LexRank* (Erkan and Radev, 2004) : An unsupervised multi-document summarizer based on the concept of eigenvector centrality in a graph of sentences to set up the edge weights;

5. *Approximate Discourse Graph* (ADG) (Christensen et al., 2013) : Approximation of a discourse graph where nodes are sentences and edges (S_u, S_v) indicates sentence S_v can be placed after S_u in a coherent summary;

6. *Personalized ADG* (PADG) (Yasunaga et al., 2017) : Normalized version of ADG where sentence nodes are normalized over all edges.

3.6 Ablation Study

In order to quantify the contribution of the different components of *SemSentSum*, we try variations of our model by removing different modules one at a time. Our two main elements are the sentence encoder (*Sent*) and the graph convolutional neural network (*GCN*). When we omit *Sent*, we substitute it with the pre-trained sentence embeddings used to build our sentence semantic relation graph.

3.7 Results and Discussion

Three dimensions are used to evaluate our model *SemSentSum* : 1) the summarization performance, to assess its capability 2) the impact of the sentence semantic relation graph generation using various methods and different thresholds t^g_{sim} 3) an ablation study to analyze the importance of each component of *SemSentSum*.

Summarization Performance We compare the results of *SemSentSum* for both settings : 665 bytes and 100 words summaries. We only include models using the same parameters to compute the ROUGE-1/ROUGE-2 score and recall as metrics.

The results for 665 bytes summaries are reported in Table 1. We compare *SemSentSum* with three types of model relying on either 1) sentence or document embeddings 2) various hand-crafted features or 3) additional data.

Model	ROUGE-1	ROUGE-2
MMR	35.49	7.50
PV-DBOW+BS	36.10	6.77
PG-MMR	36.42	9.36
SVR	36.18	9.34
G-Flow	37.33	8.74
Peer 65	37.88	9.18
R2N2	38.16	9.52
TCSum	38.27	**9.66**
SemSentSum	**39.12**	9.59

Table 1: Comparison of various models using ROUGE-1/ROUGE-2 on DUC 2004 with 665 bytes summaries.

Model	ROUGE-1	ROUGE-2
FreqSum	35.30	8.11
TsSum	35.88	8.15
Cont. LexRank	35.95	7.47
Centroid	36.41	7.97
CLASSY04	37.62	8.96
CLASSY11	37.22	9.20
GreedyKL	37.98	8.53
RegSum	38.57	**9.75**
GCN+PADG	38.23	9.48
SemSentSum	**38.72**	9.69

Table 2: Comparison of various models using ROUGE-1/2 on DUC 2004 with 100 words summaries.

1. For the first category, we significantly outperform **MMR** (Bennani-Smires et al., 2018), **PV-DBOW+BS** (Mani et al., 2017) and **PG-MMR** (Lebanoff et al., 2018). Although their methods are based on embeddings to represent the meaning, it shows that using only various distance metrics or encoder-decoder architecture on these is not efficient for the task of multi-document summarization (as also shown in the Ablation Study). We hypothesize that *SemSentSum* performs better by leveraging pre-trained sentence embeddings and hence lowering the effects of data scarcity.

2. Systems based on hand-crafted features include a widely-used learning-based summarization method, built on support vector regression **SVR** (Li et al., 2007); a graph-based method based on approximating discourse graph **G-Flow** (Christensen et al., 2013); **Peer 65** which is the best peer systems participating in DUC evaluations; and the recursive neural network **R2N2** of Cao et al. (2015) that learns automatically combinations of hand-crafted features. As can be seen, among these models completely dependent on hand-crafted features, *SemSentSum* achieves highest performance on both ROUGE scores. This denotes that using different linguistic and word-based features might not be enough to capture the semantic structures, in addition to being cumbersome to craft.

3. The last type of model is shown in **TCSum** (Cao et al., 2017) and uses transfer learning from a text classifier model, based on a domain-related dataset of 30 000

documents from New York Times (sharing the same topics of the DUC datasets). In terms of ROUGE-1, *SemSentSum* significantly outperforms **TCSum** and performs similarly on ROUGE-2 score. This demonstrates that collecting more manually annotated data and training two models is unnecessary, in addition to being difficult to use in other domains, whereas *SemSentSum* is fully data driven, domain-independent and usable in realistic scenarios.

Table 2 depicts models producing 100 words summaries, all depending on hand-crafted features. We use as baselines **FreqSum** (Nenkova et al., 2006); **TsSum** (Conroy et al., 2006); traditional graph-based approaches such as **Cont. LexRank** (Erkan and Radev, 2004); **Centroid** (Radev et al., 2004); **CLASSY04** (Conroy et al., 2004); its improved version **CLASSY11** (Conroy et al., 2011) and the greedy model **GreedyKL** (Haghighi and Vanderwende, 2009). All of these models are significantly underperforming compared to *SemSentSum*. In addition, we include state-of-the-art models : **RegSum** (Hong and Nenkova, 2014) and **GCN+PADG** (Yasunaga et al., 2017). We outperform both in terms of ROUGE-1. For ROUGE-2 scores we achieve better results than **GCN+PADG** but without any use of domain-specific hand-crafted features and a much smaller and simpler model. Finally, **RegSum** achieves a similar ROUGE-2 score but computes sentence saliences based on word scores, incorporating a rich set of word-level and domain-specific features. Nonetheless, our model is competitive and does not depend on hand-crafted features due to its full data-driven nature and thus, it is not limited to a single domain.

Consequently, the experiments show that achieving good performance for multi-document summarization without hand-crafted features or additional data is clearly feasible and *SemSentSum* produces competitive results without depending on these, is domain independent, fast to train and thus usable in real scenarios.

Sentence Semantic Relation Graph Table 3 shows the results of different methods to create the sentence semantic relation graph with various thresholds t^g_{sim} for 665 bytes summaries (we obtain similar results for 100 words). A first observation is that using cosine similarity with sentence embeddings significantly outperforms all other methods for ROUGE-1 and ROUGE-2 scores, mainly because it relies on the semantic of sentences instead of their individual words. A second is that different methods evolve similarly : *PADG, Textrank, Tf-idf* behave similarly to an U-shaped curve for both ROUGE scores while *Cosine* is the only one having an inverted U-shaped curve. The reason for this behavior is a consequence of its distribution being similar to a normal distribution because it relies on the semantic instead of words, while the others are more skewed towards zero. This confirms our hypothesis that 1) having a complete graph does not allow the model to leverage much the semantic 2) a sparse graph might not contain enough information to exploit similarities. Finally, *Lexrank* and *ADG* have different trends between both ROUGE scores.

Ablation Study We quantify the contribution of each module of *SemSentSum* in Table 4 for 665 bytes summaries (we obtain similar results for 100 words). Removing the sentence encoder produces slightly lower results. This shows that the sentence semantic relation graph captures semantic attributes well, while the fine-tuned sentence embeddings obtained via the encoder help boost the performance, making these methods complementary. By disabling only the graph convolutional layer, a drastic drop in terms of performance is observed, which emphasizes that the relationship among sentences is indeed important and not present in the data itself. Therefore, our sentence semantic relation graph is able to capture sentence similarities by analyzing the semantic structures. Interestingly, if we remove the sentence encoder in addition to the graph convolutional layer, simi-

lar results are achieved. This confirms that alone, the sentence encoder is not able to compute an efficient representation of sentences for the task of multi-document summarization, probably due to the poor size of the DUC datasets. Finally, we can observe that the use of sentence embeddings only results in similar performance to the baselines, which rely on sentence or document embeddings (Bennani-Smires et al., 2018; Mani et al., 2017).

4 Related Work

The idea of using multiple embeddings has been employed at the word level. Kiela et al. (2018) use an attention mechanism to combine the embeddings for each word for the task of natural language inference. Xu et al. (2018); Bollegala et al. (2015) concatenate the embeddings of each word into a vector before feeding a neural network for the tasks of aspect extraction and sentiment analysis. To our knowledge, we are the first to combine multiple types of sentence embeddings.

Extractive multi-document summarization has been addressed by a large range of approaches. Several of them employ graph-based methods. Radev (2000) introduced a cross-document structure theory, as a basis for multi-document summarization. Erkan and Radev (2004) proposed LexRank, an unsupervised multi-document summarizer based on the concept of eigenvector centrality in a graph of sentences. Other works exploit shallow or deep features from the graph's topology (Wan and Yang, 2006; Antiqueira et al., 2009). Wan and Yang (2008) pairs graph-based methods (e.g. random walk) with clustering. Mei et al. (2010) improved results by using a reinforced random walk model to rank sentences and keep non-redundant ones. The system by Christensen et al. (2013) does sentence selection, while balancing coherence and salience and by building a graph that approximates discourse relations across sentences (Mann and Thompson, 1988).

Besides graph-based methods, other viable approaches include Maximum Marginal Relevance (Carbonell and Goldstein, 1998), which uses a greedy approach to select sentences and considers the tradeoff between relevance and redundancy ; support vector regression (Li et al., 2007) ; conditional random field (Galley, 2006) ; or hidden markov model (Conroy et al., 2004). Yet other approaches rely on n-grams regression as in Li et al.

Method	t^g_{sim}	ROUGE-1				t^g_{sim}	ROUGE-2			
		0.0	0.25	0.5	0.75		0.0	0.25	0.5	0.75
Cosine		38.49*	38.61*	**39.12**	35.54*		9.11*	9.07*	**9.59**	7.12*
Tf-idf		36.80*	36.23*	35.26*	35.71*		7.84*	7.78*	7.07*	7.46*
Textrank		35.66*	34.75*	35.41*	35.69*		7.83*	7.17*	7.20*	7.54*
Lexrank		37.04*	36.43*	36.27*	35.65*		7.90*	8.01*	7.64*	7.61*
ADG		35.48*	34.79*	34.78*	35.40*		6.96*	7.03*	7.01*	7.32*
PADG		36.81*	36.23*	35.26*	35.71*		7.84*	7.78*	7.07*	7.46*

Table 3: ROUGE-1/2 for various methods to build the sentence semantic relation graph. A score significantly different (according to a Welch Two Sample t-test, $p = 0.001$) than cosine similarity ($t^g_{sim} = 0.5$) is denoted by *.

Model	ROUGE-1	ROUGE-2
SemSentSum	**39.12**	**9.59**
- w/o Sent	38.38*	9.11*
- w/o GCN	35.88*	7.33*
- w/o GCN,Sent	35.89*	7.24*

Table 4: Ablation test. *Sent* is the sentence encoder and *GCN* the graph convolutional network. According to a Welch Two Sample t-test ($p = 0.001$), a score significantly different than *SemSentSum* is denoted by *.

(2013). More recently, Cao et al. (2015) built a recursive neural network, which tries to automatically detect combination of hand-crafted features. Cao et al. (2017) employ a neural model for text classification on a large manually annotated dataset and apply transfer learning for multi-document summarization afterward.

The work most closely related to ours is (Yasunaga et al., 2017). They create a normalized version of the approximate discourse graph (Christensen et al., 2013), based on hand-crafted features, where sentence nodes are normalized over all the incoming edges. They then employ a deep neural network, composed of a sentence encoder, three graph convolutional layers, one document encoder and an attention mechanism. Afterward, they greedily select sentences using TF-IDF similarity to detect redundant sentences. Our model differs in four ways : 1) we build our sentence semantic relation graph by using pre-trained sentence embeddings with cosine similarity, where neither heavy preprocessing, nor hand-crafted features are necessary. Thus, our model is fully data-driven and domain-independent unlike other systems. In addition, the sentence semantic relation graph could be used for other tasks than multi-document summarization, such as detecting information cascades, query-focused summarization, keyphrase extraction or information retrieval, as it is not composed of hand-crafted features. 2) *SemSentSum* is much smaller and consequently has fewer parameters as it only uses a sentence encoder and a single convolutional layer. 3) The loss function is based on ROUGE-1 F_1 score instead of recall to prevent the tendency of choosing longer sentences. 4) Our method for summary generation is also different and novel as we leverage sentence embeddings to compute the similarity between a candidate sentence and the current summary instead of TF-IDF based approaches.

5 Conclusion

In this work, we propose a method to combine two types of sentence embeddings : 1) universal embeddings, pre-trained on a large corpus such as Wikipedia and incorporating general semantic structures across sentences and 2) domain-specific embeddings, learned during training. We merge them together by using a graph convolutional network that eliminates the need of hand-crafted features or additional annotated data.

We introduce a fully data-driven model *SemSentSum* that achieves competitive results for multi-document summarization on both kind of summary length (665 bytes and 100 words summaries), without requiring hand-crafted features or additional annotated data.

As *SemSentSum* is domain-independent, we believe that our sentence semantic relation graph and model can be used for other tasks including detecting information cascades, query-focused summarization, keyphrase extraction and information retrieval. In addition, we plan to leave the weights of the sentence semantic relation graph dynamic during training, and to integrate an attention mechanism directly into the graph.

Acknowledgments

We thank Michaela Benk for proofreading and helpful advice.

References

Lucas Antiqueira, Osvaldo N. Oliveira, Luciano da Fontoura Costa, and Maria das Graças Volpe Nunes. 2009. A complex network approach to text summarization. *Information Sciences*, 179(5) :584 – 599. Special Section - Quantum Structures : Theory and Applications.

Kamil Bennani-Smires, Claudiu-Cristian Musat, Andreea Hossmann, Michael Baeriswyl, and Martin Jaggi. 2018. Simple unsupervised keyphrase extraction using sentence embeddings. *Proceedings of the 22nd Conference on Computational Natural Language Learning, CoNLL 2018, Brussels, Belgium, October 31 - November 1, 2018*, pages 221–229.

Danushka Bollegala, Takanori Maehara, and Ken ichi Kawarabayashi. 2015. Unsupervised cross-domain word representation learning. *Proc. of the Annual Conference of the Association for Computational Linguistics (ACL) and International Joint Conferences on Natural Language Processing (IJCNLP)*.

Ziqiang Cao, Wenjie Li, Sujian Li, and Furu Wei. 2017. Improving multi-document summarization via text classification. In *Proceedings of the Thirty-First AAAI Conference on Artificial Intelligence, February 4-9, 2017, San Francisco, California, USA.*, pages 3053–3059.

Ziqiang Cao, Furu Wei, Li Dong, Sujian Li, and Ming Zhou. 2015. Ranking with recursive neural networks and its application to multi-document summarization. In *Proceedings of the Twenty-Ninth AAAI Conference on Artificial Intelligence*, AAAI'15, pages 2153–2159. AAAI Press.

Jaime Carbonell and Jade Goldstein. 1998. The use of mmr, diversity-based reranking for reordering documents and producing summaries. In *Proceedings of the 21st Annual International ACM SIGIR Conference on Research and Development in Information Retrieval*, SIGIR '98, pages 335–336, New York, NY, USA. ACM.

Janara Christensen, Stephen Soderland, Oren Etzioni, et al. 2013. Towards coherent multi-document summarization. In *Proceedings of the 2013 conference of the North American chapter of the association for computational linguistics : Human language technologies*, pages 1163–1173.

Djork-Arné Clevert, Thomas Unterthiner, and Sepp Hochreiter. 2016. Fast and accurate deep network learning by exponential linear units (elus). *International Conference on Learning Representations*.

John M Conroy, Judith D Schlesinger, Jade Goldstein, and Dianne P O'leary. 2004. Left-brain/right-brain multi-document summarization. In *Proceedings of the Document Understanding Conference (DUC 2004)*.

John M Conroy, Judith D Schlesinger, Jeff Kubina, Peter A Rankel, and Dianne P O'Leary. 2011. Classy 2011 at tac : Guided and multi-lingual summaries and evaluation metrics. *TAC*, 11 :1–8.

John M. Conroy, Judith D. Schlesinger, and Dianne P. O'Leary. 2006. Topic-focused multi-document summarization using an approximate oracle score. In *Proceedings of the COLING/ACL on Main Conference Poster Sessions*, COLING-ACL '06, pages 152–159, Stroudsburg, PA, USA. Association for Computational Linguistics.

Günes Erkan and Dragomir R Radev. 2004. Lexrank : Graph-based lexical centrality as salience in text summarization. *Journal of Artificial Intelligence Research*, 22 :457–479.

Michel Galley. 2006. A skip-chain conditional random field for ranking meeting utterances by importance. In *Proceedings of the 2006 Conference on Empirical Methods in Natural Language Processing*, EMNLP '06, pages 364–372, Stroudsburg, PA, USA. Association for Computational Linguistics.

Aria Haghighi and Lucy Vanderwende. 2009. Exploring content models for multi-document summarization. In *Proceedings of Human Language Technologies : The 2009 Annual Conference of the North American Chapter of the Association for Computational Linguistics*, NAACL '09, pages 362–370, Stroudsburg, PA, USA. Association for Computational Linguistics.

Sepp Hochreiter and Jürgen Schmidhuber. 1997. Long short-term memory. *Neural Comput.*, 9(8) :1735–1780.

Kai Hong and Ani Nenkova. 2014. Improving the estimation of word importance for news multi-document summarization. pages 712–721.

Sergey Ioffe and Christian Szegedy. 2015. Batch normalization : Accelerating deep network training by reducing internal covariate shift. In *International Conference on Machine Learning*, pages 448–456.

Douwe Kiela, Changhan Wang, and Kyunghyun Cho. 2018. Dynamic meta-embeddings for improved sentence representations. *Proceedings of the 2018 Conference on Empirical Methods in Natural Language Processing (EMNLP)*.

Diederik P. Kingma and Jimmy Ba. 2015. Adam: A method for stochastic optimization. *International Conference on Learning Representations*.

Thomas N. Kipf and Max Welling. 2017. Semi-supervised classification with graph convolutional networks. *International Conference on Learning Representations*.

Logan Lebanoff, Kaiqiang Song, and Fei Liu. 2018. Adapting the neural encoder-decoder framework from single to multi-document summarization. *Proceedings of the 2018 Conference on Empirical Methods in Natural Language Processing*.

Chen Li, Xian Qian, and Yang Liu. 2013. Using supervised bigram-based ilp for extractive summarization. In *Proceedings of the 51st Annual Meeting of the Association for Computational Linguistics (Volume 1 : Long Papers)*, volume 1, pages 1004–1013.

Sujian Li, You Ouyang, Wei Wang, and Bin Sun. 2007. Multi-document summarization using support vector regression. In *In Proceedings of DUC*. Citeseer.

C. Y. Lin. 2004. ROUGE : A package for automatic evaluation of summaries. In *Proceedings of the Workshop on Text Summarization Branches Out (WAS)*, Barcelona, Spain.

Kaustubh Mani, Ishan Verma, and Lipika Dey. 2017. Multi-document summarization using distributed bag-of-words model. *arXiv preprint arXiv :1710.02745*.

William C. Mann and Sandra A. Thompson. 1988. Rhetorical structure theory : Toward a functional theory of text organization. *Text*, 8(3) :243–281.

Qiaozhu Mei, Jian Guo, and Dragomir Radev. 2010. Divrank: The interplay of prestige and diversity in information networks. In *Proceedings of the 16th ACM SIGKDD International Conference on Knowledge Discovery and Data Mining*, KDD '10, pages 1009–1018, New York, NY, USA. ACM.

R. Mihalcea and P. Tarau. 2004. TextRank : Bringing order into texts. In *Proceedings of EMNLP-04and the 2004 Conference on Empirical Methods in Natural Language Processing*.

Ani Nenkova, Lucy Vanderwende, and Kathleen McKeown. 2006. A compositional context sensitive multi-document summarizer: Exploring the factors that influence summarization. In *Proceedings of the 29th Annual International ACM SIGIR Conference on Research and Development in Information Retrieval*, SIGIR '06, pages 573–580, New York, NY, USA. ACM.

Karolina Owczarzak, John M. Conroy, Hoa Trang Dang, and Ani Nenkova. 2012. An assessment of the accuracy of automatic evaluation in summarization. In *Proceedings of Workshop on Evaluation Metrics and System Comparison for Automatic Summarization*, pages 1–9, Stroudsburg, PA, USA. Association for Computational Linguistics.

L. Page, S. Brin, R. Motwani, and T. Winograd. 1998. The pagerank citation ranking: Bringing order to the web. In *Proceedings of the 7th International World Wide Web Conference*, pages 161–172, Brisbane, Australia.

Matteo Pagliardini, Prakhar Gupta, and Martin Jaggi. 2018. Unsupervised Learning of Sentence Embeddings using Compositional n-Gram Features. In *NAACL 2018 - Conference of the North American Chapter of the Association for Computational Linguistics*.

Jeffrey Pennington, Richard Socher, and Christopher D. Manning. 2014. Glove: Global vectors for word representation. In *Empirical Methods in Natural Language Processing (EMNLP)*, pages 1532–1543.

Dragomir R. Radev. 2000. A common theory of information fusion from multiple text sources step one: Cross-document structure. In *Proceedings of the 1st SIGdial Workshop on Discourse and Dialogue - Volume 10*, SIGDIAL '00, pages 74–83, Stroudsburg,

PA, USA. Association for Computational Linguistics.

Dragomir R Radev, Hongyan Jing, Małgorzata Styś, and Daniel Tam. 2004. Centroid-based summarization of multiple documents. *Information Processing & Management*, 40(6) :919–938.

Nitish Srivastava, Geoffrey Hinton, Alex Krizhevsky, Ilya Sutskever, and Ruslan Salakhutdinov. 2014. Dropout: A simple way to prevent neural networks from overfitting. *J. Mach. Learn. Res.*, 15(1) :1929–1958.

Xiaojun Wan and Jianwu Yang. 2006. Improved affinity graph based multi-document summarization. In *Proceedings of the Human Language Technology Conference of the NAACL, Companion Volume : Short Papers*, NAACL-Short '06, pages 181–184, Stroudsburg, PA, USA. Association for Computational Linguistics.

Xiaojun Wan and Jianwu Yang. 2008. Multi-document summarization using cluster-based link analysis. In *Proceedings of the 31st Annual International ACM SIGIR Conference on Research and Development in Information Retrieval*, SIGIR '08, pages 299–306, New York, NY, USA. ACM.

Hu Xu, Bing Liu, Lei Shu, and Philip S Yu. 2018. Double embeddings and cnn-based sequence labeling for aspect extraction. *Proceedings of the 56th Annual Meeting of the Association for Computational Linguistics*.

Michihiro Yasunaga, Rui Zhang, Kshitijh Meelu, Ayush Pareek, Krishnan Srinivasan, and Dragomir R. Radev. 2017. Graph-based neural multi-document summarization. In *Proceedings of CoNLL-2017*. Association for Computational Linguistics.

Unsupervised Aspect-Based Multi-Document Abstractive Summarization

Maximin Coavoux,[2] **Hady Elsahar,[1]** **Matthias Gallé[1]**

[1]Naver Labs Europe

[2]Univ. Grenoble Alpes, CNRS, Grenoble INP, LIG

{maximin.coavoux,hady.elsahar,matthias.galle}@naverlabs.com

Abstract

User-generated reviews of products or services provide valuable information to customers. However, it is often impossible to read each of the potentially thousands of reviews: it would therefore save valuable time to provide short summaries of their contents. We address opinion summarization, a multi-document summarization task, with an unsupervised abstractive summarization neural system. Our system is based on (i) a language model that is meant to encode reviews to a vector space, and to generate fluent sentences from the same vector space (ii) a clustering step that groups together reviews about the same aspects and allows the system to generate summary sentences focused on these aspects. Our experiments on the Oposum dataset empirically show the importance of the clustering step.

1 Introduction

Nobody reads all available user-generated comments about products they might buy. Summarizing reviews in a short paragraph would save valuable time, as well as provide better insights into the main opinions of previous buyers. In addition to traditional difficulties of summarization, the specific setting of opinion summarization faces the entanglement of multiple facets in reviews: polarity (including contradictory opinions), aspects, tone (descriptive, evaluative).

Obtaining large parallel corpora for opinion summarization is costly and makes unsupervised methods attractive. Very recently, a neural method for unsupervised multi-document abstractive summarization was proposed by Chu and Liu (2019, Meansum), based on an auto-encoder which is given the average encoding of all documents at inference time. Major limitations identified by the authors of this work are factual inaccuracies and

---

*Work done at Naver Labs Europe.

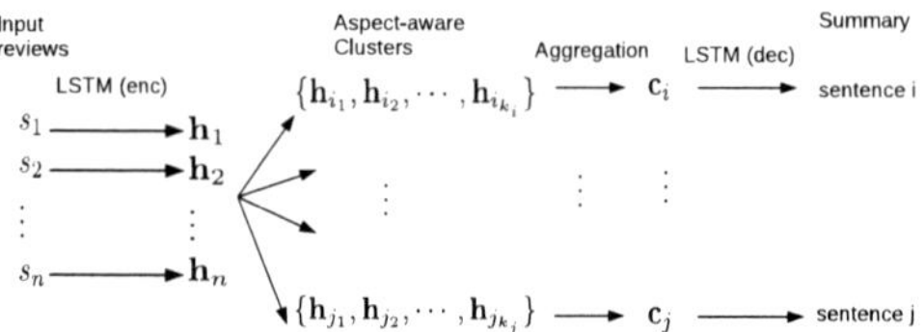

Figure 1: Aspect-aware unsupervised summarization system. The decoder LSTM shares weights with the encoder LSTM.

the inability to deal with contradictory statements. We argue that this can be attributed to feeding the decoder the summation of sentence representations in the embedding space, which is not equivalent to the average meaning representation of all the input sentences.

In this paper, we present a work in progress that investigates better ways of aggregating sentence representations in a way that preserves semantics. While available gold summaries might be expensive to acquire, we leverage more attainable training signals such as a small amount of sentiment and aspect annotations. We adopt a strategy based on a language model – used both for encoding reviews and for generating summaries – and aspect-aware sentence clustering. This clustering ensures coverage of all relevant aspects and allows the system to generate independently a sentence for each aspect mentioned in reviews. Our system proceeds by projecting reviews to a vector space, clustering them according to their main aspect, and generating one sentence for each cluster that has been discovered. Our experiments, performed on the Oposum dataset (Angelidis and Lapata, 2018), demonstrate the importance of the clustering step and assess the effect of leveraging aspect information to improve clustering.

Proceedings of the 2nd Workshop on New Frontiers in Summarization, pages 42–47

Hong Kong, China, November 4, 2019. ©2019 Association for Computational Linguistics

2 Related Work

Since obtaining large parallel corpora for opinion summarization is costly, a line of work has focused on unsupervised methods. Proposals in unsupervised opinion summarization include both extractive and abstractive methods. Unsupervised extractive summarization methods consists in selecting the most salient sentences from a text. Saliency can be quantified with the centroid method (Radev et al., 2004; Gholipour Ghalandari, 2017; Rossiello et al., 2017), which consists in computing vector representations for sentences and selecting which sentences are the closest to their centroid, and thus the most representative of the set. Other proposals make use of the PageRank algorithm (Mihalcea and Tarau, 2004; Erkan and Radev, 2004) to compute sentence saliency. The weakly supervised method of Angelidis and Lapata (2018) uses a pretrained polarity classifier and an aspect-based autoencoder to compute the saliency of reviews segments.

On the other hand, non-neural abstractive methods are based on graphs (Ganesan et al., 2010; Nayeem et al., 2018). They consist in constructing a graph whose nodes are words and extract paths that correspond to valid sentences.[1]

This work is inspired by the Meansum model (Chu and Liu, 2019), which leverages an encoder-decoder trained using self-supervision with a sentence reconstruction objective to reconstruct each of the input sentences. It performs summarization by averaging the encoded vectors of each input sentence and feeding them to the pre-trained decoder to generate a summary out of them. The main difference with that work is our use of an LSTM instead of a auto-encoder, and in particular experimenting with different ways of aggregating the documents.

3 Proposed Model

Each product p is associated with a set of reviews represented by a set of sentences $S^{(p)} = \{s_1^{(p)}, \ldots s_n^{(p)}\}$. The task consists in predicting a set of sentences (under a word budget) that contains the important information in $S^{(p)}$. Ideally, a good summary should cover all aspects (e.g. price, quality, ease of use) mentioned in reviews, and express judgements that are consistent with those in the reviews.

Overview of the approach Our approach consists in the following general pipeline:

1. Encoding: compute vector representations for sentences;

2. Clustering step: cluster sentence representations into meaningful groups (i.e. cluster together sentences that are about the same aspect);

3. Aggregation: compute a single vector representation for each cluster, from the representations of sentences in the cluster;

4. Generation step: generate a sentence for each cluster.

Each of these modules has a wide range of possible instantiations. In the next four paragraphs, we describe the architecture we implemented for each step.

3.1 RNN Language Model

The main module of our model is a standard LSTM trained with a language model objective. We construct a representation for a sentence s by running the LSTM on the sentence and retrieving the last LSTM state $\mathbf{h}$.

3.2 Sentence clustering

We use a function f_{aspect} that associates a sentence vector representation $\mathbf{h}$ to an aspect identifier $a \in \{1, \ldots, n\}$, where n is the total number of aspects. Many possibilities exist to instantiate f_{aspect}, ranging from unsupervised topic modelling (Latent Dirichlet Allocation, Blei et al., 2003), or unsupervised aspect extraction (Aspect-based Autoencoder, He et al., 2017), to weakly supervised approaches (Multi-seed Aspect Extractor, Angelidis and Lapata, 2018). In this paper, we use a supervised aspect classifier to instantiate f_{aspect}, trained jointly with the language model. This choice requires annotated data.

We score possible aspects with a single linear layer followed by a softmax activation:[2]

$$p(A = \cdot | s_i) = \mathsf{Softmax}(\mathbf{W}^{(A)} \cdot \mathbf{h}_i),$$
$$f_{aspect} = \operatorname*{argmax}_{a} p(A = a | s_i),$$

---

[1] These methods are semi-extractive: they produce sentences that are not in input reviews, but only use words that occur in them.

[2] During training, we use a sigmoid activation instead, since a segment may be annotated with several aspects, thus treating each aspect as a single binary variable.

where $\mathbf{W}^{(A)}$ is a parameter matrix, and $\mathbf{h}_i$ is the LSTM sentence encoding.

For comparison purposes, we also experiment with k-means clustering, an unsupervised method whose only hyperparameter is a predefined number of clusters.

3.3 Constructing cluster representations

For each cluster $C_a = \{(s_1, \mathbf{h}_1), (s_2, \mathbf{h}_2), \dots, (s_{k_a}, \mathbf{h}_{k_a})\}$, containing pairs made of a sentence and its vector representation, we need to compute a single representation $\mathbf{h}^{(a)}$ that retain most important information from the original sentences. To do so, we first select the most salient sentences from the cluster, and then compute the centroid of selected sentences.

Following Angelidis and Lapata (2018), we use the output of a polarity classifier to define saliency. In particular, we define the saliency score sal for a single sentence s as the prediction confidence of the classifier:

$$p(Pol = \cdot|s_i) = \mathsf{Softmax}(\mathbf{W}^{(Pol)} \cdot \mathbf{h}_i),$$
$$sal(s_i) = \max_{pol} p(Pol = pol|s_i),$$

where $\mathbf{W}^{(Pol)}$ is a parameter matrix. Finally, we prune the cluster C to the k most salient sentences $C' \subset C$, and compute their centroid:

$$\mathbf{c}_a = \frac{1}{|C'|} \sum_{(s_i, \mathbf{h}_i) \in C'} \mathbf{h}_i.$$

This method can be seen as a form of hard attention, where a few items are attended to, whereas the majority does not participate in the final representation.

3.4 Generating summary sentences

The last step of the summary construction process consists in generating a sentence per cluster. We do so by initializing the language model LSTM with the cluster representation $\mathbf{c}_a$, and performing decoding in the same fashion as a translation model (without attention).

Our decoding method is based on top-k sampling decoding (Fan et al., 2018), i.e. at each time step, we extract the k most probable next tokens, renormalize their probabilities and sample from the resulting distribution. We perform top-k sampling decoding K times. We then rerank the K generated sentences according to the cosine similarity of their representation, as computed by the LSTM, to the cluster representation $\mathbf{c}_a$. This process makes sure that non-relevant sampled sentences are rejected and is meant to improve the semantic similarity between the centroid of the cluster and the generated sentence.

3.5 Multi-Task Training Objective

We train the model using a multitask learning (MTL, Caruana, 1997) objective. We jointly optimize a language modelling objective, as well as the two supervised classification task (aspect and polarity):

$$\mathcal{L}_{\mathsf{lm}} = \sum_{i=1}^{n} -\log P(w_i|w_0^{i-1}; \theta_{\mathsf{LSTM}}),$$
$$\mathcal{L}_{\mathsf{polarity}} = -\log P(y_p|w_0^n; \theta_{\mathsf{LSTM}}, \theta_{\mathsf{polarity}}),$$
$$\mathcal{L}_{\mathsf{aspect}} = -\log P(y_a|w_0^n; \theta_{\mathsf{LSTM}}, \theta_{\mathsf{aspect}}),$$
$$\mathcal{L}_{\mathsf{MTL}} = \mathcal{L}_{\mathsf{lm}} + \mathcal{L}_{\mathsf{polarity}} + \mathcal{L}_{\mathsf{aspect}},$$

where w_0^n is a sentence, y_p is its polarity label, y_a is its aspect labels. In some experiments, we only use the language modelling objective (we optimize $\mathcal{L}_{\mathsf{lm}}$ instead of $\mathcal{L}_{\mathsf{MTL}}$). It is important to note here that while our method uses an MTL objective, it does not require aspect and polarity annotations for the input summaries but rather a small number of annotated examples for training. For the rest of the dataset (not annotated with aspect nor polarity) our model shifts training to solely a language modeling objective.

4 Experiments

Dataset We perform experiments on the Oposum dataset (Angelidis and Lapata, 2018). This dataset contains $3,461,603$ Amazon reviews for 6 types of products, extracted from the *Amazon Product Dataset* (McAuley et al., 2015). We use the raw reviews from Oposum to train the language models (separately for each product type). For each product type, small subsets of reviews are annotated with aspects (1400 sentences), polarities (330 sentences) which we use to train our polarity and aspect classifiers. We use the 10 gold summaries (per product type) additionally provided in the dataset for final evaluation. To train the sentiment and aspect classifiers, we use respectively the development and test sets from Oposum as train

Model	Bags_and_cases	Bluetooth	Boots	Keyboards	TV	Vacuums
TextRank	0.35	0.28	0.31	0.30	0.30	0.30
Mean	0.18 ±0.03	0.15 ±0.02	0.16 ±0.02	0.17 ±0.02	0.16 ±0.03	0.15 ±0.02
Kmeans	0.38 ±0.02	0.37 ±0.01	0.37 ±0.01	0.37 ±0.01	0.35 ±0.01	0.38 ±0.02
Kmeans + MTL	0.38 ±0.01	0.36 ±0.01	**0.38** ±0.02	0.35 ±0.01	0.35 ±0.02	0.36 ±0.02
Aspect + MTL	**0.4** ±0.02	**0.38** ±0.01	**0.38** ±0.01	**0.38** ±0.01	**0.37** ±0.01	**0.39** ±0.01

Table 1: ROUGE-L evaluation per product type.

Model	ROUGE-1	ROUGE-2	ROUGE-L
TextRank	0.27 ±0.02	0.03 ±0.0	0.31 ±0.02
Mean	0.12 ±0.02	0.01 ±0.01	0.16 ±0.03
Kmeans	0.32 ±0.02	0.05 ±0.01	0.37 ±0.02
Kmeans + MTL	0.31 ±0.02	0.05 ±0.01	0.36 ±0.02
Aspect + MTL	**0.33** ±0.02	0.05 ±0.01	**0.38** ±0.02
(Angelidis and Lapata, 2018)	**0.44**	**0.21**	**0.43**

Table 2: ROUGE-$\{1, 2, L\}$ metrics on the full dataset.

and development sets.[3] We split the polarity annotated sets into a train (90%) and development set (10%).

Protocol and hyperparameters To optimize the objective function in Section 3.5, at each training step, we sample a batch of sentences and perform an update on the language modelling loss ($\mathcal{L}_{\text{lm}}$), then sample a batch of sentences (from the annotated subset) and perform an update on one of the supervised classification losses ($\mathcal{L}_{\text{polarity}}$ on even steps, aspect $\mathcal{L}_{\text{aspect}}$ on odd steps).

For the language model, we use a 2-layer monodirectional LSTM with state size 1000 and randomly initialized word embeddings of size 200. Minibatches have size 10 for the language modelling objective and size 8 for aspect and polarity classification. For the k-means clustering method we set the number of clusters to 8. For the aspect-based clustering we do a grid search over different pruning sizes (16, 100). Finally, at inference time using top-k with re-ranking we set $k = 20$ and $K = 10$ (see Section 3.4). For each product type we run the training process with 2 different seeds and the inference process with 3 different seeds. The results 5 reported are the *mean* and the *std* of the 6 train/inference combinations.

External comparisons As a baseline, we use a publicly available implementation[4] (Barrios et al., 2016) of the TextRank algorithm (Mihalcea and Tarau, 2004). We also compare to the results of the extractive system of Angelidis and Lapata (2018).

Model variations We experiment with four variations of the model:

- No clustering, $\mathcal{L}_{\text{lm}}$ training objective: the summary is generated from the centroid representation of all reviews (as in the Meansum model);
- K-means, $\mathcal{L}_{\text{lm}}$ training objective;
- K-means, $\mathcal{L}_{\text{MTL}}$ objective, this setting assess whether k-means clustering provides better information when the LSTM is trained to incorporate aspect information in its representations (via MTL training);
- Aspect prediction clustering, $\mathcal{L}_{\text{MTL}}$.

5 Results and discussion

We present results in Tables 1 and 2. We report ROUGE-1, ROUGE-2 and ROUGE-L F scores (Lin, 2004) as computed by the `py-rouge` package implementation of ROUGE.[5]

First we observe that clustering reviews and generating a review sentence per cluster (Kmeans) provides a huge benefit over generating a full summary from the centroid of all reviews (Mean), as also done by the MeanSum model. Using K-means clustering with a model trained with multitask learning (Kmeans+MTL) has no effect over the quality of the summaries. Furthermore, we observe that clustering reviews based on the aspect classifier provides a small improvement (+0 to +4 ROUGE-L over K-means clustering). This model outperforms the Textrank baseline on all metrics.

We report in Table 2 the results published by Angelidis and Lapata (2018) on the Oposum dataset. Our system falls short of matching their results. However, the Oposum gold summaries are

---

[3]The provided split does not include a training set, since the authors only used the annotations for evaluation.

[4]`https://github.com/summanlp/textrank`

[5]`https://github.com/Diego999/py-rouge`

extractive, and thus are biased towards extractive methods.

Overall, we also observe that our ROUGE-2 metric is quite low in absolute value, with scores ranging around 0.05. However, those results are consistent with other published results in unsupervised abstractive summarization (on other datasets), e.g. Chu and Liu (2019). This might be related to the fact that the language model is good, so it uses on-topic words (Rouge-1) and does so in the correct order (Rouge-L); but the broader sense of what is being said might not necessarily match with reference summaries.

6   Conclusion

We have presented an unsupervised opinion summarization method, based on language modelling and aspect-based clustering. Preliminary experiments showed the benefits of clustering review sentences into meaningful groups, instead of aggregating them into a single vector as done by the MeanSum model, thus addressing an important limitation of that model. Furthermore, our experiments showed that incorporating aspect information, as predicted by a supervised classifier is beneficial to opinion summarization, and leverages only a small amount of annotated data that is easier to acquire than parallel summarization data.

References

Stefanos Angelidis and Mirella Lapata. 2018. Summarizing opinions: Aspect extraction meets sentiment prediction and they are both weakly supervised. In *Proceedings of the 2018 Conference on Empirical Methods in Natural Language Processing*, pages 3675–3686, Brussels, Belgium. Association for Computational Linguistics.

Federico Barrios, Federico López, Luis Argerich, and Rosa Wachenchauzer. 2016. Variations of the similarity function of textrank for automated summarization. *CoRR*, abs/1602.03606.

David M. Blei, Andrew Y. Ng, and Michael I. Jordan. 2003. Latent dirichlet allocation. *Journal of Machine Learning Research*, 3:993–1022.

Rich Caruana. 1997. Multitask learning. *Machine Learning*, 28(1):41–75.

Eric Chu and Peter Liu. 2019. MeanSum: a neural model for unsupervised multi-document abstractive summarization. pages 1223–1232.

Günes Erkan and Dragomir R. Radev. 2004. LexRank: Graph-based lexical centrality as salience in text summarization. *Journal of Artificial Intelligence Research*, 22(1):457–479.

Angela Fan, Mike Lewis, and Yann Dauphin. 2018. Hierarchical neural story generation. In *Proceedings of the 56th Annual Meeting of the Association for Computational Linguistics (Volume 1: Long Papers)*, pages 889–898, Melbourne, Australia. Association for Computational Linguistics.

Kavita Ganesan, ChengXiang Zhai, and Jiawei Han. 2010. Opinosis: A graph based approach to abstractive summarization of highly redundant opinions. In *Proceedings of the 23rd International Conference on Computational Linguistics (Coling 2010)*, pages 340–348, Beijing, China. Coling 2010 Organizing Committee.

Demian Gholipour Ghalandari. 2017. Revisiting the centroid-based method: A strong baseline for multi-document summarization. In *Proceedings of the Workshop on New Frontiers in Summarization*, pages 85–90, Copenhagen, Denmark. Association for Computational Linguistics.

Ruidan He, Wee Sun Lee, Hwee Tou Ng, and Daniel Dahlmeier. 2017. An unsupervised neural attention model for aspect extraction. In *Proceedings of the 55th Annual Meeting of the Association for Computational Linguistics (Volume 1: Long Papers)*, pages 388–397, Vancouver, Canada. Association for Computational Linguistics.

Chin-Yew Lin. 2004. ROUGE: A package for automatic evaluation of summaries. In *Text Summarization Branches Out*, pages 74–81, Barcelona, Spain. Association for Computational Linguistics.

Julian McAuley, Christopher Targett, Qinfeng Shi, and Anton van den Hengel. 2015. Image-based recommendations on styles and substitutes. In *Proceedings of the 38th International ACM SIGIR Conference on Research and Development in Information Retrieval*, SIGIR '15, pages 43–52, New York, NY, USA. ACM.

Rada Mihalcea and Paul Tarau. 2004. TextRank: Bringing order into text. In *Proceedings of EMNLP 2004*, pages 404–411, Barcelona, Spain. Association for Computational Linguistics.

Mir Tafseer Nayeem, Tanvir Ahmed Fuad, and Yllias Chali. 2018. Abstractive unsupervised multi-document summarization using paraphrastic sentence fusion. In *Proceedings of the 27th International Conference on Computational Linguistics*, pages 1191–1204, Santa Fe, New Mexico, USA. Association for Computational Linguistics.

Dragomir R. Radev, Hongyan Jing, Magorzata Sty, and Daniel Tam. 2004. Centroid-based summarization of multiple documents. *Information Processing and Management*, 40(6):919 – 938.

Gaetano Rossiello, Pierpaolo Basile, and Giovanni Semeraro. 2017. Centroid-based text summarization through compositionality of word embeddings. In *Proceedings of the MultiLing 2017 Workshop on Summarization and Summary Evaluation Across Source Types and Genres*, pages 12–21, Valencia, Spain. Association for Computational Linguistics.

BillSum: A Corpus for Automatic Summarization of US Legislation

Anastassia Kornilova
FiscalNote Research
Washington, DC
anastassia@fiscalnote.com

Vlad Eidelman
FiscalNote Research
Washington, DC
vlad@fiscalnote.com

Abstract

Automatic summarization methods have been studied on a variety of domains, including news and scientific articles. Yet, legislation has not previously been considered for this task, despite US Congress and state governments releasing tens of thousands of bills every year. In this paper, we introduce BillSum, the first dataset for summarization of US Congressional and California state bills (https://github.com/FiscalNote/BillSum). We explain the properties of the dataset that make it more challenging to process than other domains. Then, we benchmark extractive methods that consider neural sentence representations and traditional contextual features. Finally, we demonstrate that models built on Congressional bills can be used to summarize California bills, thus, showing that methods developed on this dataset can transfer to states without human-written summaries.

1 Introduction

The growing number of publicly available documents produced in the legal domain has led political scientists, legal scholars, politicians, lawyers, and citizens alike to increasingly adopt computational tools to discover and digest relevant information. In the US Congress, over 10,000 bills are introduced each year, with state legislatures introducing tens of thousands of additional bills. Individuals need to quickly process them, but these documents are often long and technical, making it difficult to identify the key details. While each US bill comes with a human-written summary from the Congressional Research Service (CRS),[1] similar summaries are not available in most state and local legislatures.

Automatic summarization methods aim to condense an input document into a shorter text while retaining the salient information of the original. To encourage research into automatic legislative summarization, we introduce the BillSum dataset, which contains a primary corpus of 33,422 US Congressional bills and reference summaries split into a train and a test set. Since the motivation for this task is to apply models to new legislatures, the corpus contains an additional test set of 1237 California bills and reference summaries. We establish several benchmarks and show that there is ample room for new methods that are better suited to summarize technical legislative language.

2 Background

Research into automatic summarization has been conducted in a variety of domains, such as news articles (Hermann et al., 2015), emails (Nenkova and Bagga, 2004), scientific papers (Teufel and Moens, 2002; Collins et al., 2017), and court proceedings (Grover et al., 2004; Saravanan et al., 2008; Kim et al., 2013). The later area is most similar to BillSum in terms of subject matter. However, the studies in that area either apply traditional domain-agnostic techniques or take advantage of the unique structures that are consistently present in legal proceedings (e.g precedent, law, background).[2]

While automatic summarization methods have not been applied to legislative text, previous works have used the text to automatically predict bill passage and legislators' voting behavior (Gerrish and Blei, 2011; Yano et al., 2012; Eidelman et al., 2018; Kornilova et al., 2018). However, these studies treated the document as a "bag-of-words" and did not consider the importance of individual

---

[1] http://www.loc.gov/crsinfo/

[2] Kanapala et al. (2017) provide a comprehensive overview of the works in legal summarization.

Proceedings of the 2nd Workshop on New Frontiers in Summarization, pages 48–56
Hong Kong, China, November 4, 2019. ©2019 Association for Computational Linguistics

sentences. Recently, documents from state governments have been subject to syntactic parsing for knowledge graph construction (Kalouli et al., 2018) and textual similarity analysis (Linder et al., 2018). Yet, to the best of our knowledge, BillSum is the first corpus designed, specifically for summarization of legislation.

3 Data

The BillSum dataset consists of three parts: US training bills, US test bills and California test bills. The US bills were collected from the **Govinfo** service provided by the United States Government Publishing Office (GPO).[3] Our corpus consists of bills from the 103rd-115th (1993-2016) sessions of Congress. The data was randomly split into 28,408 train bills and 5014 test bills. For California, bills from the 2015-2016 session were scraped directly from the legislature's website;[4] the summaries were written by their Legislative Counsel.

The BillSum corpus focuses on mid-length legislation from 5000 to 20,000 character in length. We chose to measure the text length in characters, instead of words or sentences, because the texts have complex structure that makes it difficult to consistently measure words. The range was chosen because on one side, short bills introduce minor changes and do not require summaries. While the CRS produces summaries for them, they often contain most of the text of the bill. On the other side, very long legislation is often composed of several large sections. The summarization problem thus becomes more akin in its formulation to multi-document summarization, a more challenging task that we leave to future work. The resulting corpus includes about 28% of all US bills, with a majority of the removed bills being shorter than 5000 characters.

For the summaries, we chose a 2000 character limit as 90% of summaries are of this length or shorter; the limit here is, also, set in characters to be consistent with our document length cut-offs. The distribution of both text and summary lengths is shown in Figure 1. Interestingly, there is little correlation between the bill and human summary length, with most summaries ranging from 1000 to 2000 characters.

For a closer comparison to other datasets, Table

[3]https://github.com/unitedstates/
congress
[4]http://leginfo.legislature.ca.gov

1 provides statistics on the number of words in the texts, after we simplify the structure of the texts.

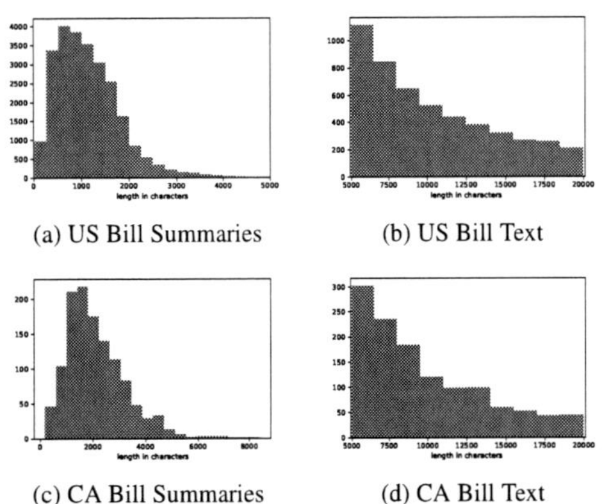

(a) US Bill Summaries   (b) US Bill Text

(c) CA Bill Summaries   (d) CA Bill Text

Figure 1: Bill Lengths

Stylistically, the BillSum dataset differs from other summarization corpora. Figure 2 presents an example Congressional bill. The nested, bulleted structure is common to most bills, where each bullet can represent a sentence or a phrase. Yet, content-wise, this is a straightforward example that states key details about the proposed grant in the outer bullets. In more challenging cases, the bill may state edits to an existing law, without whose context the change is hard to interpret, such as:

Section 4 of the Endangered Species Act of 1973 (16 U.S.C. 1533) is amended in subsection (a) in paragraph (1), by inserting "with the consent of the Governor of each State in which the endangered species or threatened species is present"

The average bill will contain both types of language, encouraging the study of both domain-specific and general summarization methods on this dataset.

4 Benchmark Methods

To establish benchmarks on summarization performance, we evaluate several extractive summarization approaches by first scoring individual sentences, then using a selection strategy to pick the best subset (Carbonell and Goldstein, 1998). While we briefly considered abstractive summarization models (Chopra et al., 2016), we found that the existing models trained on news and Wikipedia data produced ungrammatical results, and that the size of dataset is insufficient for the

		mean	min	25th	50th	75th	max
Words	US	1382	245	922	1254	1773	8463
	CA	1684	561	1123	1498	2113	3795
Sentences	US	46	7	31	41	58	372
	CA	47	12	31	42	59	137

Table 1: Text length distributions on preprocessed texts.

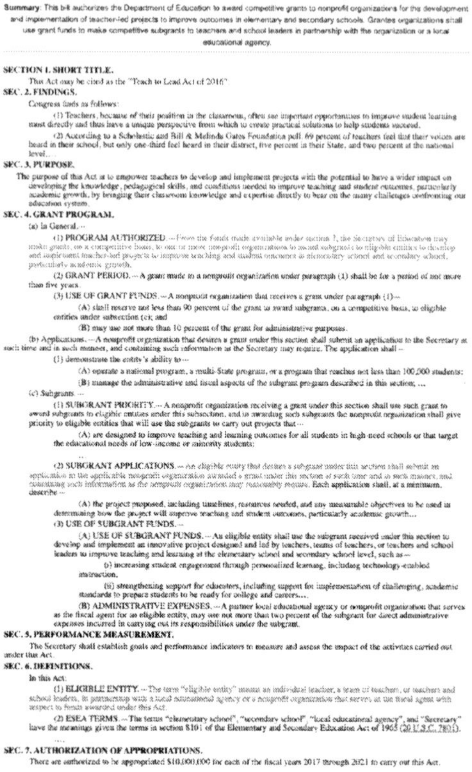

Figure 2: Example US Bill

necessary retraining. Recent works have successfully fine-tuned models for other NLP tasks to specific domains (Lee et al., 2019), but we leave to future work the exploration of similar abstractive strategies.

The scoring task is framed as a supervised learning problem. First, we create a binary label for each sentence indicating whether it belongs in the summary (Gillick et al., 2008).[5] We compute

a Rouge-2 Precision score of a sentence relative to the reference summary and simplify it to a binary value based on whether it is above or below 0.1 (Lin, 2004; Zopf et al., 2018). As an example, the sentences in the positive class are highlighted in green in Figure 2.

Second, we build several models to predict the label. For the models, we consider two aspects of a sentence: its importance in the context of the document (4.1) and its general summary-like properties (4.2).

4.1 Document Context Model (DOC)

A good summary sentence contains the main ideas mentioned in the document. Thus, researchers have designed a multitude of features to capture this property. We evaluate how several common ones transfer to our task:

The position of the sentence can determine how informative the sentence is (Seki, 2002). We encode this feature as a fraction of 'sentence position / total sentence count', to restrict this feature to the $0 - 1$ range regardless of the particular document's length. In addition, we include a binary feature for whether the sentence is near a section header.

An informative sentences will contain words that are important to a given document relative to others. Following a large percentage of previous works, we capture this property using TF-IDF (Seki, 2002; Ramos et al., 2003). First, we calculate a document-level TF-IDF weight for each word, then take the average and the maximum of these weights for a sentence as features. To relate language between sentences, "sentence-level" TF-IDF features are created using each sentence as a document for the background corpus; the average and max of the sentence's word weights are used as features.

We train a random forest ensemble model over these features with 50 estimators (Breiman, 2001).[6] This method was chosen because it best

---

[5]As noted in Section 3, it is difficult to define sentence boundaries for this task due to the bulleted structure of the documents. We simplify the text with the following heuristic: if a bullet is shorter than 10 words, we treat it as a part of the previous sentence; otherwise, we treat it as a full sentence. This cut-off was chosen by manually analyzing a sample of sentences. A more sophisticated strategy would be to check if each bullet is a sentence fragment with a syntactic parser and

then reconstruct full sentences; however, the former approach is sufficient for most documents.

[6]Implemented with `scikit-learn.org`

captured the interactions between the small number of features.

4.2 Summary Language Model (SUM)

We hypothesize that certain language is more common in summaries than in bill texts. Specifically, that summaries primarily contain general effects of the bill (e.g awarding a grant) while language detailing the administrative changes will only appear in the text (e.g inserting or modifying relatively minor language to an existing statute). Thus, a good summary should contain only the major actions.

Hong and Nenkova (2014) quantify this aspect using hand-engineered features based on the the likelihood of words appearing in summaries as opposed to the text. Later, Cao et al. (2015) built a Convolutional Neural Network (CNN) to predict if a sentence belongs in the summary and showed that this straightforward network outperforms engineered features. We follow their approach, using the BERT model as our classifier (Devlin et al., 2018). BERT can be adapted for and has achieved state-of-the-art performance on a number of NLP tasks, including binary sentiment classification.[7]

To adapt the model to our domain, we pretrain the **Bert-Large Uncased** model on the "next-sentence prediction" task using the US training dataset for 20,000 steps with a batch size of 32.[8] The pretraining stategy has been successfully applied to tune BERT for tasks in the biomedical domain (Lee et al., 2019). Using the pretrained model, the classification setup for BERT is trained on sentences and binary labels for 3 epochs over the training data.

4.3 Ensemble and Sentence Selection

To combine the signals from the DOC and SUM models, we create an ensemble averaging the two probability outputs.[9]

To create the final summary, we apply the Maximal Marginal Relevance (MMR) algorithm (Goldstein et al., 2000). MMR iteratively constructs a summary by including the highest scoring sentence with the following formula:

$$s_{next} = \max_{s \in D - S_{cur}} 0.7 * f(s) - 0.3 * sim(s, S_{cur})$$

where D is the set of all the sentences in the document, S_{cur} are the sentences in the summary so far, $f(s)$ is the sentence score from the model, sim is the cosine similarity of the sentence to S_{cur}, and 0.7 and 0.3 are constants chosen experimentally to balance the two properties. This method allows us to pick relevant sentences while minimizing redundancies. We repeat this process until we reach the length limit of 2000 characters.

5 Results

To estimate the upper bound on our approach, an oracle summarizer is created by using the true Rouge-2 Precision scores with the MMR selection strategy. In addition, we evaluate the following unsupervised baselines: **SumBasic** (Nenkova and Vanderwende, 2005), Latent Semantic Analysis (LSA) (Gong and Liu, 2001) and **TextRank** (Mihalcea and Tarau, 2004). The final results are shown in Table 2. The Rouge F-Score is used because it considers both the completeness and conciseness of the summary method.[10,11]

We evaluated the DOC, SUM, and ensemble classifiers separately. All three of our models outperform the other baselines, demonstrating that there is a "summary-like" signal in the language across bills. The SUM model outperforms the DOC model showing that a strong language model can capture general summary-like features; this result is in line with Cao et al. (2015) and Collins et al. (2017) sentence level neural network performance. However, in those studies incorporating several contextual features improved the performance, while DOC+SUM performs similarly to DOC. In future work we plan to incorporate contextual features into the neural network directly; Collins et al. (2017) showed that this strategy is effective for scientific article summarization. In addition, we plan to explore additional sentence selection strategies instead of always adding sentences to the 2000 character limit.

Next, we applied our US model to CA bills. Overall, the performance is lower than on US bills

---

[7] All code described are used directly from `https://github.com/google-research/bert`

[8] This is the pretraining procedure recommended by the authors of BERT on their github website.

[9] Additional experiments using Linear Regression with the actual Rouge-2 Precision score as the target, but found that they produced similar results.

[10] Precision and recall scores are listed in the supplemental material for additional context.

[11] Rouge scores calculated using `https://github.com/pcyin/PyRouge`

(Table 2b), but all three supervised methods perform better than the unsupervised baselines, suggesting that models built using the language of US Bills can transfer to other states. Interestingly, DOC+SUM outperforms DOC in the CA dataset, suggesting that the BERT model may have overfit to the US language. An additional reason for the drop in the performance is the difference in the structure of the summaries: In California the provided summaries state not only the proposed changes, but the relevant pieces of the existing law, as well (see Appendix B.3 for a more in-depth discussion). We hypothesize that a model trained on multi-state data would transfer better, thus we plan to expand the dataset to include all twenty-three states with human-written summaries.

Table 2: ROUGE F-scores (%) of different methods.

	Rouge-1	Rouge-2	Rouge-L
Oracle	47.97	32.14	40.89
SumBasic	30.56	15.33	23.75
LSA	32.24	14.02	23.75
TextRank	34.10	17.45	27.57
DOC	38.18	21.22	31.02
SUM	41.29	24.47	34.07
DOC + SUM	41.28	24.31	34.15

(a) Congressional Bills

	Rouge-1	Rouge-2	Rouge-L
Oracle	51.24	34.86	45.91
SumBasic	35.47	16.16	30.10
LSA	35.05	16.34	30.10
TextRank	35.81	18.10	30.10
DOC	37.32	18.72	31.87
SUM	38.67	20.59	33.11
DOC + SUM	39.26	21.16	33.77

(b) CA Bills

5.1 Summary Language Analysis

The success of the SUM model suggests that certain language is more summary-like. Following a study by Hong and Nenkova (2014) on news summarization, we apply KL-divergence based metrics to quantify which words were more summary-like. The metrics are calculated by:

1. Calculate the probability of unigrams appearing in the bill text and in the summaries ($P_t(w)$ and $P_s(w)$ respectively).

2. Calculate KL scores as : $KL_w(S|T) = P_s(w) * \ln \frac{P_s(w)}{P_t(w)}$ and the opposite.

A large value of $KL(S|T)$ indicates that the word is summary-like and $KL(T|S)$ indicates a text-like word. Table 3 shows the most summary-like and text-like words in bills and resolutions. For both document types, the summary-like words tend to be verbs or department names; the text-like words mostly refer to types of edits or background content (e.g "reporting the rise of.."). This follows our intuition about summaries being more action driven. While a complex model, like BERT, may capture these signals internally; understanding the significant language explicitly is important both for interpretability and for guiding future models.

Table 3: Examples of summary and text like words

Summary-like	prohibit, DOD, VA, allow, penalty, prohibit, EPA, eliminate, implement, require
Text-like	estimate, average, report, rise, section, finish, percent, debate

6 Conclusion

In this paper, we introduced BillSum, the first corpus for legislative summarization. This is a challenging summarization dataset due to the technical nature and complex structure of the bills. We have established several baselines and demonstrated that there is a large gap in performance relative to the oracle, showing that the problem has ample room for further development. We have also shown that summarization methods trained on US Bills transfer to California bills - thus, the summarization methods developed on this dataset could be used for legislatures without human written summaries.

References

Leo Breiman. 2001. Random forests. *Mach. Learn.*, 45(1):5–32.

Ziqiang Cao, Furu Wei, Sujian Li, Wenjie Li, Ming Zhou, and WANG Houfeng. 2015. Learning summary prior representation for extractive summarization. In *Proceedings of the 53rd Annual Meeting of the Association for Computational Linguistics and the 7th International Joint Conference on Natural Language Processing (Volume 2: Short Papers)*, volume 2, pages 829–833.

Jaime Carbonell and Jade Goldstein. 1998. The use of mmr, diversity-based reranking for reordering documents and producing summaries. In *Proceedings of the 21st Annual International ACM SIGIR Conference on Research and Development in Information Retrieval*, SIGIR '98, pages 335–336, New York, NY, USA. ACM.

Sumit Chopra, Michael Auli, and Alexander M. Rush. 2016. Abstractive sentence summarization with attentive recurrent neural networks. In *Proceedings of the 2016 Conference of the North American Chapter of the Association for Computational Linguistics: Human Language Technologies*, pages 93–98. Association for Computational Linguistics.

Ed Collins, Isabelle Augenstein, and Sebastian Riedel. 2017. A supervised approach to extractive summarisation of scientific papers. *arXiv preprint arXiv:1706.03946*.

Jacob Devlin, Ming-Wei Chang, Kenton Lee, and Kristina Toutanova. 2018. Bert: Pre-training of deep bidirectional transformers for language understanding.

Vlad Eidelman, Anastassia Kornilova, and Daniel Argyle. 2018. How predictable is your state? leveraging lexical and contextual information for predicting legislative floor action at the state level. *arXiv preprint arXiv:1806.05284*.

Sean Gerrish and David M Blei. 2011. Predicting legislative roll calls from text. In *Proceedings of the 28th international conference on machine learning (icml-11)*, pages 489–496.

Daniel Gillick, Benoit Favre, and Dilek Hakkani-Tür. 2008. The icsi summarization system at tac 2008. In *TAC*.

Jade Goldstein, Vibhu Mittal, Jaime Carbonell, and Mark Kantrowitz. 2000. Multi-document summarization by sentence extraction. In *Proceedings of the 2000 NAACL-ANLPWorkshop on Automatic Summarization - Volume 4*, NAACL-ANLP-AutoSum '00, pages 40–48, Stroudsburg, PA, USA. Association for Computational Linguistics.

Yihong Gong and Xin Liu. 2001. Generic text summarization using relevance measure and latent semantic analysis. In *Proceedings of the 24th annual international ACM SIGIR conference on Research and development in information retrieval*, pages 19–25. ACM.

Claire Grover, Ben Hachey, and Ian Hughson. 2004. The HOLJ corpus. supporting summarisation of legal texts. In *COLING 2004 5th International Workshop on Linguistically Interpreted Corpora*, pages 47–54, Geneva, Switzerland. COLING.

Karl Moritz Hermann, Tomas Kocisky, Edward Grefenstette, Lasse Espeholt, Will Kay, Mustafa Suleyman, and Phil Blunsom. 2015. Teaching machines to read and comprehend. In *Advances in Neural Information Processing Systems*, pages 1693–1701.

Kai Hong and Ani Nenkova. 2014. Improving the estimation of word importance for news multi-document summarization. In *Proceedings of the 14th Conference of the European Chapter of the Association for Computational Linguistics*, pages 712–721.

Aikaterini-Lida Kalouli, Leo Vrana, Vigile Marie Fabella, Luna Bellani, and Annette Hautli-Janisz. 2018. Cousbi: A structured and visualized legal corpus of us state bills. In *LREC 2018*, pages 7–14.

Ambedkar Kanapala, Sukomal Pal, and Rajendra Pamula. 2017. Text summarization from legal documents: a survey. *Artificial Intelligence Review*, pages 1–32.

Mi-Young Kim, Ying Xu, and Randy Goebel. 2013. Summarization of legal texts with high cohesion and automatic compression rate. In *New Frontiers in Artificial Intelligence*, pages 190–204, Berlin, Heidelberg. Springer Berlin Heidelberg.

Anastassia Kornilova, Daniel Argyle, and Vlad Eidelman. 2018. Party matters: Enhancing legislative embeddings with author attributes for vote prediction. *arXiv preprint arXiv:1805.08182*.

Jinhyuk Lee, Wonjin Yoon, Sungdong Kim, Donghyeon Kim, Sunkyu Kim, Chan Ho So, and Jaewoo Kang. 2019. Biobert: a pre-trained biomedical language representation model for biomedical text mining. *CoRR*, abs/1901.08746.

Chin-Yew Lin. 2004. Rouge: A package for automatic evaluation of summaries. *Text Summarization Branches Out*.

Fridolin Linder, Bruce A. Desmarais, Matthew Burgess, and Eugenia Giraudy. 2018. Text as policy: Measuring policy similarity through bill text reuse. *SSRN*.

Rada Mihalcea and Paul Tarau. 2004. Textrank: Bringing order into text. In *Proceedings of the 2004 conference on empirical methods in natural language processing*.

Ani Nenkova and Amit Bagga. 2004. Facilitating email thread access by extractive summary generation. *AMSTERDAM STUDIES IN THE THEORY AND HISTORY OF LINGUISTIC SCIENCE*, page 287.

Ani Nenkova and Lucy Vanderwende. 2005. The impact of frequency on summarization. *Microsoft Research, Redmond, Washington, Tech. Rep. MSR-TR-2005*, 101.

Juan Ramos et al. 2003. Using tf-idf to determine word relevance in document queries. In *Proceedings of the first instructional conference on machine learning*, volume 242, pages 133–142.

Murali Saravanan, Balaraman Ravindran, Assistant Professor, and Dr Raman. 2008. Automatic identification of rhetorical roles using conditional random fields for legal document summarization. *J. Artif. Intell. Law*.

Yohei Seki. 2002. Sentence extraction by tf/idf and position weighting from newspaper articles.

Simone Teufel and Marc Moens. 2002. Summarizing scientific articles: experiments with relevance and rhetorical status. *Computational linguistics*, 28(4):409–445.

Tae Yano, Noah A Smith, and John D Wilkerson. 2012. Textual predictors of bill survival in congressional committees. In *Proceedings of the 2012 Conference of the North American Chapter of the Association for Computational Linguistics: Human Language Technologies*, pages 793–802. Association for Computational Linguistics.

Markus Zopf, Eneldo Loza Mencía, and Johannes Fürnkranz. 2018. Which scores to predict in sentence regression for text summarization? In *Proceedings of the 2018 Conference of the North American Chapter of the Association for Computational Linguistics: Human Language Technologies, Volume 1 (Long Papers)*, pages 1782–1791. Association for Computational Linguistics.

A   Additional ROUGE Scores

As discussed in the Results section, F-Scores encourage a balance between comprehensiveness and conciseness. However, as it is useful to analyze the precision and recall scores separately, both are presented in Table 4 for US Bills and in Table 5 for CA Bills. All tested methods favor recall, since they consistently generate a 2000 character summary, instead of stopping early when a concise summary may be sufficient. For both datasets, the difference in Recall between the Oracle and DOC+SUM summarizer is a lot smaller than for Recall; which suggests that a lot of useful summary content can be found with an extractive method. In future work, we will focus on extracting more granular snippets to improve precision.

B   Additional Bill Examples

We highlight several example bills to showcase the different types of bills found in the dataset.

B.1   Complex Structure Example

In the Data section, we discussed some of the challenges with processing bills: complex formatting and technical language. Figure 3 is an excerpt from a particularly difficult example:

Table 4: ROUGE Scores of Congressional Bills

	Rouge-1	Rouge-2	Rouge-L
Oracle	41.42	27.77	39.41
SumBasic	24.35	11.54	22.15
LSA	27.00	12.99	24.70
TextRank	29.44	14.99	26.65
DOC	31.80	17.50	29.34
SUM	34.79	20.45	32.32
DOC + SUM	35.15	20.42	32.65

(a) Precision Scores

	Rouge-1	Rouge-2	Rouge-L
Oracle	65.98	46.18	62.38
SumBasic	47.55	21.97	43.14
LSA	46.13	22.61	43.05
TextRank	46.64	25.36	42.11
DOC	54.95	32.80	50.67
SUM	58.03	36.79	53.87
DOC + SUM	57.35	36.39	53.22

(b) Recall Scores

Table 5: ROUGE Scores of California Bills

	Rouge-1	Rouge-2	Rouge-L
Oracle	41.42	27.77	39.41
SumBasic	33.72	16.30	30.41
LSA	34.84	17.24	31.69
TextRank	36.66	19.28	32.61
DOC	36.44	19.10	33.14
SUM	38.15	21.23	34.52
DOC + SUM	39.14	22.07	35.87

(a) Precision Scores

	Rouge-1	Rouge-2	Rouge-L
Oracle	65.98	46.18	62.38
SumBasic	40.47	17.89	36.36
LSA	38.23	17.28	34.61
TextRank	37.79	18.97	33.50
DOC	41.17	20.53	37.19
SUM	42.21	22.20	38.04
DOC + SUM	42.17	22.59	38.24

(b) Recall Scores

- The text interleaves several layers of bullets. Lines 3, 15, 27 represent the same level (points (3) and (4) omitted for space); lines 16, 17, 19 and 21 go together, as well. These multiple levels need to be handled carefully,

SEC. 4. WOMEN'S BUSINESS CENTER PROGRAM.

(a) Women's Business Center Financial Assistance. — Section 29 of the Small Business Act (15 U.S.C. 656) is amended

(1) in subsection (a)—

(A) by striking paragraph (4);

(B) by redesignating paragraphs (2) and (3) as paragraphs (3) and (4), respectively;

(C) by inserting after paragraph (1) the following:

"(2) the term 'eligible entity' means —

"(A) a private nonprofit organization;

"(B) a State, regional, or local economic development organization;

"(C) a development, credit, or finance corporation chartered by a State;

"(D) a junior or community college, as defined in section 312(f) of the Higher Education Act of 1965; or

"(E) any combination of entities listed in subparagraphs (A) through (D);" and

(D) by adding at the end the following:

"(5) the term 'women's business center' means a project conducted by an eligible entity under this section.";

(2) in subsection (b)—

(A) by redesignating paragraphs (1), (2), and (3) as subparagraphs (A), (B), and (C), respectively;

(B) by striking "The Administration" and all that follows through "5-year projects" and inserting the following:

"(1) IN GENERAL. The Administration may provide financial assistance to an eligible entity to conduct a project,

(C) by striking "The projects shall" and inserting the following:

"(2) USE OF FUNDS — The project shall be designed to provide training and counseling that meets the needs of women, especially socially or economically disadvantaged women, and shall"; and

(D) by adding at the end the following:

"(3) AMOUNT OF FINANCIAL ASSISTANCE. —

"(A) IN GENERAL. — Except as provided in subparagraph (B), the amount of financial assistance provided under this subsection to an eligible entity per project year shall be not more than $250,000.

"(B) ADDITIONAL FINANCIAL ASSISTANCE. —

"(i) IN GENERAL. — The Administration may award financial assistance under this subsection to an eligible entity in an amount that is more than $250,000 in a given project year if the Administrator determines that the eligible entity

"(I) obtained more than $250,000 in non-Federal contributions for that project year in accordance with subsection (c);

(5) by striking subsection (f) and inserting the following:

"(f) Applications And Criteria For Initial Financial Assistance —

"(1) APPLICATION.—Each eligible entity desiring financial assistance under subsection (b) shall submit to the Administrator an application that contains—

"(A) a certification that the eligible entity—

"(i) has designated an executive director or program manager, who may be compensated using financial assistance under subsection (b) or other sources, to manage the women's business center for which assistance under subsection (f) is sought;

Figure 3: US H.R.1680 (115th)

or the summarizer will extract snippets that can not be interpreted without context.

- Lines 22-26 both introduce new language for the law and use the bulleted structure.

- Line 27 states that the existing "subsection (f)" is being removed and replaced. While lines 28 onward state the new text, the meaning of the change relative to the current text is not clear.

The human-written summary for this bill was:

(Sec. 4)"Women's business center" shall mean a project conducted by any of the following eligible entities:

- *a private nonprofit organization;*

- *a state, regional, or local economic development organization;*

- *a state-chartered development, credit, or finance corporation;*

- *a junior or community college; or*

- *any combination of these entities.*

The SBA may award up to $250,000 of financial assistance to eligible entities per project year to conduct projects designed to provide training and counseling meeting the needs of women, especially socially and economically disadvantaged women.

Most of the relevant details are capture in the text between lines 8-14 and 20-24. For examples similar to this one, the summary language is extracted almost directly from the text, but, parsing them correctly from the original structure is a non-trivial task.

B.2 Paraphrase Example

For a subset of the bills, the CRS will paraphrase the technical language. In these cases, extractive summarization methods are particularly limited. Consider the example in Figure 4 and its summary:

This bill amends the Endangered Species Act of 1973 to revise the process by which the Department of the Interior or the Department of Commerce, as appropriate, reviews petitions to list a species on the endangered or threatened species list. Specifically, the bill establishes a process for the appropriate department to declare a petition backlog and discharge the petitions when there is a backlog.

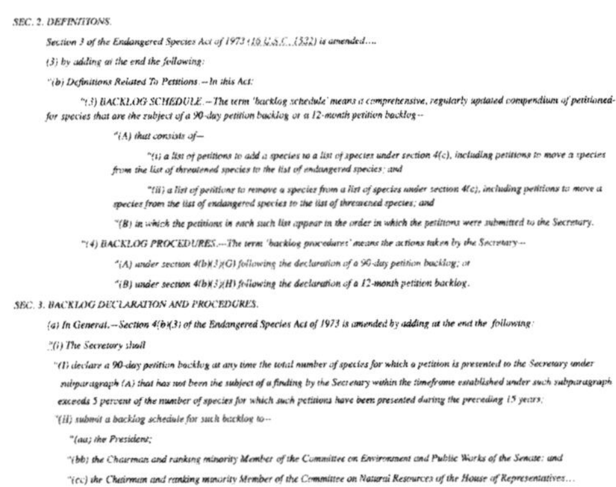

SEC. 2. DEFINITIONS.

Section 3 of the Endangered Species Act of 1973 (16 U.S.C. 1532) is amended...

(3) by adding at the end the following:

"(b) Definitions Related To Petitions.—In this Act:

"(3) BACKLOG SCHEDULE —The term 'backlog schedule' means a comprehensive, regularly updated compendium of petitioned-for species that are the subject of a 90-day petition backlog or a 12-month petition backlog—

"(A) that consists of—

"(i) a list of petitions to add a species to a list of species under section 4(c), including petitions to move a species from the list of threatened species to the list of endangered species; and

"(ii) a list of petitions to remove a species from a list of species under section 4(c), including petitions to move a species from the list of endangered species to the list of threatened species; and

"(B) in which the petitions in each such list appear in the order in which the petitions were submitted to the Secretary.

"(4) BACKLOG PROCEDURES.—The term 'backlog procedures' means the actions taken by the Secretary—

"(A) under section 4(b)(3)(G) following the declaration of a 90-day petition backlog; or

"(B) under section 4(b)(3)(B) following the declaration of a 12-month petition backlog.

SEC. 3. BACKLOG DECLARATION AND PROCEDURES.

(a) In General.—Section 4(b)(3) of the Endangered Species Act of 1973 is amended by adding at the end the following:

"(I) The Secretary shall—

"(I) declare a 90-day petition backlog at any time the total number of species for which a petition is presented to the Secretary under subparagraph (A) that has not been the subject of a finding by the Secretary within the timeframe established under such subparagraph exceeds 5 percent of the number of species for which such petitions have been presented during the preceding 15 years;

"(II) submit a backlog schedule for such backlog to—

"(aa) the President;

"(bb) the Chairman and ranking minority Member of the Committee on Environment and Public Works of the Senate; and

"(cc) the Chairman and ranking minority Member of the Committee on Natural Resources of the House of Representatives...

Figure 4: US H.R.6355 (115th)

While the bill elaborates of the "'process", the summary states that one was created. This type of summary would be hard to construct by a purely extractive method.

B.3 California Example

The California bills follow the same general patterns as US bills, but the format of some summaries is different. In Figure 5: the summary, first, explains the existing law, then explains the change. The additional context is useful, and in the future we may build a system that references the existing law to create better summaries.

Existing law requires that a bicycle operated during darkness upon a highway, a sidewalk where bicycle operation is not prohibited by the local jurisdiction, or a bikeway, as defined, be equipped with a red reflector on the rear that is visible from a distance of 500 feet to the rear when directly in front of lawful upper beams of headlamps on a motor vehicle. A violation of this requirement is an infraction.

This bill would instead require that a bicycle operated under those circumstances be equipped with a red reflector or a solid or flashing red light with a built-in reflector on the rear that is visible from a distance of 500 feet to the rear when directly in front of lawful upper beams of headlamps on a motor vehicle. By revising the definition of a crime, the bill would impose a state-mandated local program. The bill would also include a statement of legislative findings and declarations.
The California Constitution requires the state to reimburse local agencies and school districts for certain costs mandated by the state. Statutory provisions establish procedures for making that reimbursement.

Figure 5: California Bill Summary

An Editorial Network for Enhanced Document Summarization

Edward Moroshko [*] **Guy Feigenblat, Haggai Roitman, David Konopnicki**
Electrical Engineering Dept.   IBM Research AI
Technion – Israel Institute of Technology   Haifa University Campus
Haifa, Israel   Haifa, Israel
`edward.moroshko@gmail.com` `{guyf,haggai,davidko}@il.ibm.com`

Abstract

We suggest a new idea of *Editorial Network –* a mixed extractive-abstractive summarization approach, which is applied as a post-processing step over a given sequence of extracted sentences. We further suggest an effective way for training the "editor" based on a novel soft-labeling approach. Using the CNN/DailyMail dataset we demonstrate the effectiveness of our approach compared to state-of-the-art extractive-only or abstractive-only baselines.

1 Introduction

Automatic text summarizers condense a given piece of text into a shorter version (the summary). This is done while trying to preserve the main essence of the original text and keeping the generated summary as readable as possible.

Existing summarization methods can be classified into two main types, either *extractive* or *abstractive*. Extractive methods select and order text fragments (e.g., sentences) from the original text source. Such methods are relatively simpler to develop and keep the extracted fragments untouched, allowing to preserve important parts, e.g., keyphrases, facts, opinions, etc. Yet, extractive summaries tend to be less fluent, coherent and readable and may include superfluous text.

Abstractive methods apply natural language paraphrasing and/or compression on a given text. A common approach is based on the encoder-decoder (seq-to-seq) paradigm (Sutskever et al., 2014), with the original text sequence being encoded while the summary is the decoded sequence.

While such methods usually generate summaries with better readability, their quality declines over longer textual inputs, which may lead to a higher redundancy (Paulus et al., 2017). Moreover, such methods are sensitive to vocabulary size, making them more difficult to train and generalize (See et al., 2017).

A common approach for handling long text sequences in abstractive settings is through *attention* mechanisms, which aim to imitate the attentive reading behaviour of humans (Chopra et al., 2016). Two main types of attention methods may be utilized, either *soft* or *hard*. Soft attention methods first locate salient text regions within the input text and then bias the abstraction process to prefer such regions during decoding (Cohan et al., 2018; Gehrmann et al., 2018; Hsu et al., 2018; Nallapati et al., 2016; Li et al., 2018; Pasunuru and Bansal, 2018; Tan et al., 2017). On the other hand, hard attention methods perform abstraction only on text regions that were initially selected by some extraction process (Chen and Bansal, 2018; Nallapati et al., 2017; Liu et al., 2018).

Compared to previous works, whose final summary is either entirely extracted or generated using an abstractive process, in this work, we suggest a new idea of *"Editorial Network"* (EditNet) – a *mixed extractive-abstractive* summarization approach. A summary generated by *EditNet* may include sentences that were either extracted, abstracted or of both types. Moreover, per considered sentence, *EditNet* may decide not to take either of these decisions and completely reject the sentence.

Using the CNN/DailyMail dataset we demonstrate that, *EditNet*'s summarization quality is highly competitive to that obtained

---

[*] Work was done during a summer internship in IBM Research AI

Proceedings of the 2nd Workshop on New Frontiers in Summarization, pages 57–63
Hong Kong, China, November 4, 2019. ©2019 Association for Computational Linguistics

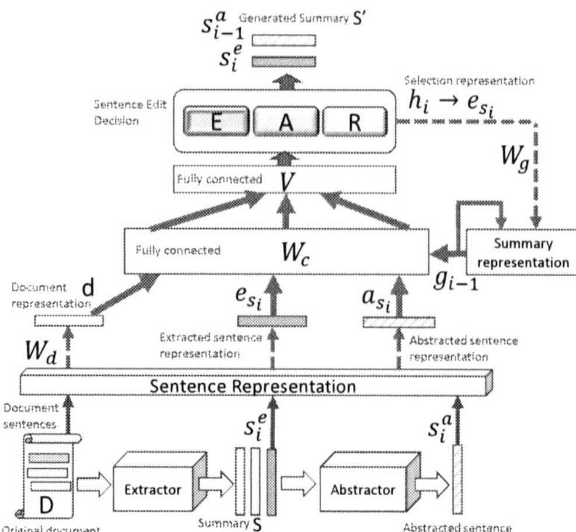

Figure 1: Editorial Network (*EditNet*)

Editor's automatic summary:
E: what was supposed to be a fantasy sports car ride at walt disney world speedway turned deadly when a lamborghini crashed into a guardrail. A: *the crash took place sunday at the exotic driving experience[a]*. A: *the lamborghini 's passenger , gary terry , died at the scene[b]*. R: ~~petty holdings , which operates the exotic driving experience at walt disney world speedway , released a statement sunday night about the crash.~~

---

[a] Original extracted sentence: "the crash took place sunday at the exotic driving experience , which bills itself as a chance to drive your dream car on a racetrack".

[b] Original extracted sentence: "the lamborghini 's passenger , 36-year-old gary terry of davenport , florida , died at the scene , florida highway patrol said"

Ground truth summary:
the crash occurred at the exotic driving experience at walt disney world speedway. officials say the driver , 24-year-old tavon watson , lost control of a lamborghini. passenger gary terry , 36 , died at the scene.

Figure 2: An example mixed summary (annotated with the editor's decisions) taken from the CNN/DM dataset

by both state-of-the-art abstractive-only and extractive-only baselines.

2 Editorial Network

Figure 1 depicts the architecture of *EditNet*. *EditNet* is applied as a post-processing step over a given input summary whose sentences were initially selected by some extractor. The key idea behind *EditNet* is to create an automatic editing process to enhance summary quality.

Let S denote a summary which was extracted from a given text (document) D. The editorial process is implemented by iterating over sentences in S according to the selection order of the extractor. For each sentence in S, the "editor" may make three possible decisions. The first decision is to keep the extracted sentence untouched (represented by label E in Figure 1). The second alternative is to rephrase the sentence (represented by label A in Figure 1). Such a decision, for example, may represent the editor's wish to simplify or compress the original source sentence. The last possible decision is to completely reject the sentence (represented by label R in Figure 1). For example, the editor may wish to ignore a superfluous or duplicate information expressed in the current sentence. An example mixed summary generated by our approach is depicted in Figure 2 in the appendix, further emphasizing the various editor's decisions.

2.1 Implementing the editor's decisions

For a given sentence $s \in D$, we now denote by s^e and s^a its original (extracted) and paraphrased (abstracted) versions. To obtain s^a we use an abstractor, whose details will be shortly explained (see Section 2.2). Let $e_s \in \mathbb{R}^n$ and $a_s \in \mathbb{R}^n$ further denote the corresponding sentence representations of s^e and s^a, respectively. Such representations allow to compare both sentence versions on the same grounds.

Recall that, for each sentence $s_i \in S$ (in order) the editor makes one of the three possible decisions: extract, abstract or reject s_i. Therefore, the editor may modify summary S by paraphrasing or rejecting some of its sentences, resulting in a mixed extractive-abstractive summary S'.

Let l be the number of sentences in S. In each step $i \in \{1, 2, \ldots, l\}$, in order to make an educated decision, the editor considers both sentence representations e_{s_i} and a_{s_i} as its input, together with two additional auxiliary representations. The first auxiliary representation is that of the whole document D itself, hereinafter denoted $d \in \mathbb{R}^n$. Such a representation provides a *global context* for decision making. Assuming document D has N sentences, let $\bar{e} = \frac{1}{N} \sum_{s \in D} e_s$. Following (Chen and Bansal, 2018; Wu and Hu, 2018a), d is then calculated as follows: $d = tanh\left(W_d \bar{e} + b_d\right)$, where $W_d \in \mathbb{R}^{n \times n}$ and $b_d \in \mathbb{R}^n$ are learnable parameters.

The second auxiliary representation is that of

the summary that was generated by the editor so far, denoted at step i as $g_{i-1} \in \mathbb{R}^n$, with $g_0 = \vec{0}$. Such a representation provides a *local context* for decision making. Given the four representations as an input, the editor's decision for sentence $s_i \in S$ is implemented using two fully-connected layers, as follows:

$$softmax\left(V tanh\left(W_c[e_{s_i}, a_{s_i}, g_{i-1}, d] + b_c\right) + b\right), \tag{1}$$

where $[\cdot]$ denotes the vectors concatenation, $V \in \mathbb{R}^{3 \times m}$, $W_c \in \mathbb{R}^{m \times 4n}$, $b_c \in \mathbb{R}^m$ and $b \in \mathbb{R}^3$ are learnable parameters.

In each step i, therefore, the editor chooses the action $\pi_i \in \{\mathsf{E}, \mathsf{A}, \mathsf{R}\}$ with the highest likelihood (according to Eq. 1), further denoted $p(\pi_i)$. Upon decision, in case it is either E or A, the editor appends the corresponding sentence version (i.e., either s_i^e or s_i^a) to S'; otherwise, the decision is R and sentence s_i is discarded. Depending on its decision, the current summary representation is further updated as follows:

$$g_i = g_{i-1} + tanh\left(W_g h_i\right), \tag{2}$$

where $W_g \in \mathbb{R}^{n \times n}$ are learnable parameters, g_{i-1} is the summary representation from the previous decision step; and $h_i \in \{e_{s_i}, a_{s_i}, \vec{0}\}$, depending on which decision is made.

Such a network architecture allows to capture various complex interactions between the different inputs. For example, the network may learn that given the global context, one of the sentence versions may allow to produce a summary with a better coverage. As another example, based on the interaction between both sentence versions with either of the local or global contexts (and possibly among the last two), the network may learn that both sentence versions may only add superfluous or redundant information to the summary, and therefore, decide to reject both.

2.2 Extractor and Abstractor

As a proof of concept, in this work, we utilize the extractor and abstractor that were previously used in (Chen and Bansal, 2018), with a slight modification to the latter, motivated by its specific usage within our approach. We now only highlight important aspects of these two sub-components and kindly refer the reader to (Chen and Bansal, 2018) for the full implementation details.

The extractor of (Chen and Bansal, 2018) consists of two main sub-components. The first is an *encoder* which encodes each sentence $s \in D$ into e_s using an hierarchical representation[1]. The second is a *sentence selector* using a *Pointer-Network* (Vinyals et al., 2015). For the latter, let $P(s)$ be the selection likelihood of sentence s.

The abstractor of (Chen and Bansal, 2018) is basically a standard encoder-aligner-decoder with a copy mechanism (See et al., 2017). Yet, instead of applying it directly only on a single given extracted sentence $s_i^e \in S$, we apply it on a "chunk" of three consecutive sentences[2] (s_-^e, s_i^e, s_+^e), where s_-^e and s_+^e denote the sentence that precedes and succeeds s_i^e in D, respectively. This in turn, allows to generate an abstractive version of s_i^e (i.e., s_i^a) that benefits from a wider local context. Inspired by previous soft-attention methods, we further utilize the extractor's sentence selection likelihoods $P(\cdot)$ for enhancing the abstractor's attention mechanism, as follows. Let $C(w_j)$ denote the abstractor's original attention value of a given word w_j occurring in (s_-^e, s_i^e, s_+^e); we then recalculate this value to be $C'(w_j) = \frac{C(w_j) \cdot P(s)}{Z}$, with $w_j \in s$ and $s \in \{s_-^e, s_i^e, s_+^e\}$; $Z = \sum_{s' \in \{s_-^e, s_i^e, s_+^e\}} \sum_{w_j \in s'} C(w_j) \cdot P(s')$ denotes the normalization term.

2.3 Sentence representation

Recall that, in order to compare s_i^e with s_i^a, we need to represent both sentence versions on as similar grounds as possible. To achieve that, we first replace s_i^e with s_i^a within the original document D. By doing so, we basically treat sentence s_i^a as if it was an ordinary sentence within D, where the rest of the document remains untouched. We then obtain s_i^a's representation by encoding it using the extractor's encoder in a similar way in which sentence s_i^e was originally supposed to be encoded. This results in a representation a_{s_i} that provides a comparable alternative to e_{s_i}, whose encoding is expected to be effected by similar contextual grounds.

2.4 Network training

We conclude this section with the description of how we train the editor using a novel soft labeling approach. Given text S (with l extracted sentences), let $\pi = (\pi_1, \ldots, \pi_l)$ denote its editing decisions

---

[1] Such a representation is basically a combination of a temporal convolutional model followed by a biLSTM encoder.

[2] The first and last chunks would only have two consecutive sentences.

(sequence). We define the following "soft" cross-entropy loss:

$$\mathcal{L}(\pi|S) = -\frac{1}{l} \sum_{s_i \in S} \sum_{\pi_i \in \{E,A,R\}} y(\pi_i) \log p(\pi_i),$$

(3)

where, for a given sentence $s_i \in S$, $y(\pi_i)$ denotes its soft-label for decision.

We next explain how each soft-label $y(\pi_i)$ is estimated. To this end, we utilize a given summary quality metric $r(S')$ which can be used to evaluate the quality of any given summary S' (e.g., ROUGE (Lin, 2004)). Overall, for a given text input S with l sentences, there are 3^l possible summaries S' to consider. Let $\pi^* = (\pi_1^*, \ldots, \pi_l^*)$ denote the best decision sequence which results in the summary which maximizes $r(\cdot)$. For $i \in \{1, 2, \ldots, l\}$, let $\bar{r}(\pi_1^*, \ldots, \pi_{i-1}^*, \pi_i)$ denote the average $r(\cdot)$ value obtained by decision sequences that start with the prefix $(\pi_1^*, \ldots, \pi_{i-1}^*, \pi_i)$. Based on π^*, the soft label $y(\pi_i)$ is then calculated[3] as follows:

$$y(\pi_i) = \frac{\bar{r}(\pi_1^*, \ldots, \pi_{i-1}^*, \pi_i)}{\sum_{\pi_j \in \{E,A,R\}} \bar{r}(\pi_1^*, \ldots, \pi_{i-1}^*, \pi_j)}$$

(4)

3 Evaluation

3.1 Dataset and Setup

We trained, validated and tested our approach using the non-annonymized version of the CNN/DailyMail dataset (Hermann et al., 2015). Following (Nallapati et al., 2016), we used the story highlights associated with each article as its ground truth summary. We further used the F-measure versions of ROUGE-1, ROUGE-2 and ROUGE-L as our evaluation metrics (Lin, 2004).

The extractor and abstractor were trained similarly to (Chen and Bansal, 2018) (including the same hyperparameters). The Editorial Network (hereinafter denoted *EditNet*) was trained according to Section 2.4, using the ADAM optimizer with a learning rate of 10^{-4} and a batch size of 32. Following (Dong et al., 2018; Wu and Hu, 2018a), we set the reward metric to be $r(\cdot) = \alpha R\text{-}1(\cdot) + \beta R\text{-}2(\cdot) + \gamma R\text{-}L(\cdot)$; with $\alpha = 0.4$, $\beta = 1$ and $\gamma = 0.5$, which were further suggested by (Wu and Hu, 2018a).

We further applied the *Teacher-Forcing* approach (Lamb et al., 2016) during training, where we considered the true-label instead of the

---

[3]For $i = 1$ we have: $\bar{r}(\pi_1^*, \ldots, \pi_0^*, \pi_1) = \bar{r}(\pi_1)$.

Table 1: Quality evaluation using ROUGE F-measure (ROUGE-1, ROUGE-2, ROUGE-L) on CNN/DailyMail non-annonymized dataset

	R-1	R-2	R-L
Extractive			
Lead-3	40.00	17.50	36.20
SummaRuNNer (Nallapati et al., 2017)	39.60	16.20	35.30
EditNet$_E$	38.43	18.07	35.37
Refresh (Narayan et al., 2018)	40.00	18.20	36.60
Rnes w/o coherence (Wu and Hu, 2018b)	41.25	18.87	37.75
BanditSum (Dong et al., 2018)	41.50	18.70	37.60
Latent (Zhang et al., 2018)	41.05	18.77	37.54
rnn-ext+RL (Chen and Bansal, 2018)	41.47	18.72	37.76
NeuSum (Zhou et al., 2018)	41.59	19.01	37.98
BERTSUM (Liu, 2019)	43.25	20.24	39.63
Abstractive			
Pointer-Generator (See et al., 2017)	39.53	17.28	36.38
KIGN+Prediction-guide (Li et al., 2018)	38.95	17.12	35.68
Multi-Task(EG+QG) (Guo et al., 2018)	39.81	17.64	36.54
EditNet$_A$	40.00	17.73	37.53
rnn-ext+abs+RL (Chen and Bansal, 2018)	40.04	17.61	37.59
RL+pg+cbdec (Jiang and Bansal, 2018)	40.66	17.87	37.06
Saliency+Entail. (Pasunuru and Bansal, 2018)	40.43	18.00	37.10
Inconsistency loss (Hsu et al., 2018)	40.68	17.97	37.13
Bottom-up (Gehrmann et al., 2018)	41.22	18.68	38.34
DCA (Celikyilmaz et al., 2018)	41.69	19.47	37.92
Mixed Extractive-Abstractive			
EditNet	41.42	19.03	38.36

editor's decision (including when updating g_i at each step i according to Eq. 2). Following (Chen and Bansal, 2018), we set $m = 512$ and $n = 512$. We trained for 20 epochs, which has taken about 72 hours on a single GPU. We chose the best model over the validation set for testing. Finally, all components were implemented in Python 3.6 using the pytorch 0.4.1 package.

3.2 Results

Table 1 compares the quality of *EditNet* with that of several state-of-the-art extractive-only or abstractive-only baselines. This includes the extractor (*rnn-ext-RL*) and abstractor (*rnn-ext-abs-RL*) components of (Chen and Bansal, 2018) that we utilized for implementing *EditNet* [4].

We further report the quality of *EditNet* when it was being enforced to take an extract-only or abstract-only decision, denoted hereinafter as *EditNet$_E$* and *EditNet$_A$*, respectively. The comparison of *EditNet* to both *EditNet$_E$* and *EditNet$_A$* variants provides a strong empirical proof that, by utilizing an hybrid decision approach, a

---

[4]The *rnn-ext-RL* extractor results reported in Table 1 are the ones that were reported by (Chen and Bansal, 2018). Training the public extractor released by these authors, we obtained the following significantly lower results: see *EditNet$_E$*

better summarization quality is obtained.

Overall, *EditNet* provides a highly competitive summary quality, where it outperforms most baselines. Interestingly, *EditNet*'s summarization quality is quite similar to that of *NeuSum* (Zhou et al., 2018). Yet, while *NeuSum* applies an extraction-only approach, summaries generated by *EditNet* include a mixture of sentences that have been either extracted or abstracted.

Two models outperform *EditNet*, *BERTSUM* (Liu, 2019) and *DCA* (Celikyilmaz et al., 2018). The *BERTSUM* model gains an impressive accuracy, yet it is an extractive model that utilizes many attention layers running in parallel with millions of parameters (Devlin et al., 2019). *DCA* gains a comparable quality to *EditNet*, it outperforms on R-2 and slightly on R-1. The contextual encoder of *DCA* is comprised of several *LSTM* layers one on top of the other with varied number of agents (hyper-tuned) that transmit messages to each other. Considering the complexity of these models, and the slow down that can incur during training and inference, we think that *EditNet* still provides a useful, high quality and relatively simple extension on top of standard encoder aligned decoder architectures.

On average, 56% and 18% of *EditNet*'s decisions were to abstract (A) or reject (R), respectively. Moreover, on average, per summary, *EditNet* keeps only 33% of the original (extracted) sentences, while the rest (67%) are abstracted ones. This demonstrates that, *EditNet* has a high capability of utilizing abstraction, while being also able to maintain or reject the original extracted text whenever it is estimated to provide the best benefit for the summary's quality.

4 Conclusions and Future Work

We have proposed *EditNet* – a novel alternative summarization approach that instead of solely applying extraction or abstraction, mixes both together. Moreover, *EditNet* implements a novel sentence rejection decision, allowing to "correct" initial sentence selection decisions which are predicted to negatively effect summarization quality. As future work, we plan to evaluate other alternative extractor-abstractor configurations and try to train the network end-to-end. We further plan to explore reinforcement learning (RL) as an alternative decision making approach.

References

Asli Celikyilmaz, Antoine Bosselut, Xiaodong He, and Yejin Choi. 2018. Deep communicating agents for abstractive summarization. In *Proceedings of the 2018 Conference of the North American Chapter of the Association for Computational Linguistics: Human Language Technologies, Volume 1 (Long Papers)*, pages 1662–1675.

Yen-Chun Chen and Mohit Bansal. 2018. Fast abstractive summarization with reinforce-selected sentence rewriting. In *Proceedings of the 56th Annual Meeting of the Association for Computational Linguistics (Volume 1: Long Papers)*, pages 675–686. Association for Computational Linguistics.

Sumit Chopra, Michael Auli, and Alexander M. Rush. 2016. Abstractive sentence summarization with attentive recurrent neural networks. In *Proceedings of the 2016 Conference of the North American Chapter of the Association for Computational Linguistics: Human Language Technologies*, pages 93–98. Association for Computational Linguistics.

Arman Cohan, Franck Dernoncourt, Doo Soon Kim, Trung Bui, Seokhwan Kim, Walter Chang, and Nazli Goharian. 2018. A discourse-aware attention model for abstractive summarization of long documents. In *Proceedings of the 2018 Conference of the North American Chapter of the Association for Computational Linguistics: Human Language Technologies, Volume 2 (Short Papers)*, pages 615–621. Association for Computational Linguistics.

Jacob Devlin, Ming-Wei Chang, Kenton Lee, and Kristina Toutanova. 2019. Bert: Pre-training of deep bidirectional transformers for language understanding. In *Proceedings of the 2019 Conference of the North American Chapter of the Association for Computational Linguistics: Human Language Technologies, Volume 1 (Long and Short Papers)*, pages 4171–4186.

Yue Dong, Yikang Shen, Eric Crawford, Herke van Hoof, and Jackie Chi Kit Cheung. 2018. Banditsum: Extractive summarization as a contextual bandit. In *Proceedings of the 2018 Conference on Empirical Methods in Natural Language Processing, Brussels, Belgium, October 31 - November 4, 2018*, pages 3739–3748.

Sebastian Gehrmann, Yuntian Deng, and Alexander Rush. 2018. Bottom-up abstractive summarization. In *Proceedings of the 2018 Conference on Empirical Methods in Natural Language Processing*, pages 4098–4109. Association for Computational Linguistics.

Han Guo, Ramakanth Pasunuru, and Mohit Bansal. 2018. Soft layer-specific multi-task summarization with entailment and question generation. In *Proceedings of the 56th Annual Meeting of the Association for Computational Linguistics (Volume*

1: Long Papers), pages 687–697. Association for Computational Linguistics.

Karl Moritz Hermann, Tomáš Kočiský, Edward Grefenstette, Lasse Espeholt, Will Kay, Mustafa Suleyman, and Phil Blunsom. 2015. Teaching machines to read and comprehend. In *Proceedings of the 28th International Conference on Neural Information Processing Systems - Volume 1*, NIPS'15, pages 1693–1701, Cambridge, MA, USA. MIT Press.

Wan-Ting Hsu, Chieh-Kai Lin, Ming-Ying Lee, Kerui Min, Jing Tang, and Min Sun. 2018. A unified model for extractive and abstractive summarization using inconsistency loss. In *Proceedings of the 56th Annual Meeting of the Association for Computational Linguistics (Volume 1: Long Papers)*, pages 132–141. Association for Computational Linguistics.

Yichen Jiang and Mohit Bansal. 2018. Closed-book training to improve summarization encoder memory. In *Proceedings of the 2018 Conference on Empirical Methods in Natural Language Processing*, pages 4067–4077. Association for Computational Linguistics.

Alex M Lamb, Anirudh Goyal ALIAS PARTH GOYAL, Ying Zhang, Saizheng Zhang, Aaron C Courville, and Yoshua Bengio. 2016. Professor forcing: A new algorithm for training recurrent networks. In *Advances In Neural Information Processing Systems*, pages 4601–4609.

Chenliang Li, Weiran Xu, Si Li, and Sheng Gao. 2018. Guiding generation for abstractive text summarization based on key information guide network. In *Proceedings of the 2018 Conference of the North American Chapter of the Association for Computational Linguistics: Human Language Technologies, Volume 2 (Short Papers)*, pages 55–60. Association for Computational Linguistics.

Chin-Yew Lin. 2004. Rouge: A package for automatic evaluation of summaries. In *Text summarization branches out: Proceedings of the ACL-04 workshop*, volume 8. Barcelona, Spain.

Peter J Liu, Mohammad Saleh, Etienne Pot, Ben Goodrich, Ryan Sepassi, Lukasz Kaiser, and Noam Shazeer. 2018. Generating wikipedia by summarizing long sequences. *arXiv preprint arXiv:1801.10198*.

Yang Liu. 2019. Fine-tune bert for extractive summarization. *arXiv preprint arXiv:1903.10318*.

Ramesh Nallapati, Feifei Zhai, and Bowen Zhou. 2017. Summarunner: A recurrent neural network based sequence model for extractive summarization of documents. In *Proceedings of the Thirty-First AAAI Conference on Artificial Intelligence, February 4-9, 2017, San Francisco, California, USA.*, pages 3075–3081.

Ramesh Nallapati, Bowen Zhou, Cícero Nogueira dos Santos, Çaglar Gülçehre, and Bing Xiang. 2016. Abstractive text summarization using sequence-to-sequence rnns and beyond. In *Proceedings of the 20th SIGNLL Conference on Computational Natural Language Learning, CoNLL 2016, Berlin, Germany, August 11-12, 2016*, pages 280–290.

Shashi Narayan, Shay B. Cohen, and Mirella Lapata. 2018. Ranking sentences for extractive summarization with reinforcement learning. In *Proceedings of the 2018 Conference of the North American Chapter of the Association for Computational Linguistics: Human Language Technologies, NAACL-HLT 2018, New Orleans, Louisiana, USA, June 1-6, 2018, Volume 1 (Long Papers)*, pages 1747–1759.

Ramakanth Pasunuru and Mohit Bansal. 2018. Multi-reward reinforced summarization with saliency and entailment. In *Proceedings of the 2018 Conference of the North American Chapter of the Association for Computational Linguistics: Human Language Technologies, Volume 2 (Short Papers)*, pages 646–653. Association for Computational Linguistics.

Romain Paulus, Caiming Xiong, and Richard Socher. 2017. A deep reinforced model for abstractive summarization. *CoRR*, abs/1705.04304.

Abigail See, Peter J. Liu, and Christopher D. Manning. 2017. Get to the point: Summarization with pointer-generator networks. In *Proceedings of the 55th Annual Meeting of the Association for Computational Linguistics, ACL 2017, Vancouver, Canada, July 30 - August 4, Volume 1: Long Papers*, pages 1073–1083.

Ilya Sutskever, Oriol Vinyals, and Quoc V. Le. 2014. Sequence to sequence learning with neural networks. In *Proceedings of the 27th International Conference on Neural Information Processing Systems - Volume 2*, NIPS'14, pages 3104–3112, Cambridge, MA, USA. MIT Press.

Jiwei Tan, Xiaojun Wan, and Jianguo Xiao. 2017. Abstractive document summarization with a graph-based attentional neural model. In *Proceedings of the 55th Annual Meeting of the Association for Computational Linguistics (Volume 1: Long Papers)*, pages 1171–1181. Association for Computational Linguistics.

Oriol Vinyals, Meire Fortunato, and Navdeep Jaitly. 2015. Pointer networks. In *Advances in Neural Information Processing Systems*, pages 2692–2700.

Yuxiang Wu and Baotian Hu. 2018a. Learning to extract coherent summary via deep reinforcement learning. In *Proceedings of the Thirty-Second AAAI Conference on Artificial Intelligence, (AAAI-18), the 30th innovative Applications of Artificial Intelligence (IAAI-18), and the 8th AAAI Symposium on Educational Advances in Artificial Intelligence (EAAI-18), New Orleans, Louisiana, USA, February 2-7, 2018*, pages 5602–5609.

Yuxiang Wu and Baotian Hu. 2018b. Learning to extract coherent summary via deep reinforcement learning. In *Proceedings of the Thirty-Second AAAI Conference on Artificial Intelligence, (AAAI-18), the 30th innovative Applications of Artificial Intelligence (IAAI-18), and the 8th AAAI Symposium on Educational Advances in Artificial Intelligence (EAAI-18), New Orleans, Louisiana, USA, February 2-7, 2018*, pages 5602–5609.

Xingxing Zhang, Mirella Lapata, Furu Wei, and Ming Zhou. 2018. Neural latent extractive document summarization. In *Proceedings of the 2018 Conference on Empirical Methods in Natural Language Processing*, pages 779–784. Association for Computational Linguistics.

Qingyu Zhou, Nan Yang, Furu Wei, Shaohan Huang, Ming Zhou, and Tiejun Zhao. 2018. Neural document summarization by jointly learning to score and select sentences. In *Proceedings of the 56th Annual Meeting of the Association for Computational Linguistics (Volume 1: Long Papers)*, pages 654–663. Association for Computational Linguistics.

Towards Annotating and Creating Sub-Sentence Summary Highlights

Kristjan Arumae♠, Parminder Bhatia♢, Fei Liu♠

♠Computer Science Department, University of Central Florida
♢Amazon, USA

{arumae,parmib}@amazon.com   feiliu@cs.ucf.edu

Abstract

Highlighting is a powerful tool to pick out important content and emphasize. Creating summary highlights at the sub-sentence level is particularly desirable, because sub-sentences are more concise than whole sentences. They are also better suited than individual words and phrases that can potentially lead to disfluent, fragmented summaries. In this paper we seek to generate summary highlights by annotating summary-worthy sub-sentences and teaching classifiers to do the same. We frame the task as jointly selecting important sentences and identifying a single most informative textual unit from each sentence. This formulation dramatically reduces the task complexity involved in sentence compression. Our study provides new benchmarks and baselines for generating highlights at the sub-sentence level.

1 Introduction

Highlighting at an appropriate level of granularity is important to emphasize salient content in an unobtrusive manner. A small collection of keywords may be insufficient to deliver the main points of an article, while highlighting whole sentences often provide superfluous information. In domains such as newswire, scholarly publications, legal and policy documents (Kim et al., 2010; Sadeh et al., 2013; Hasan and Ng, 2014), people are tempted to write long and complicated sentences. It is particularly desirable to pick out only *important sentence parts* as opposed to whole sentences.

Generating highlights at the sub-sentence level has not been thoroughly investigated in the past. A related thread of research is extractive and compressive summarization (Daumé III and Marcu, 2002; Zajic et al., 2007; Martins and Smith, 2009; Filippova, 2010; Berg-Kirkpatrick et al., 2011; Thadani and McKeown, 2013; Wang et al., 2013; Li et al., 2013, 2014; Durrett et al., 2016).

The methods select representative sentences from source documents, then delete nonessential words and constituents to form compressed summaries. Nonetheless, making multiple interdependent decisions on word deletion can render summaries ungrammatical and fragmented. In this paper, we investigate an alternative formulation that can dramatically reduce the task complexity involved in sentence compression.

We frame the task as jointly selecting representative sentences from a document and identifying a *single* most informative textual unit from each sentence to create sub-sentence highlights. This formulation is inspired by rhetorical structure theory (RST; Mann and Thompson, 1988) where sub-sentence highlights resemble the *nuclei* which are text spans essential to express the writer's purpose. The formulation also mimics human behavior on picking out important content. If multiple parts of a sentence are important, a human uses a single stroke to highlight them all, up to the whole sentence. If only a part of the sentence is relevant, she only picks out that particular sentence part.

Generating sub-sentence highlights is advantageous over abstraction (See et al., 2017; Chen and Bansal, 2018; Gehrmann et al., 2018; Lebanoff et al., 2018; Celikyilmaz et al., 2018) in several aspects. The highlights can be overlaid on the source document, allowing them to be interpreted in context. The number of highlights is controllable by limiting sentence selection. In contrast, adjusting summary length in an end-to-end, abstractive system can be difficult. Further, highlights are guaranteed to be true-to-the-original, while system abstracts can sometimes "hallucinate" facts and distort the original meaning. Our contributions in this work include the following:

- we introduce a new task formulation of creating sub-sentence summary highlights, then describe

Proceedings of the 2nd Workshop on New Frontiers in Summarization, pages 64–69
Hong Kong, China, November 4, 2019. ©2019 Association for Computational Linguistics

(i):	marseille , france -lrb- cnn -rrb- the french prosecutor leading an investigation into the crash of germanwings flight 9525 insisted wednesday that he was not aware of any video footage from on board the plane .
(ii):	marseille , france -lrb- cnn -rrb- the french prosecutor leading an investigation into the crash of germanwings flight 9525 insisted wednesday that he was not aware of any video footage from on board the plane .
(iii):	marseille , france -lrb- cnn -rrb- the french prosecutor leading an investigation into the crash of germanwings flight 9525 insisted [8] wednesday that he was not aware of any video footage from on board the plane . [22]

Figure 1: An illustration of label smoothing. Words aligned to the abstract are colored *orange*; gap words are colored *turquoise*.

an annotation scheme to obtain binary sentence labels for extraction, as well as start and end indices to mark the most important textual unit of a positively labeled sentence;

- we examine the feasibility of using neural extractive summarization with a multi-termed objective to identify summary sentences and their most informative sub-sentence units. Our study provides new benchmarks and baselines for highlighting at the sub-sentence level.

2 Annotating Sub-Sentence Highlights

We propose to derive gold-standard sub-sentence highlights from human-written abstracts that often accompany the documents (Hermann et al., 2015). However, the challenge still exists, because abstracts are very loosely aligned with source documents and they contain unseen words and phrases. We define *a summary-worthy sub-sentence unit* as the longest consecutive subsequence that contains content of the abstract. We obtain gold-standard labels for sub-sentence units by first establishing word alignments between the document and abstract, then smoothing word labels to generate sub-sentence labels.

Word Alignment The attention matrix of neural sequence-to-sequence models provides a powerful and flexible mechanism for word alignment. Let $S=\{w_i\}_{i=1}^{M}$ be a sequence of words denoting the document, and $T=\{w_t\}_{t=1}^{N}$ denoting the abstract. The attention weight $\alpha_{t,i}$ indicates the amount of attention received by the i-th document word in order to generate the t-th abstract word. All attention values (α) can be automatically learned from parallel training data. After the model is trained, we identify *a single document word* that receives the most attention for generating each abstract word, as denoted in Eq. (1) and illustrated by Figure 1 (i). This step produces a set of source words containing the content of the abstract but possibly with

distinct word forms.[1]

$$w_i^{(t)} = \arg\max_{i \in \mathsf{M}} \alpha_{t,i} \quad \forall t \qquad (1)$$

Smoothing Our goal is to identify sub-sentence units containing content of the abstract by smoothing word labels obtained in the previous step. We extract a single most informative textual unit from a sentence. As a first attempt, we obtain start and end indices of sub-sentence units using heuristics, which are described as follows:

- connecting two selected words if there is a small gap (<5 words) between them. For example, in Figure 1 (ii), the gap between "*crash*" and "*germanwings*" is bridged by labelling all gap words as selected;

- the longest consecutive subsequence after filling gaps is chosen as the most important unit of the sentence. In Figure 1 (iii), we select the longest segment containing 22 words. When a tie occurs, we choose the segment appearing first;

- creating gold-standard labels for sentences and sub-sentence units. If a segment is the most informative, i.e., longest subsequence of a sentence and >5 words, we record its start and end indices. If a segment is selected, its containing sentence is labelled as 1, otherwise 0.

2.1 Dataset and Statistics

We conduct experiments on the CNN/DM dataset released by See et al. (2017) containing news articles and human abstracts. We choose the pointer-generator networks described in the same work to obtain attention matrices used for word alignment. The model was trained on the training split of CNN/DM, then applied to all train/valid/test splits to generate gold-standard sub-sentence highlights. At test time, we compare system highlights with

---

[1] Aligning multiple document words with a single abstract word is possible by retrieving document words whose attention weights exceed a threshold. But the method can be data- and model-dependent, increasing the variability of alignment.

	Sentences		**Gold-Standard Highlights**			**Human Abstracts**	
	#TotalSents	%PosSents	#Sents	#Tokens	%CompR	#Sents	#Tokens
Train	5,312,010	24.42	4.51	51.46	0.47	3.68	56.47
Valid	211,022	30.85	4.87	57.11	0.47	4.00	62.73
Test	182,663	29.63	4.72	54.47	0.46	3.79	59.56

Table 1: Data statistics are broken into three categories. *Sentences* indicate the number of total sentences as well as the rate of positive labels. *Gold-Standard Highlights* reflect document-level details of our new ground truth labels. Compression rate ("CompR") indicates the percentage of a positive labeled sentence was covered by the segment. Finally *Human Abstracts* provides a comparison against CNN/DailyMail ground truth summaries.

gold-standard highlights and human abstracts, respectively, to validate system performance.

In Table 1, we present data statistics of the gold-standard sub-sentence highlights. We observe that gold-standard highlights and human abstracts are of comparable length in terms of tokens. On average, 28% of document sentences are labelled as positive. Among these, 47% of the words belong to gold-standard sub-sentence highlights. In our processed dataset we retain important document level information such as original sentence placement and document ID. We consider each document sentence as a data instance, and introduce a neural model to predict (i) a binary sentence level label, and (ii) start and end indices of a consecutive subsequence for a positive sentence. We are particularly interested in predicting start and end indices to encourage sub-sentence segments to remain self-contained. Finally, we leverage the document ID to re-combine model output to still generate summaries at the document level.

3 Models

We provide initial modeling for our data with a single state-of-the-art architecture. The purpose is to build meaningful representations that allow for joint prediction of summary-worthy sentences and their sub-sentence units. Our model receives an input sequence as an individualized sentence denoted as $S=\{w_i^s\}_{i=1}^{\mathsf{M}}$, where s denotes the sentence index in the original document. The model learns to predict the sentence label and start/end index of a sub-sentence unit based on contextualized representations.

For each token w_i^s we leverage a combined representation E_{tok}, $E_{\text{s-pos}}$, and $E_{\text{d-pos}}$, i.e., a token embedding, sentence level positional embedding, and a document level positional embedding. Here *s-pos* denotes the token position in a sentence, *d-pos* denotes the sentence position in a document, and $E(w_i^s) \in \mathbb{R}^d$. We justify the last embedding by

noting that the sentence position within that document plays an important role since generally there is a higher probability of positive labels towards the beginning. The final input representation is an element-wise addition of all embeddings (Eq. (2)). This input is encoded using a bi-directional transformer (Vaswani et al., 2017; Devlin et al., 2018), denoted as $\mathbf{h}$.

$$E(w_i^s) := E_{\text{tok}}(w_i^s) + E_{\text{s-pos}}(w_i^s) + E_{\text{d-pos}}(w_i^s) \quad (2)$$

3.1 Objectives

We use the transformer output to generate three labels: sentence, start and end positions of the sub-sentence unit. First we obtain the sequence representation via the [CLS] token.[2] We apply a linear transformation to this vector and a softmax layer to obtain a binary label for the entire sentence.

For the indexing objective we transform the encoder output, $\mathbf{h}$, to account for start and end index classification. $\mathbf{a} = \text{MLP}_{\text{start/end}}(\mathbf{h}) \in \mathbb{R}^{\mathsf{M} \times 2}$. Again we make use of a single linear transformation, here it is applied across the encoder temporally giving each time-step two channels. The two channels are individually passed through a softmax layer to produce two distributions, for the start and end index. Finally we use a combined loss term which is trained end-to-end using a cross entropy objective:

$$\mathcal{L} = \lambda(\mathcal{L}_{\text{start}} + \mathcal{L}_{\text{end}}) + \mathcal{L}_{\text{sent}}. \quad (3)$$

For negatively labeled sentences $\mathcal{L}_{\text{start}}$ and $\mathcal{L}_{\text{end}}$ are not utilized during training. λ is a coefficient balancing between two task objectives.

3.2 Experimental Setup

The encoder hidden state dimension is set at 768, with 12 layers and 12 attention heads (BERT$_{\text{BASE}}$ uncased). We utilize dropout (Srivastava et al., 2014) with $p = 0.1$, and λ is empirically set to 0.1.

---

[2] [CLS] is fine-tuned as a class label for the entire sequence, and always positioned at $\mathbf{h}_1$

	ROUGE-1			**ROUGE-2**			**ROUGE-L**		
Model	P	R	F_1	P	R	F_1	P	R	F_1
Oracle (sent.)	36.63	69.52	46.58	20.24	37.76	25.55	25.59	47.84	32.34
Oracle (segm.)	59.71	50.95	53.82	34.42	29.60	**31.16**	43.23	36.89	38.95
Pointer Gen. (See et al., 2017)	–	–	39.53	–	–	17.28	–	–	36.38
QASumm+NER (Arumae and Liu, 2019)	–	–	25.89	–	–	11.65	–	–	22.06
ABSTRACT Sent	30.91	48.61	34.84	13.31	21.40	15.09	20.14	31.44	22.55
Sent + posit.	31.31	56.53	37.72	14.45	26.70	**17.53**	20.51	37.05	24.63
Segm	32.58	44.97	34.73	13.79	19.36	14.75	21.36	29.03	22.51
Segm + posit.	33.11	52.74	37.99	14.96	24.30	**17.26**	21.69	34.41	24.75
SUB-SENT Sent	38.93	58.49	42.81	28.88	44.49	31.96	32.92	50.14	36.32
Sent + posit.	39.97	68.59	47.02	31.38	55.31	**37.19**	34.58	60.30	40.86
Segm	41.31	54.27	42.83	30.29	40.38	31.43	34.81	46.01	36.07
Segm + posit.	42.43	64.09	47.43	32.75	50.40	**36.76**	36.43	55.58	40.80

Table 2: ROUGE results on CNN/DM test set at both sentence and sub-sentence level. The top two rows test gold-standard sentences and sub-sentences against human abstracts. Additionally we show results of an abstractive (See et al., 2017) and an extractive summarizer (Arumae and Liu, 2019) whose CNN/DM results are macro-averaged. The bottom two sections showcase our models. We report results at sentence and sub-sentence level and report those with and without $E_{\text{d-pos}}$ embeddings (*+posit.*). These results are further broken down to reflect evaluation against human abstracts and our own gold standard segments.

We use Adam (Kingma and Ba, 2014) as our optimizer with a learning rate of $3e^{-5}$, and implement early stopping against the validation split. Devlin et al. (2018) suggest that fine-tuning takes only a few epochs with large datasets. Training was conducted on a GeForce GTX 1080 Ti GPU, and each model took at most three days to converge with a maximum epoch time of 12 hours.

At inference time we only extract start and end indices when the sentence label is positive. Additionally if the system produced an end index occurring before the start index we ignore it and select the argmax of the distribution for end indexes which are located after the start index.

4 Results

In Table 2 we report results on the CNN/DM test set evaluated by ROUGE (Lin, 2004). We examine to what extent our summary sentences and sub-sentence highlights, annotated using the strategy presented in §2, have matched the content of human abstracts. These are the *oracle* results for sentences and segments, respectively. Despite that abstracts can contain unseen words, we observe that 70% of the abstract words are covered by gold-standard sentences, and 51% of abstract words are included in sub-sentence units, suggesting the effectiveness of our annotation method on capturing summary-worthy content.

We proceed by evaluating our method against state-of-the-art extractive and abstractive summarization systems. Arumae and Liu (2019) present an approach to extract summary segments using question-answering as supervision signal, assuming a high quality summary can serve as document surrogate to answer questions. See et al. (2017) present pointer-generator networks, an abstractive summarization model and a reliable baseline for being both state-of-the-art, and also a vital tool for guiding our data creation. We show that the performance of oracle summaries is superior to these baselines in terms of R-2, with sub-sentence highlights achieving the highest R-2 F-score of 31%, suggesting extracting sub-sentence highlights is a promising direction moving forward.

4.1 Modeling

Our models are shown in the bottom two sections of Table 2. We obtain system-predicted whole sentences (*Sent*) and sub-sentence segments (*Segm*); then evaluate them against both human abstracts (ABSTRACT) and gold-standard highlights (SUB-SENT). We test the efficacy of document positional embeddings (Eq. (2)), denoted as *+posit.*

Using R-2 as a defining metric, our model outperforms or performs competitively with both the abstractive and extractive baselines. We find that the use of document level positional embeddings is beneficial and that for both summary types, models with these embeddings have a competitive edge against those without. Notably sub-sentence level ROUGE scores consistently outmatch sentence level values. These results are nontrivial, as segment level modeling is highly challenging, often resulting in increased precision but drastically reduced recall (Cheng and Lapata, 2016).

Our model (+*posit*) positively labeled 22.27% of sentences, with an average summary length of 3.54 sentences. The segment model crops selected sentences, exhibiting a compression ratio of 0.77. Comparing to gold-standard ratio of 0.47, there is a 67.4% increase, pointing to future work on highlighting sub-sentence segments.

5 Conclusion

We introduced a new task and dataset to study sub-sentence highlight extraction. We have shown the dataset provides a new upper bound for evaluation metrics, and that the use of sub-sentence segments provides more concise summaries over full sentences. Furthermore, we evaluated our data using a state-of-the-art neural architecture to show the modeling capabilities using this data.

Acknowledgments

We thank the anonymous reviewers for their valuable suggestions. This research was supported in part by the National Science Foundation grant IIS-1909603.

References

Kristjan Arumae and Fei Liu. 2019. Guiding extractive summarization with question-answering rewards. In *Proceedings of the North American Chapter of the Association for Computational Linguistics (NAACL)*.

Taylor Berg-Kirkpatrick, Dan Gillick, and Dan Klein. 2011. Jointly learning to extract and compress. In *Proceedings of the Annual Meeting of the Association for Computational Linguistics (ACL)*.

Asli Celikyilmaz, Antoine Bosselut, Xiaodong He, and Yejin Choi. 2018. Deep communicating agents for abstractive summarization. In *Proceedings of the North American Chapter of the Association for Computational Linguistics (NAACL)*.

Yen-Chun Chen and Mohit Bansal. 2018. Fast abstractive summarization with reinforce-selected sentence rewriting. In *Proceedings of the Annual Meeting of the Association for Computational Linguistics (ACL)*.

Jianpeng Cheng and Mirella Lapata. 2016. Neural summarization by extracting sentences and words. In *Proceedings of the 54th Annual Meeting of the Association for Computational Linguistics (Volume 1: Long Papers)*, volume 1, pages 484–494.

Hal Daumé III and Daniel Marcu. 2002. A noisy-channel model for document compression. In *Proceedings of the Annual Meeting of the Association for Computational Linguistics (ACL)*.

Jacob Devlin, Ming-Wei Chang, Kenton Lee, and Kristina Toutanova. 2018. Bert: Pre-training of deep bidirectional transformers for language understanding. *arXiv preprint arXiv:1810.04805*.

Greg Durrett, Taylor Berg-Kirkpatrick, and Dan Klein. 2016. Learning-based single-document summarization with compression and anaphoricity constraints. In *Proceedings of the Association for Computational Linguistics (ACL)*.

Katja Filippova. 2010. Multi-sentence compression: Finding shortest paths in word graphs. In *Proceedings of the International Conference on Computational Linguistics (COLING)*.

Sebastian Gehrmann, Yuntian Deng, and Alexander M. Rush. 2018. Bottom-up abstractive summarization. In *Proceedings of the Conference on Empirical Methods in Natural Language Processing (EMNLP)*.

Kazi Saidul Hasan and Vincent Ng. 2014. Automatic keyphrase extraction: A survey of the state of the art. In *Proceedings of the Annual Meeting of the Association for Computational Linguistics (ACL)*.

Karl Moritz Hermann, Tomas Kocisky, Edward Grefenstette, Lasse Espeholt, Will Kay, Mustafa Suleyman, and Phil Blunsom. 2015. Teaching machines to read and comprehend. In *Proceedings of Neural Information Processing Systems (NIPS)*.

Su Nam Kim, Olena Medelyan, Min-Yen Kan, and Timothy Baldwin. 2010. SemEval-2010 task 5: Automatic keyphrase extraction from scientific articles. In *Proceedings of the 5th International Workshop on Semantic Evaluation*.

Diederik P Kingma and Jimmy Ba. 2014. Adam: A method for stochastic optimization. *arXiv preprint arXiv:1412.6980*.

Logan Lebanoff, Kaiqiang Song, and Fei Liu. 2018. Adapting the neural encoder-decoder framework from single to multi-document summarization. In *Proceedings of the Conference on Empirical Methods in Natural Language Processing (EMNLP)*.

Chen Li, Fei Liu, Fuliang Weng, and Yang Liu. 2013. Document summarization via guided sentence compression. In *Proceedings of the 2013 Conference on Empirical Methods in Natural Language Processing (EMNLP)*.

Chen Li, Yang Liu, Fei Liu, Lin Zhao, and Fuliang Weng. 2014. Improving multi-document summarization by sentence compression based on expanded constituent parse tree. In *Proceedings of the Conference on Empirical Methods on Natural Language Processing (EMNLP)*.

Chin-Yew Lin. 2004. Rouge: A package for automatic evaluation of summaries. *Text Summarization Branches Out*.

William C. Mann and Sandra A. Thompson. 1988. Rhetorical structure theory: Toward a functional theory of text organization. *Text*, 8(3):243–281.

Andre F. T. Martins and Noah A. Smith. 2009. Summarization with a joint model for sentence extraction and compression. In *Proceedings of the ACL Workshop on Integer Linear Programming for Natural Language Processing*.

Norman Sadeh, Alessandro Acquisti, Travis Breaux, Lorrie Cranor, Aleecia McDonald, Joel Reidenberg, Noah Smith, Fei Liu, Cameron Russel, Florian Schaub, and Shomir Wilson. 2013. The usable privacy policy project: Combining crowdsourcing, machine learning and natural language processing to semi-automatically answer those privacy questions users care about. Technical Report CMU-ISR-13-119, Carnegie Mellon University.

Abigail See, Peter J. Liu, and Christopher D. Manning. 2017. Get to the point: Summarization with pointer-generator networks. In *Proceedings of the Annual Meeting of the Association for Computational Linguistics (ACL)*.

Nitish Srivastava, Geoffrey Hinton, Alex Krizhevsky, Ilya Sutskever, and Ruslan Salakhutdinov. 2014. Dropout: a simple way to prevent neural networks from overfitting. *The Journal of Machine Learning Research*, 15(1):1929–1958.

Kapil Thadani and Kathleen McKeown. 2013. Sentence compression with joint structural inference. In *Proceedings of CoNLL*.

Ashish Vaswani, Noam Shazeer, Niki Parmar, Jakob Uszkoreit, Llion Jones, Aidan N Gomez, Ł ukasz Kaiser, and Illia Polosukhin. 2017. Attention is all you need. In I. Guyon, U. V. Luxburg, S. Bengio, H. Wallach, R. Fergus, S. Vishwanathan, and R. Garnett, editors, *Advances in Neural Information Processing Systems 30*, pages 5998–6008. Curran Associates, Inc.

Lu Wang, Hema Raghavan, Vittorio Castelli, Radu Florian, and Claire Cardie. 2013. A sentence compression based framework to query-focused multi-document summarization. In *Proceedings of ACL*.

David Zajic, Bonnie J. Dorr, Jimmy Lin, and Richard Schwartz. 2007. Multi-candidate reduction: Sentence compression as a tool for document summarization tasks. *Information Processing and Management*.

SAMSum Corpus: A Human-annotated Dialogue Dataset
for Abstractive Summarization

Bogdan Gliwa, Iwona Mochol, Maciej Biesek, Aleksander Wawer (iD)
Samsung R&D Institute Poland
{b.gliwa, i.mochol, m.biesek, a.wawer}@samsung.com

Abstract

This paper introduces the **SAMSum Corpus**, a new dataset with abstractive dialogue summaries. We investigate the challenges it poses for automated summarization by testing several models and comparing their results with those obtained on a corpus of news articles. We show that model-generated summaries of dialogues achieve higher ROUGE scores than the model-generated summaries of news – in contrast with human evaluators' judgement. This suggests that a challenging task of abstractive dialogue summarization requires dedicated models and non-standard quality measures. To our knowledge, our study is the first attempt to introduce a high-quality chat-dialogues corpus, manually annotated with abstractive summarizations, which can be used by the research community for further studies.

1   Introduction and related work

The goal of the summarization task is condensing a piece of text into a shorter version that covers the main points succinctly. In the abstractive approach important pieces of information are presented using words and phrases not necessarily appearing in the source text. This requires natural language generation techniques with high level of semantic understanding (Chopra et al., 2016; Rush et al., 2015; Khandelwal et al., 2019; Zhang et al., 2019; See et al., 2017; Chen and Bansal, 2018; Gehrmann et al., 2018).

Major research efforts have focused so far on summarization of single-speaker documents like news (e.g., Nallapati et al. (2016)) or scientific publications (e.g., Nikolov et al. (2018)). One of the reasons is the availability of large, high-quality news datasets with annotated summaries, e.g., CNN/Daily Mail (Hermann et al., 2015; Nallapati et al., 2016). Such a comprehensive dataset for dialogues is lacking.

The challenges posed by the abstractive dialogue summarization task have been discussed in the literature with regard to AMI meeting corpus (McCowan et al., 2005), e.g. Banerjee et al. (2015), Mehdad et al. (2014), Goo and Chen (2018). Since the corpus has a low number of summaries (for 141 dialogues), Goo and Chen (2018) proposed to use assigned topic descriptions as gold references. These are short, label-like goals of the meeting, e.g., *costing evaluation of project process; components, materials and energy sources; chitchat.* Such descriptions, however, are very general, lacking the messenger-like structure and any information about the speakers.

To benefit from large news corpora, Ganesh and Dingliwal (2019) built a dialogue summarization model that first converts a conversation into a structured text document and later applies an attention-based pointer network to create an abstractive summary. Their model, trained on structured text documents of CNN/Daily Mail dataset, was evaluated on the Argumentative Dialogue Summary Corpus (Misra et al., 2015), which, however, contains only 45 dialogues.

In the present paper, we further investigate the problem of abstractive dialogue summarization. With the growing popularity of online conversations via applications like Messenger, WhatsApp and WeChat, summarization of chats between a few participants is a new interesting direction of summarization research. For this purpose we have created the **SAMSum Corpus**[1] which contains over 16k chat dialogues with manually annotated summaries. The dataset is freely available for the research community[2].

The paper is structured as follows: in Section 2

---

[1] The name is a shortcut for **Samsung Abstractive Messenger Summarization**

[2] The dataset will be published on ELRA language resources catalogue.

Proceedings of the 2nd Workshop on New Frontiers in Summarization, pages 70–79
Hong Kong, China, November 4, 2019. ©2019 Association for Computational Linguistics

Dataset	Train	Validation	Test
CNN/DM	287 227	13 368	11 490
SAMSum	14 732	818	819

Table 1: Datasets sizes

we present details about the new corpus and describe how it was created, validated and cleaned. Brief description of baselines used in the summarization task can be found in Section 3. In Section 4, we describe our experimental setup and parameters of models. Both evaluations of summarization models, the automatic with ROUGE metric and the linguistic one, are reported in Section 5 and Section 6, respectively. Examples of models' outputs and some errors they make are described in Section 7. Finally, discussion, conclusions and ideas for further research are presented in sections 8 and 9.

2 SAMSum Corpus

Initial approach. Since there was no available corpus of messenger conversations, we considered two approaches to build it: (1) using existing datasets of documents, which have a form similar to chat conversations, (2) creating such a dataset by linguists.

In the first approach, we reviewed datasets from the following categories: chatbot dialogues, SMS corpora, IRC/chat data, movie dialogues, tweets, comments data (conversations formed by replies to comments), transcription of meetings, written discussions, phone dialogues and daily communication data. Unfortunately, they all differed in some respect from the conversations that are typically written in messenger apps, e.g. they were too technical (IRC data), too long (comments data, transcription of meetings), lacked context (movie dialogues) or they were more of a spoken type, such as a dialogue between a petrol station assistant and a client buying petrol.

As a consequence, we decided to create a chat dialogue dataset by constructing such conversations that would epitomize the style of a messenger app.

Process of building the dataset. Our dialogue summarization dataset contains natural messenger-like conversations created and written down by linguists fluent in English. The style and register of conversations are diversified – dialogues could be informal, semi-formal or formal, they may contain slang phrases, emoticons and typos. We asked linguists to create conversations similar to those they write on a daily basis, reflecting the proportion of topics of their real-life messenger conversations. It includes chit-chats, gossiping about friends, arranging meetings, discussing politics, consulting university assignments with colleagues, etc. Therefore, this dataset does not contain any sensitive data or fragments of other corpora.

Each dialogue was created by one person. After collecting all of the conversations, we asked language experts to annotate them with summaries, assuming that they should (1) be rather short, (2) extract important pieces of information, (3) include names of interlocutors, (4) be written in the third person. Each dialogue contains only one reference summary.

Validation. Since the SAMSum corpus contains dialogues created by linguists, the question arises whether such conversations are really similar to those typically written via messenger apps. To find the answer, we performed a validation task. We asked two linguists to doubly annotate 50 conversations in order to verify whether the dialogues could appear in a messenger app and could be summarized (i.e. a dialogue is not too general or unintelligible) or not (e.g. a dialogue between two people in a shop). The results revealed that 94% of examined dialogues were classified by both annotators as good i.e. they do look like conversations from a messenger app and could be condensed in a reasonable way. In a similar validation task, conducted for the existing dialogue-type datasets (described in the Initial approach section), the annotators agreed that only 28% of the dialogues resembled conversations from a messenger app.

Cleaning data. After preparing the dataset, we conducted a process of cleaning it in a semiautomatic way. Beforehand, we specified a format for written dialogues with summaries: a colon should separate an author of utterance from its content, each utterance is expected to be in a separate line. Therefore, we could easily find all deviations from the agreed structure – some of them could be automatically fixed (e.g. when instead of a colon, someone used a semicolon right after the interlocutor's name at the beginning of an utterance), others were passed for verification to linguists. We also tried to correct typos in interlocutors' names (if one person has several utterances, it happens that, before one of them, there is a typo in his/her name) – we used the Levenshtein distance to find very similar names (possibly with typos e.g. 'George' and 'Goerge') in a single conversation, and those cases with very similar names were passed to linguists for verification.

Description. The created dataset is made of 16369 conversations distributed uniformly into 4 groups based on the number of utterances in conversations: 3-6, 7-12, 13-18 and 19-30. Each utterance contains the name of the speaker. Most conversations consist of dialogues between two interlocutors (about 75% of all conversations), the rest is between three or more people. Table 1 presents the size of the dataset split used in our experiments. The example of a dialogue from this corpus is shown in Table 2.

Dialogue
Blair: Remember we are seeing the wedding planner after work
Chuck: Sure, where are we meeting her?
Blair: At Nonna Rita's
Chuck: Can I order their seafood tagliatelle or are we just having coffee with her? I've been dreaming about it since we went there last month
Blair: Haha sure why not
Chuck: Well we both remmber the spaghetti pomodoro disaster from our last meeting with Diane
Blair: Omg hahaha it was all over her white blouse
Chuck: :D
Blair: :P
Summary
Blair and Chuck are going to meet the wedding planner after work at Nonna Rita's. The tagliatelle served at Nonna Rita's are very good.

Table 2: Example of a dialogue from the collected corpus

3 Dialogues baselines

The baseline commonly used in the news summarization task is Lead-3 (See et al., 2017), which takes three leading sentences of the document as the summary. The underlying assumption is that the beginning of the article contains the most

Model	n	R-1	R-2	R-L
LEAD	3	31.40	8.68	29.42
	4	31.87	8.93	29.91
	5	32.02	9.53	**30.07**
MIDDLE	3	28.04	6.57	26.13
	4	30.08	7.96	28.10
	5	29.91	8.12	27.97
LONGEST	3	**32.46**	10.27	29.92
	4	32.19	**10.35**	29.91
	5	31.61	10.21	29.55
LONGER -THAN	10	28.31	9.69	26.72
	20	29.36	10.23	27.59
	30	29.61	10.28	27.71
MOST-ACTIVE -PERSON	n/a	26.54	8.55	24.57

Table 3: Baselines for the dialogues summarization

significant information. Inspired by the Lead-n model, we propose a few different simple models:

- MIDDLE-n, which takes n utterances from the middle of the dialogue,

- LONGEST-n, treating only n longest utterances in order of length as a summary,

- LONGER-THAN-n, taking only utterances longer than n characters in order of length (if there is no such long utterance in the dialogue, takes the longest one),

- MOST-ACTIVE-PERSON, which treats all utterances of the most active person in the dialogue as a summary.

Results of the evaluation of the above models are reported in Table 3. There is no obvious baseline for the task of dialogues summarization. We expected rather low results for Lead-3, as the beginnings of the conversations usually contain greetings, not the main part of the discourse. However, it seems that in our dataset greetings are frequently combined with question-asking or information passing (sometimes they are even omitted) and such a baseline works even better than the MIDDLE baseline (taking utterances from the middle of a dialogue). Nevertheless, the best dialogue baseline turns out to be the LONGEST-3 model.

4 Experimental setup

This section contains a description of setting used in the experiments carried out.

4.1 Data preparation

In order to build a dialogue summarization model, we adopt the following strategies: (1) each candidate architecture is trained and evaluated on the dialogue dataset; (2) each architecture is trained on the train set of CNN/Daily Mail joined together with the train set of the dialogue data, and evaluated on the dialogue test set.

In addition, we prepare a version of dialogue data, in which utterances are separated with a special token called the separator (artificially added token e.g. '<EOU>' for models using word embeddings, '|' for models using subword embeddings). In all our experiments, news and dialogues are truncated to 400 tokens, and summaries – to 100 tokens. The maximum length of generated summaries was not limited.

4.2 Models

We carry out experiments with the following summarization models (for all architectures we set the beam size for beam search decoding to 5):

- **Pointer generator network** (See et al., 2017). In the case of *Pointer Generator*, we use a default configuration[3], changing only the minimum length of the generated summary from 35 (used in news) to 15 (used in dialogues).

- **Transformer** (Vaswani et al., 2017). The model is trained using OpenNMT library[4]. We use the same parameters for training both on news and on dialogues[5], changing only the minimum length of the generated summary – 35 for news and 15 for dialogues.

- **Fast Abs RL** (Chen and Bansal, 2018). It is trained using its default parameters[6]. For dialogues, we change the convolutional word-level sentence encoder (used in extractor part) to only use kernel with size equal 3 instead of 3-5 range. It is caused by the fact

that some of utterances are very short and the default setting is unable to handle that.

- **Fast Abs RL Enhanced**. The additional variant of the *Fast Abs RL* model with slightly changed utterances i.e. to each utterance, at the end, after artificial separator, we add names of all other interlocutors. The reason for that is that *Fast Abs RL* requires text to be split into sentences (as it selects sentences and then paraphrase each of them). For dialogues, we divide text into utterances (which is a natural unit in conversations), so sometimes, a single utterance may contain more than one sentence. Taking into account how this model works, it may happen that it selects an utterance of a single person (each utterance starts with the name of the author of the utterance) and has no information about other interlocutors (if names of other interlocutors do not appear in selected utterances), so it may have no chance to use the right people's names in generated summaries.

- **LightConv and DynamicConv** (Wu et al., 2019). The implementation is available in fairseq[7] (Ott et al., 2019). We train lightweight convolution models in two manners: (1) learning token representations from scratch; in this case we apply BPE tokenization with the vocabulary of 30K types, using fastBPE implementation[8] (Sennrich et al., 2015); (2) initializing token embeddings with pre-trained language model representations; as a language model we choose GPT-2 small (Radford et al., 2019).

4.3 Evaluation metrics

We evaluate models with the standard ROUGE metric (Lin, 2004), reporting the F_1 scores (with stemming) for ROUGE-1, ROUGE-2 and ROUGE-L following previous works (Chen and Bansal, 2018; See et al., 2017). We obtain scores using the `py-rouge` package[9].

5 Results

The results for the news summarization task are shown in Table 4 and for the dialogue summarization – in Table 5. In both domains, the best models' ROUGE-1 exceeds 39, ROUGE-2 – 17 and

---

[3] `https://github.com/abisee/pointer-generator`
[4] `https://github.com/OpenNMT/OpenNMT-py`
[5] `http://opennmt.net/OpenNMT-py/Summarization.html`
[6] `https://github.com/ChenRocks/fast_abs_rl`

[7] `https://github.com/pytorch/fairseq`
[8] `https://github.com/glample/fastBPE`
[9] `https://pypi.org/project/py-rouge/`

ROUGE-L – 36. Note that the strong baseline for news (Lead-3) is outperformed in all three metrics only by one model. In the case of dialogues, all tested models perform better than the baseline (LONGEST-3).

In general, the Transformer-based architectures benefit from training on the joint dataset: news+dialogues, even though the news and the dialogue documents have very different structures. Interestingly, this does not seem to be the case for the *Pointer Generator* or *Fast Abs RL* model.

The inclusion of a separation token between dialogue utterances is advantageous for most models – presumably because it improves the discourse structure. The improvement is most visible when training is performed on the joint dataset.

Having compared two variants of the *Fast Abs RL* model – with original utterances and with enhanced ones (see Section 4.2), we conclude that enhancing utterances with information about the other interlocutors helps achieve higher ROUGE values.

The largest improvement of the model performance is observed for *LightConv* and *DynamicConv* models when they are complemented with pretrained embeddings from the language model *GPT-2*, trained on enormous corpora.

It is also worth noting that some models (*Pointer Generator*, *Fast Abs RL*), trained only on the dialogues corpus (which has 16k dialogues), reach similar level (or better) in terms of ROUGE metrics than models trained on the CNN/DM news dataset (which has more than 300k articles). Adding pretrained embeddings and training on the joined dataset helps in achieving significantly higher values of ROUGE for dialogues than the best models achieve on the CNN/DM news dataset.

According to ROUGE metrics, the best performing model is *DynamicConv* with *GPT-2* embeddings, trained on joined news and dialogue data with an utterance separation token.

6 Linguistic verification of summaries

ROUGE is a standard way of evaluating the quality of machine generated summaries by comparing them with reference ones. The metric based on n-gram overlapping, however, may not be very informative for abstractive summarization, where paraphrasing is a keypoint in producing high-quality sentences. To quantify this conjecture, we

Model	R-1	R-2	R-L
Lead-3 baseline	40.24	17.44	34.90
Pointer Generator	38.72	16.67	35.59
Fast Abs RL	**40.99**	**17.72**	**38.30**
Transformer	38.72	16.89	35.74
LightConv	39.44	17.20	36.20
DynamicConv	39.46	17.33	36.29
LightConv + GPT2 emb	39.52	17.31	36.15
DynamicConv + GPT2 emb	39.94	17.56	36.51

Table 4: Model evaluation on the news corpus test set

manually evaluated summaries generated by the models for 150 news and 100 dialogues. We asked two linguists to mark the quality of every summary on the scale of -1, 0, 1, where -1 means that a summarization is poor, extracts irrelevant information or does not make sense at all, 1 – it is understandable and gives a brief overview of the text, and 0 stands for a summarization that extracts only a part of relevant information, or makes some mistakes in the produced summary.

We noticed a few annotations (7 for news and 4 for dialogues) with opposite marks (i.e. one annotator judgement was -1, whereas the second one was 1) and decided to have them annotated once again by another annotator who had to resolve conflicts. For the rest, we calculated the linear weighted Cohen's kappa coefficient (McHugh, 2012) between annotators' scores. For news examples, we obtained agreement on the level of 0.371 and for dialogues – 0.506. The annotators' agreement is higher on dialogues than on news, probably because of structures of those data – articles are often long and it is difficult to decide what the key-point of the text is; dialogues, on the contrary, are rather short and focused mainly on one topic.

For manually evaluated samples, we calculated ROUGE metrics and the mean of two human ratings; the prepared statistics is presented in Table 6. As we can see, models generating dialogue summaries can obtain high ROUGE results, but their outputs are marked as poor by human annotators. Our conclusion is that the ROUGE metric corresponds with the quality of generated summaries for news much better than for dialogues, confirmed by Pearson's correlation between human evaluation and the ROUGE metric, shown

Model	Train data	Separator	R-1	R-2	R-L
LONGEST-3 baseline	n/a	n/a	32.46	10.27	29.92
Pointer Generator	dialogues	no	38.55	14.14	34.85
Pointer Generator	dialogues	yes	40.08	15.28	36.63
Fast Abs RL	dialogues	no	40.96	17.18	39.05
Fast Abs RL Enhanced	dialogues	no	41.95	18.06	39.23
Transformer	dialogues	no	36.62	11.18	33.06
Transformer	dialogues	yes	37.27	10.76	32.73
LightConv	dialogues	no	33.19	11.14	30.34
DynamicConv	dialogues	no	33.79	11.19	30.41
DynamicConv	dialogues	yes	33.69	10.88	30.93
LightConv + GPT-2 emb.	dialogues	no	41.81	16.34	37.63
DynamicConv + GPT-2 emb.	dialogues	no	41.79	16.44	37.54
DynamicConv + GPT-2 emb.	dialogues	yes	41.54	16.29	37.07
Pointer Generator	news + dialogues	no	35.04	13.25	32.42
Pointer Generator	news + dialogues	yes	37.27	14.42	34.36
Fast Abs RL	news + dialogues	no	41.03	16.93	39.05
Fast Abs RL Enhanced	news + dialogues	no	41.87	17.47	39.53
Transformer	news + dialogues	no	41.91	18.25	38.77
Transformer	news + dialogues	yes	42.37	18.44	39.27
LightConv	news + dialogues	no	40.29	17.28	36.81
DynamicConv	news + dialogues	no	40.66	17.41	37.20
DynamicConv	news + dialogues	yes	41.07	17.11	37.27
LightConv + GPT-2 emb.	news + dialogues	no	44.47	19.75	40.07
DynamicConv + GPT-2 emb.	news + dialogues	no	44.69	20.28	40.76
DynamicConv + GPT-2 emb.	news + dialogues	yes	**45.41**	**20.65**	**41.45**

Table 5: Model evaluation on the dialogues corpus test set

in Table 7.

7 Difficulties in dialogue summarization

In a structured text, such as a news article, the information flow is very clear. However, in a dialogue, which contains discussions (e.g. when people try to agree on a date of a meeting), questions (one person asks about something and the answer may appear a few utterances later) and greetings, most important pieces of information are scattered across the utterances of different speakers. What is more, articles are written in the third-person point of view, but in a chat everyone talks about themselves, using a variety of pronouns, which further complicates the structure. Additionally, people talking on messengers often are in a hurry, so they shorten words, use the slang phrases (e.g. 'u r gr8' means 'you are great') and make typos. These phenomena increase the difficulty of performing dialogue summarization.

Table 8 and 9 show a few selected dialogues, together with summaries produced by the best tested models:

- *DynamicConv + GPT-2* embeddings with a separator (trained on news + dialogues),

- *DynamicConv + GPT-2* embeddings (trained on news + dialogues),

- *Fast Abs RL* (trained on dialogues),

- *Fast Abs RL Enhanced* (trained on dialogues),

- *Transformer* (trained on news + dialogues).

One can easily notice problematic issues. Firstly, the models frequently have difficulties in associating names with actions, often repeating the same name, e.g., for Dialogue 1 in Table 8, *Fast Abs RL* generates the following summary: 'lilly and lilly are going to eat salmon'. To help the model deal with names, the utterances are enhanced by adding information about the other interlocutors – *Fast Abs RL enhanced* variant de-

		#examples	mean	median	R-1	R-2	R-L
NEWS	overall	100	0.18	0.5	39.76	16.55	36.23
	Fast Abs RL	50	0.33	0.5	42.33	18.28	38.82
	DynamicConv	50	0.03	0.25	37.19	14.81	33.64
DIALOGUES	overall	150	-0.503	-0.5	43.53	19.94	40.66
	Fast Abs RL	50	-0.55	-0.75	42.16	19.28	40.37
	Fast Abs RL Enhanced	50	-0.63	-1.0	39.79	16.59	37.05
	DynamicConv + GPT-2 emb.	50	-0.33	-0.5	48.63	23.95	44.57

Table 6: Statistics of human evaluation of summaries' quality and ROUGE evaluation of those summaries

	ROUGE-1		ROUGE-2		ROUGE-L	
	corr	p-value	corr	p-value	corr	p-value
NEWS	0.47	1e-6	0.44	6e-6	0.48	1e-6
DIALOGUES	0.32	7.7e-5	0.30	1.84e-4	0.32	8.1e-5

Table 7: Pearson's correlations between human judgement and ROUGE metric

scribed in Section 4.2. In this case, after enhancement, the model generates a summary containing both interlocutors' names: 'lily and gabriel are going to pasta...'. Sometimes models correctly choose speakers' names when generating a summary, but make a mistake in deciding who performs the action (the subject) and who receives the action (the object), e.g. for Dialogue 4 *Dynamic-Conv + GPT-2 emb. w/o sep.* model generates the summary 'randolph will buy some earplugs for maya', while the correct form is 'maya will buy some earplugs for randolph'.

A closely related problem is capturing the context and extracting information about the arrangements after the discussion. For instance, for Dialogue 4, the *Fast Abs RL* model draws a wrong conclusion from the agreed arrangement. This issue is quite frequently visible in summaries generated by *Fast Abs RL*, which may be the consequence of the way it is constructed; it first chooses important utterances, and then summarizes each of them separately. This leads to the narrowing of the context and loosing important pieces of information.

One more aspect of summary generation is deciding which information in the dialogue content is important. For instance, for Dialogue 3 *DynamicConv + GPT-2 emb. with sep.* generates a correct summary, but focuses on a piece of information different than the one included in the reference summary. In contrast, some other models – like *Fast Abs RL enhanced* – select both of the

pieces of information appearing in the discussion. On the other hand, when summarizing Dialogue 5, the models seem to focus too much on the phrase 'it's the best place', intuitively not the most important one to summarize.

8 Discussion

This paper is a step towards abstractive summarization of dialogues by (1) introducing a new dataset, created for this task, (2) comparison with news summarization by the means of automated (ROUGE) and human evaluation.

Most of the tools and the metrics measuring the quality of text summarization have been developed for a single-speaker document, such as news; as such, they are not necessarily the best choice for conversations with several speakers.

We test a few general-purpose summarization models. In terms of human evaluation, the results of dialogues summarization are worse than the results of news summarization. This is connected with the fact that the dialogue structure is more complex – information is spread in multiple utterances, discussions, questions, more typos and slang words appear there, posing new challenges for summarization. On the other hand, dialogues are divided into utterances, and for each utterance its author is assigned. We demonstrate in experiments that the models benefit from the introduction of separators, which mark utterances for each person. This suggests that dedicated models having some architectural changes, taking into ac-

Dialogue 1	Dialogue 2
1. lilly: sorry, i'm gonna be late	1. randolph: honey
2. lilly: don't wait for me and order the food	2. randolph: are you still in the pharmacy?
3. gabriel: no problem, shall we also order something for you?	3. maya: yes
4. gabriel: so that you get it as soon as you get to us?	4. randolph: buy me some earplugs please
5. lilly: good idea	5. maya: how many pairs?
6. lilly: pasta with salmon and basil is always very tasty here	6. randolph: 4 or 5 packs
	7. maya: i'll get you 5
	8. randolph: thanks darling
REF: lilly will be late. gabriel will order pasta with salmon and basil for her.	**REF:** maya will buy 5 packs of earplugs for randolph at the pharmacy.
L3: 6, 3, 4 [38/17/38] **DS:** lilly and gabriel are going to order pasta with salmon and basil [62/42/62] **D:** lilly and gabriel are going to order pasta with salmon and basil [62/42/62] **F:** lilly will be late . she will order the food . lilly and lilly are going to eat salmon and basil [55/39/55] **FE:** lilly will be late . lilly and gabriel are going to pasta with salmon and basil is always tasty . [63/47/63] **T:** lilly will order the food as soon as she gets to gabriel [31/17/23]	**L3:** 2, 4, 8 [36/8/36] **DS:** randolph and maya are going to buy some earplugs for randolph. [43/19/43] **D:** randolph will buy some earplugs for maya. [63/24/42] **F:** maya is in the pharmacy . maya will get 5 . [48/21/48] **FE:** randolph is in the pharmacy . randolph will buy some earplugs for randolph . maya will get 5 . [64/38/64] **T:** randolph will buy some earplugs for randolph . maya will get 5 pairs . [58/36/42]

Table 8: Examples of dialogues (Part 1). REF – reference summary, L3 – LONGEST-3 baseline, DS – Dynamic-Conv + GPT-2 emb. with sep., D – DynamicConv + GPT-2 emb., F – Fast Abs RL, FE – Fast Abs RL Enhanced, T – Transformer. For L3, three longest utterances are listed. Rounded ROUGE values [R-1/R-2/R-L] are given in square brackets.

count the assignation of a person to an utterance in a systematic manner, could improve the quality of dialogue summarization.

We show that the most popular summarization metric ROUGE does not reflect the quality of a summary. Looking at the ROUGE scores, one concludes that the dialogue summarization models perform better than the ones for news summarization. In fact, this hypothesis is not true – we performed an independent, manual analysis of summaries and we demonstrated that high ROUGE results, obtained for automatically-generated dialogue summaries, correspond with lower evaluation marks given by human annotators. An interesting example of the misleading behavior of the ROUGE metrics is presented in Table 9 for Dialogue 4, where a wrong summary – 'paul and cindy don't like red roses.' – obtained all ROUGE values higher than a correct summary – 'paul asks cindy what color flowers should buy.'.

Despite lower ROUGE values, news summaries were scored higher by human evaluators. We conclude that when measuring the quality of model-generated summaries, the ROUGE metrics are more indicative for news than for dialogues, and a new metric should be designed to measure the quality of abstractive dialogue summaries.

9 Conclusions

In our paper we have studied the challenges of abstractive dialogue summarization. We have addressed a major factor that prevents researchers from engaging into this problem: the lack of a proper dataset. To the best of our knowledge, this is the first attempt to create a comprehensive resource of this type which can be used in future research. The next step could be creating an even more challenging dataset with longer dialogues that not only cover one topic, but span over

Dialogue 3	Dialogue 4
1. ashleigh: looks like we're going to the cinema!! 2. ashleigh: <file_gif> 3. peter: you got the job?? 4. ashleigh: i got hte job! :d 5. peter: <file_gif> 6. ashleigh: <file_gif>	1. paul: what color flowers should i get 2. cindy: any just not yellow 3. paul: ok, pink? 4. cindy: no maybe red 5. paul: just tell me what color and what type ok? 6. cindy: ugh, red roses!
REF: ashleigh got the job.	**REF:** paul will buy red roses following cindy's advice.
L3: 1, 4, 3 [33/18/33] **DS:** ashleigh and peter are going to the cinema. [33/0/33] **D:** ashleigh got hte job. [75/33/75] **F:** ashleigh and ashleigh are going to the cinema. peter got the job . [50/29/50] **FE:** ashley and peter are going to the cinema together . ashleigh got the job. [47/40/47] **T:** ashleigh got the job at the cinema . peter and ashleigh are going there . [47/40/47]	**L3:** 5, 1, 2 [13/0/13] **DS:** paul and cindy don't like red roses. [47/13/35] **D:** paul asks cindy what color flowers should buy. [35/0/24] **F:** cindy is going to buy red roses [50/29/38] **FE:** cindy is buying red roses . cindy will buy red . [56/38/44] **T:** cindy does n't know what color should get. cindy does not know what to do [8/0/8]

Dialogue 5
1. eve: where are we meeting?   2. charlie: at the entrance   3. nicole: yes, it's the best place. we would't find each other inside, it'll be too crowded   4. eve: ok!
REF: eve, charlie and nicole are meeting at the entrance.   **L3:** 3, 1, 2 [43/11/43]   **DS:** eve, charlie and nicole are meeting at the entrance. [100/100/100]   **D:** eve, charlie and nicole are meeting at the entrance. [100/100/100]   **F:** charlie is at the entrance . it 's the best place . [42/24/42]   **FE:** charlie is at the entrance . nicole and charlie are going to find each other inside . [58/18/42]   **T:** eve and nicole are meeting at the entrance . it 's the best place to meet . [67/55/67]

Table 9: Examples of dialogues (Part 2). REF – reference summary, L3 – LONGEST-3 baseline, DS – Dynamic-Conv + GPT-2 emb. with sep., D – DynamicConv + GPT-2 emb., F – Fast Abs RL, FE – Fast Abs RL Enhanced, T – Transformer. For L3, three longest utterances are listed. Rounded ROUGE values [R-1/R-2/R-L] are given in square brackets.

numerous different ones.

As shown, summarization of dialogues is much more challenging than of news. In order to perform well, it may require designing dedicated tools, but also new, non-standard measures to capture the quality of abstractive dialogue summaries in a relevant way. We hope to tackle these issues in future work.

Acknowledgments

We would like to express our sincere thanks to Tunia Błachno, Oliwia Ebebenge, Monika Jędras and Małgorzata Krawentek for their huge contribution to the corpus collection – without their ideas, management of the linguistic task and verification of examples we would not be able to create this paper. We are also grateful for the reviewers' helpful comments and suggestions.

References

Siddhartha Banerjee, Prasenjit Mitra, and Kazunari Sugiyama. 2015. Abstractive meeting summarization using dependency graph fusion. In *Proceedings of the 24th International Conference on World Wide Web*, pages 5–6.

Yen-Chun Chen and Mohit Bansal. 2018. Fast abstractive summarization with reinforce-selected sentence rewriting. In *Proceedings of the 56th Annual Meeting of the Association for Computational Linguistics*, pages 675–686.

Sumit Chopra, Michael Auli, and Alexander M. Rush. 2016. Abstractive sentence summarization with attentive recurrent neural networks. In *Proceedings of the 2016 Conference of the North American Chapter of the Association for Computational Linguistics: Human Language Technologies*, pages 93–âĂŞ98.

Prakhar Ganesh and Saket Dingliwal. 2019. Abstractive summarization of spoken and written conversation. *arXiv:1902.01615*.

Sebastian Gehrmann, Yuntian Deng, and Alexander Rush. 2018. Bottom-up abstractive summarization. In *Proceedings of the 2018 Conference on Empirical Methods in Natural Language Processing*, pages 4098–4109.

Chih-Wen Goo and Yun-Nung Chen. 2018. Abstractive dialogue summarization with sentence-gated modeling optimized by dialogue acts. *2018 IEEE Spoken Language Technology Workshop (SLT)*, pages 735–742.

Karl M. Hermann, TomÃąs KociskÃ¡, Edward Grefenstette, Lasse Espeholt, Will Kay, Mustafa Suleyman, and Phil Blunsom. 2015. Teaching machines to read and comprehend. *CoRR*, abs/1506.03340.

Urvashi Khandelwal, Kevin Clark, Dan Jurafsky, and Lukasz Kaiser. 2019. Sample efficient text summarization using a single pre-trained transformer. *CoRR*, abs/1905.08836.

Chin-Yew Lin. 2004. ROUGE: A package for automatic evaluation of summaries. In *Text Summarization Branches Out*, pages 74–81, Barcelona, Spain. Association for Computational Linguistics.

I. McCowan, J. Carletta, W. Kraaij, S. Ashby, S. Bourban, M. Flynn, M. Guillemot, T. Hain, J. Kadlec, V. Karaiskos, M. Kronenthal, G. Lathoud, M. Lincoln, A. Lisowska, W. Post, Dennis Reidsma, and P. Wellner. 2005. The ami meeting corpus. In *Proceedings of Measuring Behavior 2005, 5th International Conference on Methods and Techniques in Behavioral Research*, pages 137–140.

Mary L. McHugh. 2012. Interrater reliability: the kappa statistic. *Biochemia medica*, 22(3):276–282.

Yashar Mehdad, Giuseppe Carenini, and Raymond T. Ng. 2014. Abstractive summarization of spoken and written conversations based on phrasal queries. In *Proceedings of the 52nd Annual Meeting of the Association for Computational Linguistics*, volume 1, pages 1220–1230.

Amita Misra, Pranav Anand, Jean Fox Tree, and Marilyn Walker. 2015. Using summarization to discover argument facets in online idealogical dialog. In *The North American Chapter of the Association for Computational Linguistics (NAACL)*.

Ramesh Nallapati, Bowen Zhou, Cicero Nogueira dos Santos, Caglar Gulcehre, and Bing Xiang. 2016. Abstractive text summarization using sequence-to-sequence rnns and beyond. In *Computational Natural Language Learning*.

Nikola Nikolov, Michael Pfeiffer, and Richard Hahnloser. 2018. Data-driven summarization of scientific articles. In *Proceedings of the Eleventh International Conference on Language Resources and Evaluation (LREC 2018)*.

Myle Ott, Sergey Edunov, Alexei Baevski, Angela Fan, Sam Gross, Nathan Ng, David Grangier, and Michael Auli. 2019. fairseq: A fast, extensible toolkit for sequence modeling. In *Proceedings of the 2019 Conference of the North American Chapter of the Association for Computational Linguistics (Demonstrations)*, pages 48–53.

Alec Radford, Jeff Wu, Rewon Child, David Luan, Dario Amodei, and Ilya Sutskever. 2019. Language models are unsupervised multitask learners.

Alexander M. Rush, Sumit Chopra, and Jason Weston. 2015. A neural attention model for abstractive sentence summarization. In *Proceedings of the 2015 Conference on Empirical Methods in Natural Language Processing*, pages 379–389.

Abigail See, Peter J. Liu, and Christopher D. Manning. 2017. Get to the point: Summarization with pointer-generator networks. In *Proceedings of the 55th Annual Meeting of the Association for Computational Linguistics*, volume 1, pages 1073–1083.

Rico Sennrich, Barry Haddow, and Alexandra Birch. 2015. Neural machine translation of rare words with subword units. *CoRR*, abs/1508.07909.

Ashish Vaswani, Noam Shazeer, Niki Parmar, Jakob Uszkoreit, Llion Jones, Aidan N. Gomez, Lukasz Kaiser, and Illia Polosukhin. 2017. Attention is all you need. In *Advances in Neural Information Processing Systems 30*, pages 5998–6008.

Felix Wu, Angela Fan, Alexei Baevski, Yann Dauphin, and Michael Auli. 2019. Pay less attention with lightweight and dynamic convolutions. In *International Conference on Learning Representations*.

Haoyu Zhang, Jianjun Xu, and Ji Wang. 2019. Pretraining-based natural language generation for text summarization. *CoRR*, abs/1902.09243.

A Closer Look at Data Bias in Neural Extractive Summarization Models

Ming Zhong,* Danqing Wang,* Pengfei Liu,* Xipeng Qiu†, Xuanjing Huang
Shanghai Key Laboratory of Intelligent Information Processing, Fudan University
School of Computer Science, Fudan University
825 Zhangheng Road, Shanghai, China
{mzhong18,dqwang18,pfliu14,xpqiu,xjhuang}@fudan.edu.cn

Abstract

In this paper, we take stock of the current state of summarization datasets and explore how different factors of datasets influence the generalization behaviour of neural extractive summarization models. Specifically, we first propose several properties of datasets, which matter for the generalization of summarization models. Then we build the connection between priors residing in datasets and model designs, analyzing how different properties of datasets influence the choices of model structure design and training methods. Finally, by taking a typical dataset as an example, we rethink the process of the model design based on the experience of the above analysis. We demonstrate that when we have a deep understanding of the characteristics of datasets, a simple approach can bring significant improvements to the existing state-of-the-art model.

1 Introduction

Neural network-based models have achieved great success on summarization tasks (See et al., 2017; Celikyilmaz et al., 2018; Jadhav and Rajan, 2018). Current studies on summarization either explore the possibility of optimization in terms of **networks' structures** (Zhou et al., 2018; Chen and Bansal, 2018; Gehrmann et al., 2018), the improvement in terms of **training schemas** (Wang et al., 2019; Narayan et al., 2018; Wu and Hu, 2018; Chen and Bansal, 2018), or the information fusion with large **pre-trained knowledge** (Peters et al., 2018; Devlin et al., 2018; Liu, 2019; Dong et al., 2019). More recently, Zhong et al. (2019) conducts a comprehensive analysis on why existing summarization systems perform so well from above three aspects. Despite their success, a relatively missing topic[1]

is to analyze and understand the impact on the models' generalization ability from a dataset perspective. With the emergence of more and more summarization datasets (Sandhaus, 2008; Nallapati et al., 2016; Cohan et al., 2018; Grusky et al., 2018), the time is ripe for us to bridge the gap between the insufficient understanding of the nature of *datasets* themselves and the increasing improvement of the *learning methods*.

In this paper, we take a step towards addressing this challenge by taking neural extractive summarization models as an interpretable testbed, investigating how to quantify the characteristics of datasets. As a result, we could explain the behaviour of our models and design new ones. Specifically, we seek to answer two main questions:

Q1: In the summarization task, different datasets present diverse characteristics, so *what is the bias introduced by these dataset choices and how does it influence the model's generalization ability?* We explore two types of factors: *constituent factors* and *style factors*, and analyze how they affect the generalization of neural summarization models respectively. These factors can help us diagnose the weakness of existing models.

Q2: *How different properties of datasets influence the choices of model structure design and training schemas?* We propose some measures and examine their abilities to explain how different model architectures, training schemas, and pre-training strategies react to various properties of datasets.

Our contributions can be summarized as follows:

Main Contributions 1) For the summarization task itself, we diagnose the weakness of existing learning methods in terms of networks' structures, training schemas, and pre-trained knowledge. Some observations could instruct future researchers

---

*These three authors contributed equally.

†Corresponding author.

[1]Concurrent with our work, (Jung et al., 2019) makes a similar analysis on datasets biases and presents three factors which matter for the text summarization task.

Proceedings of the 2nd Workshop on New Frontiers in Summarization, pages 80–89
Hong Kong, China, November 4, 2019. ©2019 Association for Computational Linguistics

Factors of Datasets	Measures	Model designs
Constituent[4.1]	Positional coverage rate [4.1.1] Content coverage rate [4.1.2]	Architecture designs [6.2] Pre-trained strategies [6.2]
Style [4.2]	Density [4.2.1] Compression [4.2.2]	Training schemas [6.1]

Table 1: Organization structure of this paper: four measures presented in this paper and choices of model designs they have influence on.

for a new state-of-the-art performance. 2) We show that a comprehensive understanding of the dataset's properties guides us to design a more reasonable model. We hope to encourage future research on how characteristics of datasets influence the behavior of neural networks.

We summarize our observations as follows: 1) Existing models under-utilize the nature of the training data. We demonstrate that a simple training method on CNN/DM (dividing training set based on domain) can achieve significant improvement. 2) BERT is not a panacea and will fail in some situation. The improvement brought by BERT is related to the *style factor* defined in this paper. 3) It is difficult to handle the hard cases (defined by *style factor*) via architecture design and pre-training knowledge under the extractive framework. 4) Based on the sufficient understanding of the nature of datasets, a more reasonable data partitioning (based on *constituent factors*) method can be mined.

2 Related Work

We briefly outline connections and differences to following related lines of research.

Neural Extractive Summarization Recently, neural network-based models have achieved great success in extractive summarization. (Celikyilmaz et al., 2018; Jadhav and Rajan, 2018; Liu, 2019). Existing works on text summarization can roughly fall into one of three classes: exploring *networks' structures* with suitable bias (Cheng and Lapata, 2016; Nallapati et al., 2017; Zhou et al., 2018); introducing new *training schemas* (Narayan et al., 2018; Wu and Hu, 2018; Chen and Bansal, 2018) and incorporating large *pre-trained knowledge* (Peters et al., 2018; Devlin et al., 2018; Liu, 2019; Dong et al., 2019). Instead of exploring the possibility for a new state-of-the-art along one of above three lines, in this paper, we aim to bridge the gap between the lack of understanding of the characteristics for the datasets and the increasing development of above three learning methods.

Concurrent with our work, (Jung et al., 2019) conducts a quite similar analysis on datasets biases and proposes three factors which matter for the text summarization task. One major difference between these two works is that we additionally focus on how dataset biases influence the designs of models.

Understanding the Generalization Ability of Neural Networks While neural networks have shown superior generalization ability, yet it remains largely unexplained. Recently, some researchers begin to take a step towards understanding the generalization behaviour of neural networks from the perspective of network architectures or optimization procedure (Schmidt et al., 2018; Baluja and Fischer, 2017; Zhang et al., 2016; Arpit et al., 2017). Different from these work, in this paper, we claim that interpreting the generalization ability of neural networks is built on a good understanding of the characteristic of the data.

3 Learning Methods and Datasets

3.1 Learning Methods

Generally, given a dataset $\mathcal{D}$, different learning methods are trying to explain the data in diverse ways, which show different generalization behaviours. Existing learning methods for extractive summarization systems vary in architectures designs, pre-trained strategies and training schemas.

Architecture Designs Architecturally speaking, most of existing extractive summarization systems consists of three major modules: **sentence encoder**, **document encoder** and **decoder**.

In this paper, our architectural choices vary with two types of document encoders: `LSTM`[2] (Hochreiter and Schmidhuber, 1997) and `Transformer` (Vaswani et al., 2017) while we keep the sentence encoder (convolutional neural networks) and decoder (sequence labeling) unchanged[3]. The base

---

[2] We use the implementation of He et al. (2017).

[3] Since they do not show significant influence on our explored experiments.

model in all experiments refers to Transformer equipped with sequence labelling.

Pre-trained Strategies   To explore how different pre-trained strategies influence the model, we take two types of pre-trained knowledge into consideration: we choose Word2vec (Mikolov et al., 2013) as an investigated exemplar for non-contextualized word embeddings and adopt BERT as a contextualized word pre-trainer (Devlin et al., 2018).

Training Schemas   In general, we train a monolithic model to fit the dataset, but in particular, when the data itself has some special properties, we can introduce different training methods to fully exploit all the information contained in the data.

1. **Multi-domain Learning** The basic idea of multi-domain learning in this paper is to introduce domain tag as a low-dimension vector which can augment learned representations. Domain-aware model will make it possible to learn domain-specific features.

2. **Meta-learning** we also try to make models aware of different distribution by meta-learning. Specifically, for each iteration, we sample several domains as meta-train and the other as meta-test. The meta-test gradients will be combined with the meta-train gradients and finally update the model.

3.2 Datasets

We explore four mainstream news articles summarization datasets (CNN/DM, Newsroom, NYT50 and DUC2002) which are various in their publications. We also modify two large-scale scientific paper datasets (arXiv and PubMed) to investigate characteristics for different domains. Detailed statistics are illustrated in Table 2.

4 Quantifying Characteristics of Text Summarization Datasets

In this paper, we present four measures to quantify the characteristics of summarization datasets, which can be abstracted into two types: *constituent factor* and *style factors*.

4.1 Constituent Factors

Motivation   When the neural summarization model determines whether a sentence should be extracted, the representation of the sentence consists of two components: position representation[4], which indicates the position of the sentence in the document; content representation, which contains the semantic information of the sentence.

Therefore, we define the position and content information of the sentence as constituent factors, aiming to explore how the selected sentences in the test set relate to the training set in terms of position and content information.

4.1.1 Positional Information

Positional Value (P-Value)   Given a document $D = s_1, \cdots, s_n$, for each sentence s_i with label $y_i = 1$, we introduce the notion of positional value $p_i \in 1, \cdots, K$, whose value is the output of the mapping function $p_i = \mathrm{f}(i)$.

Positional Coverage Rate (PCR)   Taking positional value p as a discrete random variable, we can define the discrete probability distribution of p over a dataset $\mathcal{D}$,

$$P(p = u) = \frac{N_u}{N_{sent}} \tag{1}$$

where N_u denotes the number of sentence with $p = u$ and N_{sent} represents the number of sentences with $y_i = 1$ in dataset $\mathcal{D}$.

Based on above definition, for any two datasets $\mathcal{D}^A$ and $\mathcal{D}^B$, we could quantify the proximity of their positional value distribution

$$\eta_p(\mathcal{D}^A, \mathcal{D}^B) = -log(\mathrm{KL}(P^A || P^B)) \tag{2}$$

where $\mathrm{KL}(\cdot)$ denotes KL-divergence function. P^A and P^B represent two position value distribution over two datasets. The datasets with similar positional value distribution usually have large PCR η_p.

4.1.2 Content Information

Content Value (C-Value)   Given a dataset $\mathcal{D}$, we want to find the patterns that appear most frequently in the ground truth[5] of $\mathcal{D}$ and score them. For each sentence in gound truth, we remove the stop words and punctuation, replace all numbers with "0", and perform lemmatization on each token. After the pre-processing, we treat n-gram ($n > 1$) as the pattern in $\mathcal{D}$ and calculate the score $\varphi(pt_i, \mathcal{D})$ for

---

[4]The position representation is obtained from the model structure in LSTM and by positional embedding in Transformer.

[5]Ground truth is extracted by the greedy algorithm in Nallapati et al. (2017)

	Statistics			Measures		Lead-k			Ext-Oralce		
	Train	**Valid**	**Test**	**Density**	**Compres.**	**R-1**	**R-2**	**R-L**	**R-1**	**R-2**	**R-L**
CNN/DM (3)	287,227	13,368	11,490	3.70	13.76	40.24	17.53	36.29	56.55	33.40	53.03
arXiv (6)	187,324	6,218	6,217	2.19	5.59	35.37	9.25	30.93	52.44	22.72	46.15
PubMed (5)	87,897	4,946	5,031	2.04	2.28	36.09	11.49	32.13	46.19	19.91	40.83
DUC2002 (6)	-	-	567	4.43	5.52	47.65	23.19	43.92	62.15	37.30	58.33
NYT50 (4)	96,826	4,000	3,452	4.64	15.33	38.54	19.90	35.27	63.97	43.51	60.70
Newsroom (2)	995,041	108,837	108,862	8.60	35.07	34.19	23.42	31.41	54.97	41.28	51.62

Table 2: Detailed statistics of six datasets. Density and Compression are *style factors* in Section 4.2. Lead-k indicates ROUGE score of the first k sentences in the document and Ext-Oracle indicates ROUGE score of sentences in the ground truth, they represent the lower and upper bound of extractive models respectively. The figure in parentheses after the datasets denotes the number of sentences extracted in Lead-k, which is close to the average number of Ext-Oracle labels.

each pattern as follows:

$$\varphi(pt_i, \mathcal{D}) = \frac{N_{pt_i}}{\sum\limits_{pt_j \in \mathcal{D}} N_{pt_j}} \quad (3)$$

where N_{pt_i} denotes the number of i-th pattern.

Content Coverage Rate (CCR) We introduce the notion of η_c to measure the degree of contents' overlap between training and test set in which the sentences with ground truth labels reside in.

$$\text{Sim}(i, j) = \varphi(pt_i, \phi_{tr}) * \varphi(pt_j, \phi_{te}) \quad (4)$$

$$\eta_c(\mathcal{D}_{tr}, \mathcal{D}_{te}) = \sum_{pt_i \in \phi_{tr}} \sum_{pt_j \in \phi_{te}} \text{Sim}(i, j) \quad (5)$$

where ϕ denotes the set[6] of patterns which is helpful to pick out ground truth sentences. $\text{Sim}(\cdot)$ measures the similarity of two patterns, $\mathcal{D}_{tr}$ and $\mathcal{D}_{te}$ represent the training set and test set of $\mathcal{D}$ respectively.

4.2 Style Factors

Motivation Different from constituent factors, style factors influence the generalization ability of summarization models by adjusting the learning difficulty of samples' features.

For this type of factor, we did not propose a new measure, but adopt the indicators DENSITY, COMPRESSION proposed by (Grusky et al., 2018)[7] We claim that the contribution here is to focus on the understanding of these metrics and explore the reasons why they affect the performance of summarization models, which is missing from previous work. More importantly, only when we understand how these metrics affect the performance of the

models can we use them to explain some of the differences in model generalization.

4.2.1 Density

Density is used to qualitatively measure the degree to which a summary is derivative of a document (Grusky et al., 2018). Specifically, given a document D and its corresponding summary S, Density(D,S) measures the percentage of words in the summary that are from document.

$$\text{Density}(D, S) = \frac{1}{|S|} \sum_{f \in \mathcal{F}(D,S)} |f|^2 \quad (6)$$

where $|\cdot|$ denotes the number of words. $\mathcal{F}(D, S)$ is a set of extractive fragments, which characterize the the longest shared token sequence.

4.2.2 Compression

Compression is used to characterize the word ratio between the document and summary (Grusky et al., 2018).

$$\text{Compression}(d, s) = |D| / |S| \quad (7)$$

5 Investigating Influence of Proposed Factors on Summarization Models

5.1 Constituent Factors

5.1.1 Exp-I: Breaking Down the Test set

For the P-Value, the threshold set can be denoted as $\{t_0 = 0, t_1, \cdots, t_K = \infty\}$. We calculate $Pos(i)$ for each sentence s_i:

$$Pos(i) = \begin{cases} i & 0 \leq i < t_1 \text{ or } i \geq t_{K-1} \\ \frac{i}{n} \cdot t_{K-1} & others \end{cases} \quad (8)$$

and define $p_i = k$ if $t_{k-1} \leq Pos(i) < t_k$. The $Pos(i)$ considers both absolute and relevant position of the sentence in the document. In

---

[6] We choose 100 bigrams and trigrams as the set.

[7] DENSITY and COMPRESSION was originally used to describe the diversity between datasets in the construction of new datasets.

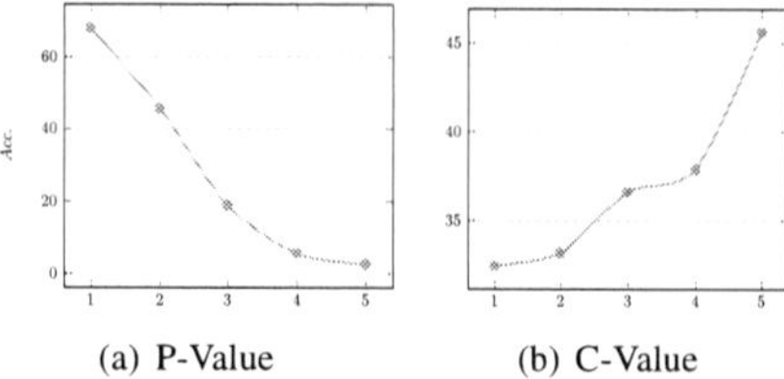

(a) P-Value   (b) C-Value

Figure 1: The accuracy on CNN/DM dataset, test set is broken down based on P-Value and C-Value.

the experiment, we make $K = 5$ and choose $\{0, 3, 7, 15, 35, \infty\}$ for the threshold set.

For the C-Value, we calculate the score for each sentence based on the pattern score from training set.

$$\varphi(s_i, \mathcal{D}) = \sum_{pt_j \in s_i} \varphi(pt_j, \mathcal{D}_{tr}) \qquad (9)$$

where s_i denotes sentence in the ground truth of test set. The score indicates the degree of overlap between the sentence and important patterns of the training set. We then sort all the sentences in ascending order by score and divide them into five intervals with the same number of sentences.

As shown in Figure 1, when the sentence is in the front of the document or contains more salient patterns, the accuracy of the model to extract sentences is higher. The phenomenon means that our proposed P-Value and C-Value reflect position distribution and content information of a specific dataset to a certain extent, and the model does learn *constituent factors* and uses them to determine whether a sentence is selected.

5.1.2 Exp-II: Cross-dataset Generalization

From the above experiments, we can see that P-Value and C-Value are sufficient to characterize some attributes in a specific dataset, but beyond that, we seek to understand the differences between mainstream datasets through PCR and CCR.

We calculate PCR/CCR score and measure the performance of the base model by ROUGE-2 score on five datasets. We can see from Table 3 that the training and test set of the same dataset always have the highest PCR/CCR score, which indicates the distribution between them is the closest based on *constituent factors*. Furthermore, model performance is also in accord with this trend. Consistency presented by the experiment, on the one hand, illustrates that there are significant shifts between different datasets, which results in performance differences of the model in cross-dataset setting, on

	Dataset	CNNDM	arXiv	Pubmed	NYT50	Newsr.
PCR	CNNDM	1.41	0.56	0.38	0.75	0.70
	arXiv	0.51	2.38	0.68	0.15	0.28
	Pubmed	0.38	0.66	3.79	0.08	0.41
	NYT50	1.27	0.22	0.23	1.46	1.28
	Newsr.	1.02	0.30	0.40	0.79	4.57
CCR	CNNDM	3.69	0.07	0.89	1.32	1.56
	arXiv	0.05	10.04	0.47	0.03	0.16
	Pubmed	0.72	0.62	11.03	0.51	2.03
	NYT50	1.34	0.07	0.75	3.13	2.12
	Newsr.	1.27	0.21	2.09	1.41	4.21
R-2	CNNDM	18.71	9.55	11.60	21.72	15.89
	arXiv	11.46	16.91	16.21	15.10	15.93
	PubMed	9.68	15.56	16.46	10.39	12.16
	NYT50	17.01	9.62	11.98	25.39	20.52
	Newsr.	17.38	9.42	12.23	20.21	24.59

Table 3: Results of cross-dataset PCR(η^p), CCR(η^c) and ROUGE-2 score. Each cell η_{ij}^p and η_{ij}^c denotes the coverage rate between training dataset (rows) and test dataset (columns). Each cell R-2$_{ij}$ denotes model performance in cross-dataset setting.

the other hand, it reflects that position distribution and content information are the key factors of such dataset-shift.

After verifying the validity of PCR and CCR, we utilize them to estimate the distance between the real distribution of datasets. For instance, news articles datasets (CNN/DM, NTY50 and Newsroom) and scientific paper datasets (arXiv and PubMed) both have lower scores in terms of two metrics, that is to say, there is a larger shift between them, which is also in line with our knowledge. Based on the estimation, we can understand more deeply the impact of different datasets on the generalization ability of various neural extractive summarization models.

5.2 Style Factors

We integrate training set, validation set and test set as a whole set and divide it into three parts according to the density or compression of each article and name them "low", "medium" and "high". For example, articles in "density, high" represents these articles have a higher density in the entire dataset. Based on above operation, we break down the test set and attempt to analyze how style factors influence the model performance.

Exploration of Density Density represents the overlap between the summary and the original text, so the samples with high density are more friendly to extractive models. Consequently, it is easy for us to understand the higher the density, the higher the

84

	Metrics	Low	Medium	High
	R-1	35.07	41.63	**46.48**
DENSITY	R-2	11.22	17.87	**26.39**
	R-L	31.19	37.69	**43.21**
	F1	33.81	38.02	**38.38**
	R-1	**44.95**	41.32	36.41
COMPRES.	R-2	**21.74**	18.61	15.10
	R-L	**41.09**	37.61	32.98
	F1	**39.82**	37.01	32.23

Table 4: The performance of our base model on CNN/DM dataset, test set is broken down based on DENSITY and COMPRESSION

ROUGE score in Table 4. However, the F_1 value of prediction is also positively correlated with the density, which means that density is closely related to the learning difficulty.

		1	2	3	Total
Low	ψ	0.18	0.15	0.13	0.46
	Pct	8.5%	7.0%	6.0%	21.5%
Medium	ψ	0.24	0.20	0.17	0.61
	Pct	9.0%	7.6%	6.4%	23.0%
High	ψ	0.32	0.27	0.22	0.81
	Pct	10.8%	9.1%	7.5%	27.4%

Table 5: Experiment about DENSITY, Pct denotes the percentage of $\psi(s_i, S)$ to $\sum_{s_i \in D} \psi(s_i, S)$. The first three sentences contain more salient information in samples with higher density.

In order to comprehend this correlation, we conduct the following experiment. Given an article and summary pair, we assign a score $\psi(s_i, S)$ to each sentence in article to indicate how much sailent information is contained in the sentence.

$$\psi(s_i, S) = \mathrm{LCS}(s_i, S) / |s_i| \qquad (10)$$

where $\mathrm{LCS}(s_i, S)$ denotes the longest common subsequence length (not counting stop words and punctuation) of the sentence and summary. We calculate the percentage of $\psi(s_i, S)$ to $\sum_{s_i \in D} \psi(s_i, S)$ and present the results of the three highest-scoring sentences in Table 5. Obviously, in samples with high density, the salient information is more concentrated in a few sentences, making it easier for the model to extract correct sentences.

Therefore, for dataset with high density, we can try to introduce external knowledge into the model, which helps the model better understand the semantic information, and thus easier to capture sentences with salient patterns. In addition, models with external knowledge should have better gen-

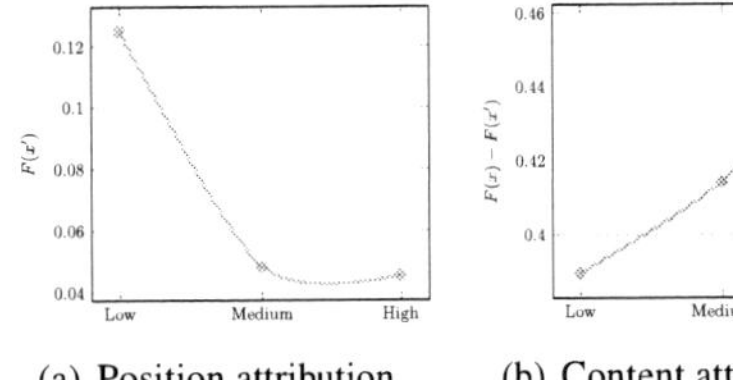

(a) Position attribution   (b) Content attribution

Figure 2: The position and content attribution on CNN/DM, the test set is broken down based on COMPRESSION.

eralization ablity when transferred to high-density dataset. These inferences will be verified in Section 6.1 and 6.2.1.

Exploration of Compression Documents with high compression tend to have fewer sentences because summaries usually have a similar length in the same dataset. So the results of compression in Table 4 are in line with our expectations, how the model represents long documents to get good performance in text summarization task remains a challenge (Celikyilmaz et al., 2018).

Unlike the exploration of density, we attempt to understand how the model extracts sentences when faced with different compression samples. We utilize an attribution technique called Integrated Gradients (IG) (Sundararajan et al., 2017) to separate the position and content information of each sentence. The setting of *input x* and *baseline x'* in this paper is close to Mudrakarta et al. (2018)[8], but it is worth noting that our base model adds positional embedding to each sentence, so *input x* and *baseline x'* both have positional information.

We tend to think that $F(x')$ denotes the attribution of positional information, and $F(x) - F(x')$ denotes the attribution of content information when model makes decisions, where $F : \mathbb{R}^n \to [0, 1]$ represents a deep network. Figure 2 illustrates that as compression increases, the help provided by positional information is gradually reduced and content information becomes more important to the model. In other words, the model can perceive the compression and decide whether to pay more attention to positional information or important patterns, this observation is helpful for us to design models or study their generalization ability in Section 6.2.1.

---

[8]Using empty documents (a sequence of word embeddings corresponding to padding value) as *baseline x'*.

Models	DENSITY			COMPRESSION			All
	Low	Medium	High	Low	Medium	High	
LSTM	11.17	17.75	25.84	21.66	18.25	14.73	18.58
- Word2Vec	0.08 ↓	0.36 ↓	0.57 ↓	0.51 ↓	0.32 ↓	0.18 ↓	0.35 ↓
+ BERT	0.44 ↑	0.80 ↑	1.46 ↑	1.19 ↑	0.80 ↑	0.68 ↑	0.92 ↑
Transformer	11.15	17.84	26.17	22.00	18.34	14.65	18.71
- Word2Vec	0.10 ↓	0.30 ↓	0.54 ↓	0.48 ↓	0.12 ↓	0.30 ↓	0.31 ↓
+ BERT	0.52 ↑	0.77 ↑	1.28 ↑	0.98 ↑	0.86 ↑	0.79 ↑	0.88 ↑

Table 6: Performance of models equipped with different types of knowledge on CNN/DM dataset. BERT here removes the gradient as a way of introducing external knowledge.

6 Bridge the Gap between Dataset Bias and Model Design Prior

In this section we investigate how different properties of datasets influence the choices of model structures, pre-trained strategies, and training schemas.

Idea of Experiment Design Through the above analysis in Section 4, the *constituent factors* reflect the relationship between diverse data distributions and *style factors* directly affect the learning difficulty of samples' features. Based on the different attributes of the above two types of factors, we designed the following investigation accordingly: for the *style factor*, we not only investigate the influence of different model architectures and pre-trained strategies on it, but utilize it to explain the generalization behaviour of the models. For the *constituent factors*, we discuss their effects on different training strategies, such as multi-domain learning and meta-learning, because these learning modes are all about how to better model various types of distributions.

6.1 *Style Factors* Bias

In this section, we study **whether the samples with different learning difficulties described by the** *style factors* **can be well handled through the improvement of structure or the introducing of pre-training knowledge or we need to extend our model in other ways**.

Table 6 shows the breakdown performance on CNN/DM based on DENSITY and COMPRESSION. And we can observe that: 1) An obvious trend is that LSTM performs better than Transformer with increasing difficulty in sample learning (low density and high compression). For instance, LSTM performs worse than Transformer on the subset with high density, while surpasses Transformer when the density of testing examples becomes lower. 2) Generally, the introducing of pre-training word vectors can improve the overall results of the models. However, we found that increasing the learning difficulty of samples would weaken the benefits brought by pre-trained embeddings. 3) The prospects for further gains for these hard cases described by *style factor* from novel architecture design and knowledge pre-training seem quite limited, suggesting that perhaps we should explore other ways, such as generating summaries instead of extracting.

6.2 *Constituent Factors* Bias

We design our experiment towards the answer to two main questions as follows.

6.2.1 Exp-I: How do dataset properties influence the choices of training schemas?

When our training set itself contains multiple domains grouped by the *constituent factors*, how can we make full use of the datasets characteristic and find the most suitable training schemas? For example, CNN/DailyMail, as one of the most popular datasets, consists of two sub-datasets. For this question, dataset-shift discussed in Section 5.1.2 and the learning difficuculties of the dataset should be taken into consideration.

Choices of Training Schemas: We compare four training schemas: joint training, multi-domain learning[9] with explicit information (tag embedding), implicit information (BERT) and meta-learning.

Evaluation Setting: In order to more comprehensively reflect the generalization ability of different models, we conducted zero-shot transfer evaluation. Specifically, each of our models is trained on CNN/DM while evaluated both on CNN/DM (IN-DATASET) and other datasets (CROSS-DATASET).

---

[9] We view CNN and DailyMail in CNN/DM as two different domains.

Dataset	Basic			Tag			Meta			Bert		
	R-1	R-2	R-L	R-1	R-2	R-L	R-1	R-2	R-L	R-1	R-2	R-L
CNNDM	41.31	18.71	37.62	41.37	18.89	37.70	41.26	18.77	37.60	**42.27**	**19.72**	**38.62**
Arxiv	36.29	9.55	32.01	37.12	10.09	32.73	36.25	9.58	31.95	37.00	**10.22**	32.59
Pubmed	36.13	11.60	31.91	36.75	12.02	32.47	36.07	11.65	31.89	**36.93**	**12.15**	**32.71**
DUC2002	49.21	24.08	45.37	49.25	24.28	45.38	49.34	24.22	45.50	**49.77**	**24.67**	**45.87**
NYT50	41.17	21.72	37.85	40.84	21.06	37.45	41.23	21.56	37.89	**43.80**	**24.09**	**40.46**
Newsroom	28.08	15.89	25.08	26.37	13.78	23.21	28.10	15.85	25.06	**29.30**	**16.73**	**26.16**

Table 7: Results of four models under two types of evaluation settings: IN-DATASET, and CROSS-DATASET. Bold indicates the best performance of all models, red indicated the best performance other than BERT.

Table 7 shows the results of four models under two types of evaluation settings: IN-DATASET, and CROSS-DATA, and we have the following findings:

1) For IN-DATASET setting, comparing the *Tag* and the basic models, we find a very simple method that assign each sample a domain tag could achieve improvement. The reason here we claim is that domain-aware model makes full use of the nature of dataset. 2) For multi-domain and meta-learning model, we attempt to explain from the perspective of data distribution. Although meta-learning obtains worse performance under IN-DATASET setting, it yet has achieved impressive performance under CROSS-DATASET setting. Concretely, meta-learning model surpasses *Tag* model on three datasets: DUC2002, NYT50 and Newsroom, whose distribution is closer to CNN/DM based on *constituent factors* in Table 3. Correspondingly, *Tag* model uses a randomly initialized embedding for zero-shot transfer, and we suspect that this perturbation unexpectedly generalizes well on some far-distributed datasets (arXiv and PubMed). 3) BERT has shown its superior performance and nearly outperforms all competitors. However, the generalization ability of BERT is poor on arXiv, PubMed and DUC2002 compared to the performance improvement in IN-DATASET setting. In contrast, BERT shows good generalization when tranferring to datasets with high density and compression (NYT50 and Newsroom). As we have discussed in Sec. 5.2, samples with high *style factors* require model to capture salient patterns, which is exactly the improvement of introducing external knowledge from BERT.

6.2.2 Exp-II: Searching for a Good Domain

The second question we study is **what makes a good domain**? To answer this question, we define the concept of domain based not solely on the dataset, but divide the training set by directly utiliz-

Models	R-1	R-2	R-L
Transformer	41.31	18.71	37.62
+ random tag	41.19	18.52	37.57
+ domain tag	**41.41**	18.71	**37.74**
+ P-Value tag	41.38	18.71	37.67
+ C-Value tag	41.39	18.73	37.71
+ P-Value & C-Value tag	**41.41**	**18.74**	**37.74**
Liu (2019)	42.57	19.96	39.04
BERT (our implementation)	42.59	19.92	38.94
+ domain tag	42.72	19.91	39.05
+ P-Value & C-Value tag	**42.77**	**19.98**	**39.10**

Table 8: Results of experiments with tags on our base model and current state-of-the-art model. The usage of BERT here is as same as Liu (2019), which is to fine tune BERT on CNN/DM.

ing the *constituent factors*. Specifically, we explore the following different settings:

1) **Random tag:** Each sample is assigned a random "pseudo-domains" tag.

2) **Domain:** Divide training samples according to the domain (CNN or DM) they belong to .

3) **P- and C-Value:** Each sentence is assigned a tag by its corresponding P-Value and C-value scores.

We experiment with tags on our base model and the current state-of-the-art model Liu (2019). Liu (2019) and the results are presented in Table 8, we can obtain the following observations:

1) *Random partitioning does not make sense and cannot lead to the improvement of performance.* Conversely, the partitions based on the *constituent factors* have obtained the benefit. 2) This simple learning method that dividing the training set based on domain has shown considerable benefit, which can be complementary to the improvement brought by BERT. 3) The division based on the *constituent factors* (P-value & C-value) achieves the best result in the context of BERT, which implies that *for the summarization task, mining the characteristics of*

the dataset itself plays an important role.

7 Conclusion

In this paper, we conduct a data-dependent understanding of neural extractive summarization models, exploring how different factors of datasets influence these models and how to make full use of the nature of dataset so as to design a more powerful model. Experiments with in-depth analyses diagnose the weakness of existing models and provide guidelines for future research.

References

Devansh Arpit, Stanisław Jastrzebski, Nicolas Ballas, David Krueger, Emmanuel Bengio, Maxinder S Kanwal, Tegan Maharaj, Asja Fischer, Aaron Courville, Yoshua Bengio, et al. 2017. A closer look at memorization in deep networks. In *Proceedings of the 34th International Conference on Machine Learning-Volume 70*, pages 233–242. JMLR. org.

Shumeet Baluja and Ian Fischer. 2017. Adversarial transformation networks: Learning to generate adversarial examples. *arXiv preprint arXiv:1703.09387.*

Asli Celikyilmaz, Antoine Bosselut, Xiaodong He, and Yejin Choi. 2018. Deep communicating agents for abstractive summarization. In *Proceedings of the 2018 Conference of the North American Chapter of the Association for Computational Linguistics: Human Language Technologies, Volume 1 (Long Papers)*, volume 1, pages 1662–1675.

Yen-Chun Chen and Mohit Bansal. 2018. Fast abstractive summarization with reinforce-selected sentence rewriting. In *Proceedings of the 56th Annual Meeting of the Association for Computational Linguistics (Volume 1: Long Papers)*, volume 1, pages 675–686.

Jianpeng Cheng and Mirella Lapata. 2016. Neural summarization by extracting sentences and words. In *Proceedings of the 54th Annual Meeting of the Association for Computational Linguistics (Volume 1: Long Papers)*, volume 1, pages 484–494.

Arman Cohan, Franck Dernoncourt, Doo Soon Kim, Trung Bui, Seokhwan Kim, Walter Chang, and Nazli Goharian. 2018. A discourse-aware attention model for abstractive summarization of long documents. In *Proceedings of the 2018 Conference of the North American Chapter of the Association for Computational Linguistics: Human Language Technologies, Volume 2 (Short Papers)*, pages 615–621.

Jacob Devlin, Ming-Wei Chang, Kenton Lee, and Kristina Toutanova. 2018. Bert: Pre-training of deep bidirectional transformers for language understanding. *arXiv preprint arXiv:1810.04805.*

Li Dong, Nan Yang, Wenhui Wang, Furu Wei, Xiaodong Liu, Yu Wang, Jianfeng Gao, Ming Zhou, and Hsiao-Wuen Hon. 2019. Unified language model pre-training for natural language understanding and generation. *arXiv preprint arXiv:1905.03197.*

Sebastian Gehrmann, Yuntian Deng, and Alexander Rush. 2018. Bottom-up abstractive summarization. In *Proceedings of the 2018 Conference on Empirical Methods in Natural Language Processing*, pages 4098–4109.

Max Grusky, Mor Naaman, and Yoav Artzi. 2018. Newsroom: A dataset of 1.3 million summaries with diverse extractive strategies. In *Proceedings of the 2018 Conference of the North American Chapter of the Association for Computational Linguistics: Human Language Technologies, Volume 1 (Long Papers)*, volume 1, pages 708–719.

Luheng He, Kenton Lee, Mike Lewis, and Luke Zettlemoyer. 2017. Deep semantic role labeling: What works and whats next. In *Proceedings of the 55th Annual Meeting of the Association for Computational Linguistics (Volume 1: Long Papers)*, volume 1, pages 473–483.

Sepp Hochreiter and Jürgen Schmidhuber. 1997. Long short-term memory. *Neural computation*, 9(8):1735–1780.

Aishwarya Jadhav and Vaibhav Rajan. 2018. Extractive summarization with swap-net: Sentences and words from alternating pointer networks. In *Proceedings of the 56th Annual Meeting of the Association for Computational Linguistics (Volume 1: Long Papers)*, volume 1, pages 142–151.

Taehee Jung, Dongyeop Kang, Lucas Mentch, and Eduard Hovy. 2019. Earlier isn't always better: Subaspect analysis on corpus and system biases in summarization. *arXiv preprint arXiv:1908.11723.*

Yang Liu. 2019. Fine-tune BERT for extractive summarization. *CoRR*, abs/1903.10318.

Tomas Mikolov, Kai Chen, Greg Corrado, and Jeffrey Dean. 2013. Efficient estimation of word representations in vector space. *arXiv preprint arXiv:1301.3781.*

Pramod Kaushik Mudrakarta, Ankur Taly, Mukund Sundararajan, and Kedar Dhamdhere. 2018. Did the model understand the question? In *Proceedings of the 56th Annual Meeting of the Association for Computational Linguistics (Volume 1: Long Papers)*, pages 1896–1906.

Ramesh Nallapati, Feifei Zhai, and Bowen Zhou. 2017. Summarunner: A recurrent neural network based sequence model for extractive summarization of documents. In *Thirty-First AAAI Conference on Artificial Intelligence.*

Ramesh Nallapati, Bowen Zhou, Cicero dos Santos, Ça glar Gulçehre, and Bing Xiang. 2016. Abstractive text summarization using sequence-to-sequence rnns and beyond. *CoNLL 2016*, page 280.

Shashi Narayan, Shay B Cohen, and Mirella Lapata. 2018. Ranking sentences for extractive summarization with reinforcement learning. In *Proceedings of the 2018 Conference of the North American Chapter of the Association for Computational Linguistics: Human Language Technologies, Volume 1 (Long Papers)*, volume 1, pages 1747–1759.

Matthew Peters, Mark Neumann, Mohit Iyyer, Matt Gardner, Christopher Clark, Kenton Lee, and Luke Zettlemoyer. 2018. Deep contextualized word representations. In *Proceedings of the 2018 Conference of NAACL*, volume 1, pages 2227–2237.

Evan Sandhaus. 2008. The new york times annotated corpus. *Linguistic Data Consortium, Philadelphia*, 6(12):e26752.

Ludwig Schmidt, Shibani Santurkar, Dimitris Tsipras, Kunal Talwar, and Aleksander Madry. 2018. Adversarially robust generalization requires more data. In *Advances in Neural Information Processing Systems*, pages 5014–5026.

Abigail See, Peter J Liu, and Christopher D Manning. 2017. Get to the point: Summarization with pointer-generator networks. In *Proceedings of the 55th Annual Meeting of the Association for Computational Linguistics (Volume 1: Long Papers)*, volume 1, pages 1073–1083.

Mukund Sundararajan, Ankur Taly, and Qiqi Yan. 2017. Axiomatic attribution for deep networks. In *Proceedings of the 34th International Conference on Machine Learning-Volume 70*, pages 3319–3328. JMLR. org.

Ashish Vaswani, Noam Shazeer, Jakob Parmar, Llion Jones, Aidan N Gomez, Łukasz Kaiser, and Illia Polosukhin. 2017. Attention is all you need. In *Advances in NIPS*.

Danqing Wang, Pengfei Liu, Ming Zhong, Jie Fu, Xipeng Qiu, and Xuanjing Huang. 2019. Exploring domain shift in extractive text summarization. *arXiv preprint arXiv:1908.11664*.

Yuxiang Wu and Baotian Hu. 2018. Learning to extract coherent summary via deep reinforcement learning. In *Thirty-Second AAAI Conference on Artificial Intelligence*.

Chiyuan Zhang, Samy Bengio, Moritz Hardt, Benjamin Recht, and Oriol Vinyals. 2016. Understanding deep learning requires rethinking generalization. *arXiv preprint arXiv:1611.03530*.

Ming Zhong, Pengfei Liu, Danqing Wang, Xipeng Qiu, and Xuanjing Huang. 2019. Searching for effective neural extractive summarization: What works and what's next. In *Proceedings of the 57th Annual Meeting of the Association for Computational Linguistics*, pages 1049–1058, Florence, Italy. Association for Computational Linguistics.

Qingyu Zhou, Nan Yang, Furu Wei, Shaohan Huang, Ming Zhou, and Tiejun Zhao. 2018. Neural document summarization by jointly learning to score and select sentences. In *Proceedings of the 56th Annual Meeting of the Association for Computational Linguistics (Volume 1: Long Papers)*, volume 1, pages 654–663.

Global Voices: Crossing Borders in Automatic News Summarization

Khanh Nguyen[⊙] and **Hal Daumé III**[⊙♡]

University of Maryland, College Park[⊙], Microsoft Research, New York[♡]

`{kxnguyen,hal}@umiacs.umd.edu`

Abstract

We construct *Global Voices*, a multilingual dataset for evaluating cross-lingual summarization methods. We extract social-network descriptions of Global Voices news articles to cheaply collect evaluation data for into-English and from-English summarization in 15 languages. Especially, for the into-English summarization task, we crowd-source a high-quality evaluation dataset based on guidelines that emphasize accuracy, coverage, and understandability. To ensure the quality of this dataset, we collect human ratings to filter out bad summaries, and conduct a survey on humans, which shows that the remaining summaries are preferred over the social-network summaries. We study the effect of translation quality in cross-lingual summarization, comparing a translate-then-summarize approach with several baselines. Our results highlight the limitations of the ROUGE metric that are overlooked in monolingual summarization.

1 Introduction

Cross-lingual summarization is an important but highly unexplored task. The ability to summarize information written or spoken in any language at a large scale would empower humans with much more knowledge about the diverse world. Despite the fast development of automatic summarization (Allahyari et al., 2017; Dong, 2018; Gambhir and Gupta, 2017), present technology mostly focuses on monolingual summarization. There is currently lacking a standard, high-quality multilingual dataset for evaluating cross-lingual summarization methods. Two main challenges present in constructing such a dataset. First, the cost of crowsourcing human-written summaries is high. It generally takes a long time for a human to summarize a document, as they not only have to read and understand information in the article, but also have to

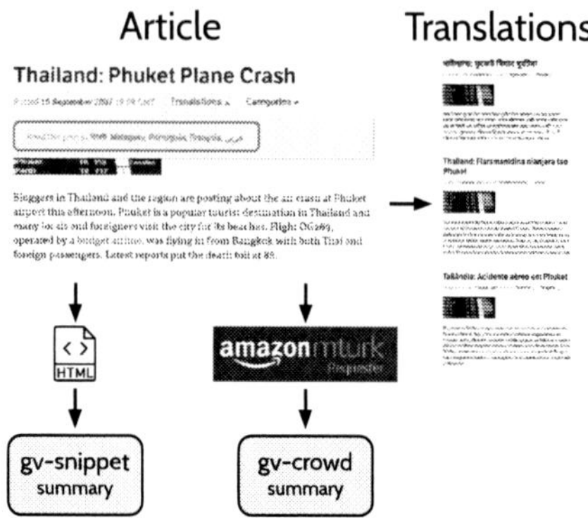

Figure 1: Data construction pipeline. We collect two types of summary: (a) the social network description of the article (`gv-snippet`) and (b) the 50-word summary written by Mechanical Turk workers following our guidelines (`gv-crowd`).

make complex decisions in sieving and paraphrasing the information. Second, it is difficult to design summarization guidelines for humans, as the task is generally not well-defined: the selection of what content is "important" in a summary is based on subjective and common-sense rules that vary among individuals and are difficult to be expressed precisely in words.

Even in monolingual summarization, there were limited attempts in constructing summarization datasets via crowd-sourcing (Over et al., 2007; Dang and Owczarzak, 2008, 2010). These datasets are mostly used for evaluation due to their small sizes. To construct large-scale training datasets, researchers mine news sources that naturally provide human-written summaries (Hermann et al., 2015; Sandhaus, 2008), or construct artificial summaries from document titles (Rush et al., 2015). Summaries collected in this way may be not best for evaluation because they are generated under unknown guidelines (or there may be no guide-

Proceedings of the 2nd Workshop on New Frontiers in Summarization, pages 90–97
Hong Kong, China, November 4, 2019. ©2019 Association for Computational Linguistics

lines at all). Previous work on cross-lingual summarization performs evaluation with human judgments (Orsan and Chiorean, 2008), or with automatic metrics and noisy source articles generated by automatic translation systems (Wan et al., 2010; Ouyang et al., 2019). The former approach is expensive and not reproducible, while the latter is prone to biases induced by translation systems that could be further amplified by summarization systems.

This paper presents *Global Voices*, a high-quality multilingual dataset of summaries of news articles. The dataset can serve as a standard benchmark in both multilingual and cross-lingual summarization. Global Voices[1] is a multilingual website that reports and translates news about unheard voices across the globe. Translation in this website is performed by the Lingua team,[2] consisting of volunteer translators. As of August 2019, Global Voices provides translations of news articles in 51 languages; many articles are translated into multiple languages. Figure 1 illustrates a sample article from Global Voices. We extract the social-network descriptions of the articles to (cheaply) construct gv-snippet, an evaluation set for multilingual and cross-lingual news summarization. Nevertheless, these descriptions usually have poor coverage over the original contents because they were written with the intention of drawing user clicks to read more about the articles. Therefore, besides gv-snippet, we construct a smaller but higher-quality dataset of human-written English summaries, called gv-crowd, based on our guidelines which explicitly emphasize accuracy, coverage and understandability. The Global Voices dataset is summarized in Table 2. It currently supports 15 languages, which span nine language genera (Romance, Barito, Indic, Slavic, Semitic, Greek, Germanic, Japanese, Bantoid) and five language families (Indo-European, Austronesian, Japanese, Niger-Congo, Afro-Asiatic).

2 Dataset Construction

Data Collection and Pre-Processing. Using Scrapy,[3] we crawl and download HTML source codes of 41,939 English articles and their translations. We use bs4[4] to extract each article's main

Language	ISO 639-1	gv-snippet	gv-crowd
Number of articles			
English	en	4,573	529
Spanish	es	3,921	487
Malagasy	mg	2,680	374
Bengali	bn	2,253	352
French	fr	2,130	352
Portuguese	pt	798	162
Russian	ru	795	139
Arabic	ar	745	191
Italian	it	718	135
Macedonian	mk	701	138
Greek	el	694	128
German	de	647	204
Japanese	ja	424	75
Swahili	sw	418	84
Dutch	nl	348	87
Other statistics			
Summarized by		GV authors	MTurkers
Summary languages		All versions	English
Summary lengths (words)		-	40-50
Article lengths (words)		150-500	150-350

Table 1: Summary of the Global Voices dataset. The dataset include articles in 15 languages. English versions of all non-English articles are included. The gv-snippet split contains social-network summaries of all articles, while the gv-crowd split contains crowd-sourced summaries of English articles.

content and remove image captions. Next, we use html2text[5] to convert the main content's HTML source code to regular text, removing web-page and image URLs. Since an article may content block-quotes written in original languages, we detect language of each paragraph and remove paragraphs that are not in the article's main language. Language detection is conducted by voting decisions of four packages: langdetect,[6] langid,[7] polyglot,[8] fastText[9] (Joulin et al., 2016a,b).

Constructing gv-snippet. This split includes articles whose English versions contain from 150 to 500 words. For each article, we extract its Open Graph description by extracting the meta tag with property og:description in the HTML source code, and use the description as the reference summary of the article. These descriptions are short text snippets that serve as captions of the articles when they appear on social networks (e.g. Facebook, Twitter).

Crowd-sourcing gv-crowd. We select English

---

[1] https://globalvoices.org/

[2] https://globalvoices.org/lingua/

[3] https://scrapy.org/

[4] https://www.crummy.com/software/BeautifulSoup/

[5] https://pypi.org/project/html2text/

[6] https://pypi.org/project/langdetect/

[7] https://github.com/saffsd/langid.py

[8] https://pypi.org/project/polyglot/

[9] https://fasttext.cc/docs/en/language-identification.html

articles that contain 150-350 words, and request workers from Mechanical Turk[10] (MT) to summarize them in 40-50 words. Each HIT[11] asks a worker to summarize five articles in 35 minutes. We recruit Turkers in Canada and the U.S.A. with Masters qualification, a HIT approval rate greater than or equal to 97%, and a number of HITs approved greater than or equal to 1,000. On average, collecting a summary costs 1.50 USD (including taxes and extra fees). We inform workers of our evaluation guidelines, which focus on three criteria:

- *Accuracy*: information in a summary should be based on the original article only. It can be paraphrased from but should not disagree with information in the article.

- *Coverage*: a summary should reflect the most important messages/stories in the original article. Each message/story should be captured as detailed as possible, without missing other important messages/stories.

- *Understandability*: a summary must be written in standard, fluent English. Readers must be able to understand the summary without reading the original article. Understanding the summary must not require any additional knowledge beyond knowledge required to understand the article.

In comparison, the DUC-2004 dataset (Over et al., 2007) only provides subtle format suggestions and leaves the summary contents almost entirely to the decisions of the writers:

> "...Imagine that to save time, rather than read through a set of complete documents, you first read a list of very short summaries of those documents and based on these summaries you choose which documents to read in their entirety. Create your very short summaries to be useful in such a scenario. A very short summary could look like a newspaper headline, be a list of important terms or phrases separated by commas, a sentence, etc. It should not contain any formatting, i.e., no indented lists, etc. Feel free to use your own words."
>
> Source: https://duc.nist.gov/duc2004

Our guideline criteria are similar to those of the TAC 2010's guided summarization task (Dang and Owczarzak, 2010) but we do not restrict the summary format using domain-specific templates.

---

[10] https://www.mturk.com/

[11] a Mechanical Turk task.

Some articles may read disrupted due to removals of images and videos, and may contain non-English texts. To ensure the summaries are based on the English texts only, we advise workers to (a) *not* web-search for the original content and (b) ignore the non-English contents. We also emphasize spelling words correctly and recommend copying difficult-to-spell words from the original articles. In the end, we collect 840 summaries for 738 articles.

Human Evaluation of gv-crowd. The summary-collecting task receives mostly positive feedback from workers. The task is widely regarded as "fun", "interesting", and "challenging". However, many workers raised concern about the strict time constraint. To evaluate the quality of the dataset, we launch another MT task in which we ask workers to rate and post-edit the summaries collected in the previous task. Each task HIT requires evaluating ten summaries in 60 minutes. We recruit workers in Canada and the U.S.A. with a HIT approval rate greater than or equal to 97%, and a number of HITs approved greater than or equal to 1,000.

Specifically, we ask workers to provide two types of ratings: *criterion-based* ratings and *overall* ratings. Each worker is instructed to first give a 1-to-5 rating of a summary in each of our three criteria (accuracy, coverage, understandability), and then to give an overall rating of the summary. We define three levels of the overall rating:

- *Bad*: the summary misrepresents the original article. It contains factual errors that disagree with the content of the article. OR it does not cover the most important message/story of the article. OR it is missing other important points that could easily be included without violating the 50-word constraint.

- *Acceptable*: the summary covers the most important message/story of the article. It does *not* contain factual errors. It is missing one or two important points that would be difficult to include in a 50-word summary.

- *Good*: the summary covers the most important message/story of the article. It does *not* contain factual errors. All important points are captured.

In addition, the worker is required to write short reasons (each in 5-25 words) to justify their ratings.

Among 840 summaries collected, 383 (45.60%) were rated as *Good*, 264 (31.43%) *Acceptable*, and 193 (22.98%) *Bad*. We observe that among the three criteria, understandability is easiest to meet while coverage is the most challenging: the mean understandability rating is 4.06 while the mean coverage rating is only 3.47; about 90% of the summaries attain understandability ratings of at least 3. By computing Pearson correlation coefficients, we find that the overall rating most strongly linearly correlates with the coverage rating (0.81) and least with the understandability rating (0.57). Common flaws identified by the human evaluators include: missing important points, factual errors, abstruse and/or verbose writing.

To construct the `gv-crowd` split, we pair each article with its highest-rated summaries[12] and excluded articles that (a) are paired with *Bad* summaries or (b) have a criterion-based rating below 3. We also ask workers to correct spelling and factual errors in the *Bad* summaries, but these post-edited summaries require further evaluation to be included in the dataset in the future. To facilitate summarization evaluation studies, we will release all the summaries accompanied with their ratings, reasons, and post-edit versions.

For a (randomly selected) subset of 50 articles, we collect *three* summaries per article to study the diversity in quality and language usage among human-written summaries of the same documents. We find that the summary quality does not vary greatly: the overall-rating difference between the highest and lowest rated summaries is at most 1 in 74% of these articles. To quantify the diversity of summaries, we calculate the *pairwise* ROUGE scores, using one summary as the reference and another as the predicted

$$\text{ROUGE}_{\text{pair}} = \frac{1}{3 \cdot 50} \sum_{i=1}^{50} \sum_{1 \leq j < k \leq 3} \text{ROUGE}(s_{i,j}, s_{i,k})$$

(1)

where $s_{i,j}$ and $s_{i,k}$ are distinct summaries of the i-th article. The $\text{ROUGE}_{\text{pair}}$-1,2,L F-1 scores are relatively low (39.44, 12.39, and 32.85, respectively), indicating that the summaries highly vary in vocabulary and sentence structure.

---

[12]For a pair of summaries, we first compare their overall ratings, then sums of three criterion-based ratings, then the individual accuracy, coverage, understandability ratings (in this specific order).

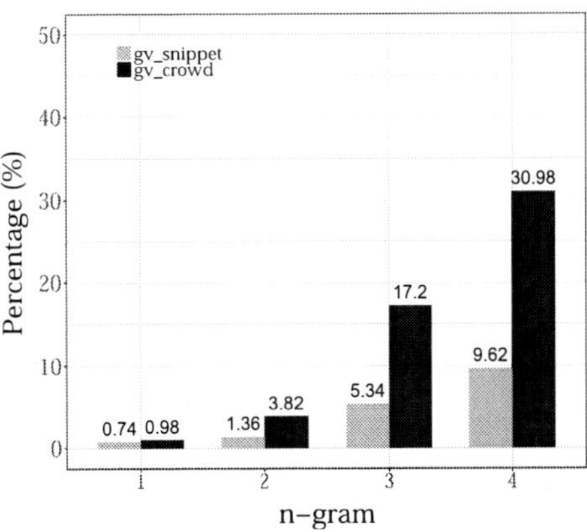

Figure 2: Average fraction of n-grams in the summary that are not seen in the original article.

Human Comparison of `gv-snippet` and `gv-crowd`. To ensure that the `gv-crowd` summaries are of higher quality than the `gv-snippet` summaries, we conduct a survey that asks MT workers to compare the two types of summary. Concretely, each worker reads an article and its `gv-snippet` and `gv-crowd` summaries. We ask the worker to specify which summary (or none) is better in each of the three criteria and is better overall. We remove partial sentences that end with "..." in the `gv-snippet` summaries to ensure that the workers rate the two types of summary mainly based on their contents, not based on any peculiar features. We also randomly shuffle the order of the summaries in a pair so that the workers cannot rely on the order to determine the summary type. Each worker is given 45 minutes to compare five summary pairs. Each summary pair is evaluated by three workers. We recruit workers with similar qualifications to those in the `gv-crowd` evaluation task.

The outcome of this survey is positive. In 22 out of the 30 articles included in the survey (75.9%), at least 2 out of 3 workers prefer the `gv-crowd` summary. Overall, 63 out of 90 workers (70.0%) prefer the `gv-crowd` summaries to its `gv-snippet` counterparts. As expected, coverage is the criterion where the `gv-crowd` summaries show most strength against the `gv-crowd` summaries, with a preference ratio of 83.3% (25/30) compared to 66.7% (20/30) of accuracy or understandability.

We also evaluate these two types of summary in terms of how novel their summaries are compared to the original articles. Figure 2 shows the

Model	Train	Validation
Translation (sentences)		
Spanish-English	4.1M	3K
French-English	5.6M	3K
German-English	151.6K	2K
Arabic-English	174.3K	2K
Summarization (pairs of documents and summaries)		
English	287.2K	13.4K

Table 2: Data used to train and validate translation and summarization models.

average fractions of novel n-grams of each type of summary. Overall, the summaries reuse most words in the articles. The `gv-crowd` summaries contain substantially more novel 3-grams and 4-grams than the `gv-snippet` summaries, partly because each sentence of a `gv-crowd` summary usually includes information from multiple sentences in the original article. On 73% of the articles in the `gv-crowd` split, the `gv-crowd` summary has higher fractions of novel n-grams than the `gv-snippet` counterpart (with $n = 1, 2, 3, 4$).

3 Experiments

We study the task of generating English summaries of non-English news articles. This task can naturally be decomposed into two subtasks: translation and summarization. We follow a *translate-then-summarize* approach where each article is first translated into English using a pre-trained machine translation model, then the translation is summarized using a pre-trained English summarization model. Data for training models in both subtasks are publicly available, allowing solving the joint task in a *zero-shot* manner, in the sense that no parallel pairs of (original document, English summary) are provided during training. On the other hand, a *summarize-then-translate* approach is practically difficult to implement because of the lack of large-scale datasets for training reliable summarization models in non-English languages.

Translation models. Our goal is to study the effect of translation quality in this task. Hence, we employ translation models trained under various amounts of resources. We conduct experiments in four source languages: Spanish (es), French (fr), German (de), and Arabic (ar). Concretely, we train the {es,fr}-en models using the large-scale CommonCrawl and News Commentary datasets, and

train the {de,ar}-en models using the low-resource multilingual TED (Duh, 2018) dataset. We apply standard machine translation pre-processing steps, normalizing and tokenizing the data with Moses scripts. We tokenize Arabic texts with the PyArabic tool (Zerrouki, 2010). Our translation models implement the Transformer architecture (Vaswani et al., 2017). The {es,fr}-en models have the same hyperparameters as those of the base Transformer architecture described in Table 3 of Vaswani et al. (2017). The {de,ar}-en models have less parameters, using 4 attention heads and a feed-forward hidden size of 1024. We train the models using the `fairseq-py` toolkit (Ott et al., 2019). Since the models are trained to perform sentence-level translation, we split the source articles into sentences, perform translation, and join the output sentences into articles. The training settings are the same as those of Vaswani et al. (2017) except that: (a) the maximum tokens in a batch is 4,000, (b) the {es,fr}-en models and the {de,ar}-en models are trained for $5 \cdot 10^4$ and $8 \cdot 10^5$ iterations, respectively, and (c) the {de,ar}-en models use a dropout ratio of 0.3. Training with an Nvidia Titan Xp GPU took place in approximately 5 hours for the smaller models and 3.5 days for the larger models.

Summarization models. We employ the state-of-the-art Bi-LSTM bottom-up abstractive summarization model (Gehrmann et al., 2018). We make use of a pre-trained instance of this model provided by OpenNMT-py (Klein et al., 2017) and trained on the CNN/DailyMail dataset (Hermann et al., 2015).

Baselines. We compare the following approaches:
- FIRST50: copies the first 50 words of the English version of the source article.
- PERFECTTRANS: directly summarizes the English version of the source article.
- TRANSTHENSUM: our approach which first translates the source article into English then summarizes the translation.

Evaluation. Translation quality is measured by corpus-level BLEU, treating each article as a data point. Summarization quality is determined by computing ROUGE-1, ROUGE-2, ROUGE-L F-1 scores.

Results. Table 3 presents our results. A qualitative example is illustrated in Figure 3. As expected, translation quality varies among different pairs of languages. The Spanish-English model

Figure 3: An example in our dataset. The source document is originally written in English and is translated into Arabic by a Global Voices translator. Our translation system translates the Arabic article into English poorly. The summarization system mostly copies segments from the translation and carries grammatical errors (underlined) from the translation to its summary. The gv-snippet summary is a mere copy of the first few sentences of the English version of the article (though this may not always be the case in other articles). On the other hand, the gv-crowd summary offers better coverage, including information in the second paragraph. Note that this article is challenging to summarize perfectly in 50 words because it features four different parallel stories at the same time. Here, the gv-crowd summarizer trades off coverage for specificity of the stories.

Method	Spanish-English	French-English	German-English	Arabic-English
Translation quality (BLEU ↑)				
Transformer	37.45	29.80	19.34	10.77
Summarization quality evaluated on gv-snippet (ROUGE-1|2|L F-1 scores ↑)				
FIRST50	63.7 | 55.1 | 61.3	64.7 | 56.2 | 62.3	65.2 | 57.1 | 63.0	62.9 | 53.5 | 60.5
PERFECTTRANS	38.0 | 22.1 | 34.0	38.1 | 21.8 | 34.0	37.7 | 21.9 | 33.6	36.8 | 20.0 | 32.7
TRANSTHENSUM	33.0 | 12.4 | 28.4	32.0 | 10.6 | 27.2	28.3 | 7.4 | 23.7	24.5 | 4.3 | 20.4
Summarization quality evaluated on gv-crowd (ROUGE-1|2|L F-1 scores ↑)				
FIRST50	46.4 | 23.4 | 40.4	46.0 | 22.8 | 40.1	47.4 | 25.7 | 40.9	45.9 | 22.9 | 40.4
PERFECTTRANS	36.1 | 13.5 | 31.3	36.7 | 13.7 | 31.7	36.6 | 14.1 | 31.6	36.9 | 14.0 | 31.9
TRANSTHENSUM	35.1 | 10.6 | 30.0	33.3 | 8.9 | 28.5	29.4 | 6.0 | 25.0	26.0 | 3.8 | 22.1

Table 3: Cross-lingual summarization results with different approaches. Translation quality is measured on the gv-snippet articles, of which the gv-crowd articles are a subset.

achieves the highest BLEU score (34.45) due to the amount of training data and the closeness between the language pair; on the other spectrum, the Arabic-English model offers poorest translations (10.77). Nevertheless, despite the large gaps in BLEU scores, we observe much smaller divergences in ROUGE-1 and ROUGE-L scores. For example, in the extreme case of Arabic-English, even when the BLEU drops by almost 90% when switch from the reference to the predicted translations, the ROUGE-L F1-score only decreases by only about 30%. This observation highlights a major limitation of ROUGE-1 and ROUGE-L: their insensitivity to the summary readability. Even though a source document may contain meaningless, ungrammatical contents (reflected by a low BLEU score), a model that summarizes by simply copying phrases can easily achieve high ROUGE-1 and ROUGE-L scores. This limitation is difficult to observe in the context of monolingual summarization because the source documents come from natural sources and thus are mostly grammatical and meaningful. Another interesting finding is that the FIRST50 baseline achieves higher ROUGE scores when evaluated on `gv-snippet` than on `gv-crowd`. This observation indicates that the `gv-snippet` summaries overlap highly with the beginning part of the articles, confirming the results from our human preference survey that these summaries generally have poorer coverage over the entire articles than the `gv-crowd` summaries.

4 Conclusion

This work introduces a dataset for evaluating multilingual and cross-lingual summarization methods in multiple languages. Future work aims to extend the dataset to more languages and construct a large-scale training dataset. Another interesting direction is to study whether multi-task learning can benefit cross-lingual summarization. To take advantage of the fact that translating the entire source article may not be necessary, it would be useful to teach models to devise more efficient translation strategies by informing them of the downstream summarization objective.

Acknowledgement

This material is based upon work supported by the National Science Foundation under Grant No. IIS-1618193. Any opinions, findings, and conclusions or recommendations expressed in this material are those of the author(s) and do not necessarily reflect the views of the National Science Foundation.

References

Mehdi Allahyari, Seyedamin Pouriyeh, Mehdi Assefi, Saeid Safaei, Elizabeth D Trippe, Juan B Gutierrez, and Krys Kochut. 2017. Text summarization techniques: a brief survey. *International Journal of Advanced Computer Science and Applications(IJACSA)*.

Hoa Trang Dang and Karolina Owczarzak. 2008. Overview of the tac 2008 update summarization task. In *TAC*.

Hoa Trang Dang and Karolina Owczarzak. 2010. Overview of tac 2010 summarization track. In *TAC*.

Yue Dong. 2018. A survey on neural network-based summarization methods. *arXiv preprint arXiv:1804.04589*.

Kevin Duh. 2018. The multitarget ted talks task. http://www.cs.jhu.edu/~kevinduh/a/multitarget-tedtalks/.

Mahak Gambhir and Vishal Gupta. 2017. Recent automatic text summarization techniques: a survey. *Artificial Intelligence Review*, 47(1):1–66.

Sebastian Gehrmann, Yuntian Deng, and Alexander M Rush. 2018. Bottom-up abstractive summarization. In *Proceedings of Empirical Methods in Natural Language Processing*.

Karl Moritz Hermann, Tomas Kocisky, Edward Grefenstette, Lasse Espeholt, Will Kay, Mustafa Suleyman, and Phil Blunsom. 2015. Teaching machines to read and comprehend. In *Advances in neural information processing systems*, pages 1693–1701.

Armand Joulin, Edouard Grave, Piotr Bojanowski, Matthijs Douze, Hérve Jégou, and Tomas Mikolov. 2016a. Fasttext.zip: Compressing text classification models. *arXiv preprint arXiv:1612.03651*.

Armand Joulin, Edouard Grave, Piotr Bojanowski, and Tomas Mikolov. 2016b. Bag of tricks for efficient text classification. *arXiv preprint arXiv:1607.01759*.

Guillaume Klein, Yoon Kim, Yuntian Deng, Jean Senellart, and Alexander M Rush. 2017. Opennmt: Open-source toolkit for neural machine translation. In *Proceedings of the Association for Computational Linguistics*.

C Orsan and Oana Andreea Chiorean. 2008. Evaluation of a cross-lingual romanian-english multi-document summariser. In *International Language Resources and Evaluation*.

Myle Ott, Sergey Edunov, Alexei Baevski, Angela Fan, Sam Gross, Nathan Ng, David Grangier, and Michael Auli. 2019. fairseq: A fast, extensible toolkit for sequence modeling. In *Conference of the North American Chapter of the Association for Computational Linguistics*.

Jessica Ouyang, Boya Song, and Kathleen McKeown. 2019. A robust abstractive system for cross-lingual summarization. In *Proceedings of the 2019 Conference of the North American Chapter of the Association for Computational Linguistics: Human Language Technologies, Volume 1 (Long and Short Papers)*, pages 2025–2031.

Paul Over, Hoa Dang, and Donna Harman. 2007. Duc in context. *Information Processing & Management*, 43(6):1506–1520.

Alexander M Rush, Sumit Chopra, and Jason Weston. 2015. A neural attention model for abstractive sentence summarization. In *Proceedings of Empirical Methods in Natural Language Processing*.

Evan Sandhaus. 2008. The new york times annotated corpus. *Linguistic Data Consortium*.

Ashish Vaswani, Noam Shazeer, Niki Parmar, Jakob Uszkoreit, Llion Jones, Aidan N Gomez, Łukasz Kaiser, and Illia Polosukhin. 2017. Attention is all you need. In *Advances in neural information processing systems*, pages 5998–6008.

Xiaojun Wan, Huiying Li, and Jianguo Xiao. 2010. Cross-language document summarization based on machine translation quality prediction. In *Proceedings of the 48th Annual Meeting of the Association for Computational Linguistics*, pages 917–926. Association for Computational Linguistics.

Taha Zerrouki. 2010. pyarabic, an arabic language library for python.

Multi-Document Summarization with Determinantal Point Processes and Contextualized Representations

Sangwoo Cho♠, Chen Li◇, Dong Yu◇, Hassan Foroosh♠, Fei Liu♠

♠Computer Science Department, University of Central Florida
◇Tencent AI Lab, Bellevue, WA, USA

swcho@knights.ucf.edu {ailabchenli, dyu}@tencent.com {foroosh,feiliu}@cs.ucf.edu

Abstract

Emerged as one of the best performing techniques for extractive summarization, determinantal point processes select the most probable set of sentences to form a summary according to a probability measure defined by modeling sentence prominence and pairwise repulsion. Traditionally, these aspects are modelled using shallow and linguistically informed features, but the rise of deep contextualized representations raises an interesting question of whether, and to what extent, contextualized representations can be used to improve DPP modeling. Our findings suggest that, despite the success of deep representations, it remains necessary to combine them with surface indicators for effective identification of summary sentences.

1 Introduction

Determinantal point processes, shortened as DPP, is one of a number of optimization techniques that perform remarkably well in summarization competitions (Hong et al., 2014). These optimization-based summarization methods include integer linear programming (Gillick and Favre, 2009), minimum dominating set (Shen and Li, 2010), maximizing submodular functions under a budget constraint (Lin and Bilmes, 2010; Yogatama et al., 2015), and DPP (Kulesza and Taskar, 2012). DPP is appealing to extractive summarization, since not only has it demonstrated promising performance on summarizing text/video content (Gong et al., 2014; Zhang et al., 2016; Sharghi et al., 2018), but it has the potential of being combined with deep neural networks for better representation and selection (Gartrell et al., 2018).

The most distinctive characteristic of DPP is its decomposition into the *quality* and *diversity* measures (Kulesza and Taskar, 2012). A *quality* measure is a positive number indicating how important a sentence is to the extractive summary. A *diversity* measure compares a pair of sentences for redundancy. If a sentence is of high quality, any *set* containing it will have a high probability score. If two sentences contain redundant information, they cannot both be included in the summary, thus any *set* containing both of them will have a low probability. DPP focuses on selecting the most probable *set* of sentences to form a summary according to sentence quality and diversity measures.

To better measure quality and diversity aspects, we draw on deep contextualized representations. A number of models have been proposed recently, including ELMo (Peters et al., 2018), BERT (Devlin et al., 2018), XLNet (Yang et al., 2019; Dai et al., 2019), RoBERTa (Liu et al., 2019) and many others. These representations encode a given text into a vector based on left and right context. With carefully designed objectives and billions of words used for pretraining, they have achieved astonishing results in several tasks including predicting entailment relationship, semantic textual similarity, and question answering. We are particularly interested in leveraging BERT for better sentence quality and diversity estimates.

This paper extends on previous work (Cho et al., 2019) by incorporating deep contextualized representations into DPP, with an emphasis on better sentence selection for extractive multi-document summarization. The major research contributions of this work include the following: (*i*) we make a first attempt to combine DPP with BERT representations to measure sentence quality and diversity and report encouraging results on benchmark summarization datasets; (*ii*) our findings suggest that it is best to model sentence *quality*, i.e., how important a sentence is to the summary, by combining semantic representations and surface indicators of the sentence, whereas pairwise sentence *dissimilarity* can be determined by semantic repre-

Proceedings of the 2nd Workshop on New Frontiers in Summarization, pages 98–103
Hong Kong, China, November 4, 2019. ©2019 Association for Computational Linguistics

sentations only; (*iii*) our analysis reveals that combining contextualized representations with surface features (e.g., sentence length, position, centrality, etc) remains necessary, as deep representations, albeit powerful, may not capture domain-specific semantics/knowledge such as word frequency.

2 DPP for Summarization

Determinantal point process (Kulesza and Taskar, 2012) defines a probability measure $\mathcal{P}$ over all subsets ($2^{|\mathcal{Y}|}$) of a ground set containing all document sentences $\mathcal{Y} = \{1, 2, \cdots, \mathsf{N}\}$. Our goal is to identify a most probable subset Y, corresponding to an extractive summary, that achieves the highest probability score. The probability measure $\mathcal{P}$ is defined as

$$\mathcal{P}(Y; L) = \frac{\det(L_Y)}{\det(L + I)}, \qquad (1)$$

$$\sum_{Y \subseteq \mathcal{Y}} \det(L_Y) = \det(L + I), \qquad (2)$$

where $\det(\cdot)$ is the determinant of a matrix; I is the identity matrix; $L \in \mathbb{R}^{\mathsf{N} \times \mathsf{N}}$ is a positive semi-definite (PSD) matrix, known as the L-ensemble; L_{ij} indicates the correlation between sentences i and j; and L_Y is a submatrix of L containing only entries indexed by elements of Y. As illustrated in Eq. (1), the probability of an extractive summary $Y \subseteq \mathcal{Y}$ is thus proportional to the determinant of the matrix L_Y.

Kulesza and Taskar (2012) introduce a decomposition of the L-ensemble matrix: $L_{ij} = q_i \cdot S_{ij} \cdot q_j$ where $q_i \in \mathbb{R}^+$ is a positive number indicating the *quality* of a sentence and S_{ij} is a measure of *similarity* between sentences i and j. The q and S model the sentence quality and pairwise similarity respectively and contribute to the L-ensemble matrix. A log-linear model is used to determine sentence quality: $q_i = \exp(\boldsymbol{\theta}^\top \mathbf{f}(i))$, where $\mathbf{f}(i)$ is a feature vector for sentence i and $\boldsymbol{\theta}$ are feature weights to be learned during DPP training. We optimize $\boldsymbol{\theta}$ by maximizing log-likelihood with gradient descent, illustrated as follows:

$$\mathcal{L}(\boldsymbol{\theta}) = \sum_{m=1}^{M} \log \mathcal{P}(\hat{Y}^{(m)}; L^{(m)}(\boldsymbol{\theta})), \qquad (3)$$

$$\nabla_{\boldsymbol{\theta}} = \sum_{m=1}^{M} \sum_{i \in \hat{Y}^{(m)}} \mathbf{f}(i) - \sum_{j} \mathbf{f}(j) K_{jj}^{(m)}, \qquad (4)$$

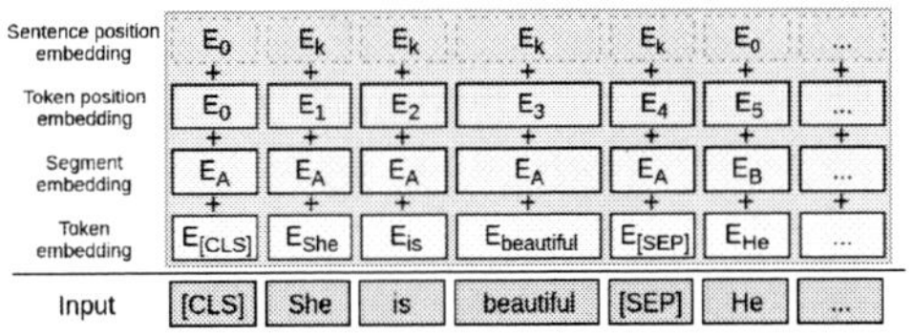

Sentence position embedding	E_0	E_k	E_k	E_k	E_k	E_0	...
	+	+	+	+	+	+	+
Token position embedding	E_0	E_1	E_2	E_3	E_4	E_5	...
	+	+	+	+	+	+	+
Segment embedding	E_A	E_A	E_A	E_A	E_A	E_B	...
	+	+	+	+	+	+	+
Token embedding	$E_{[CLS]}$	E_{She}	E_{is}	$E_{beautiful}$	$E_{[SEP]}$	E_{He}	...
Input	[CLS]	She	is	beautiful	[SEP]	He	...

Figure 1: BERT-*sim* and BERT-*imp* utilize embeddings for tokens, segments, token position in a sentence and sentence position in a document. These embeddings are element-wisely added up then fed into the model.

CNN/DM	mean	min	max
train-pos	13.95	1	318
train-neg	21.90	1	337
DUC-04	2.22	1	5
TAC-11	1.67	1	5

Table 1: Position of summary-worthy sentences in a document for single-doc (CNN/DM) and multi-doc datasets (DUC-04, TAC11). 'pos' are summary-worthy document sentences; 'neg' are sentences that are randomly sampled from the same document.

where M is the total number of training instances; $\hat{Y}^{(m)}$ is the ground-truth summary of the m-th instance; $K = L(L + I)^{-1}$ is the kernel matrix and $\mathcal{P}(\hat{Y}^{(m)}; L^{(m)}(\boldsymbol{\theta}))$ is defined by Eq. (1). We refer the reader to (Kulesza and Taskar, 2012) for details on gradient derivation (Eq. (4)). In the following we describe two BERT models to respectively estimate sentence pairwise similarity and importance. The trained models are then plugged into the DPP framework for computing S and q.

2.1 BERT Architecture

We introduce two models that fine-tune the BERT-base architecture (Devlin et al., 2018) to calculate the similarity between a pair of sentences (BERT-*sim*) and learn representations that characterize the importance of a single sentence (BERT-*imp*). Importantly, training instances for both BERT models are derived from *single-document* summarization dataset (Hermann et al., 2015) by Lebanoff et al. (2019), containing a collection of single sentences (or sentence pairs) and their associated labels. During testing, the trained BERT models are applied to single sentences and sentence pairs derived from *multi-document* input to obtain quality and similarity measures.

BERT-*sim* takes as input a pair of sentences and transforms each token in the sentence into an embedding using an embedding layer. They are then passed through the BERT-base architecture to produce a vector representing the input sentence pair. The vector, denoted by $\mathbf{u} \in \mathbb{R}^d$, is the final hidden state corresponding to the "[CLS]" token (d=768), which is used as the aggregate sequence representation. $\mathbf{u}$ is passed through a feed-forward layer with the same dimension d, followed by a dropout layer, and a final softmax prediction layer to classify whether a pair of sentences contain redundant information or not. Once the model is trained, we can apply it to a pair of sentences i and j to obtain the similarity score S_{ij}.

BERT-*imp* uses a similar architecture to predict if any single sentence is important to the summary. Once the model is trained, we can apply it to the i-th sentence to generate a vector $\mathbf{u}_i$ which is used as the feature representation $\mathbf{f}(i)$ for the i-th sentence when computing q_i.

The embedding layer, illustrated in Fig. 1, consists of several types of embeddings, respectively representing tokens, segments, the token position in a sentence and sentence position within a given document. These embeddings are element-wisely added up then fed to the model. The sentence position embeddings are incorporated in this work to capture the position of a sentence in the article. It is utilized only by BERT-*imp*, as position matters for sentence importance but not quite so for pairwise similarity. As shown in Table 1, positive sentences in the training data (see §3.1) tend to appear at the beginning of an article, consistently more so than negative sentences. Further, ground-truth summary sentences of the DUC and TAC datasets are likely to appear among the first five sentences of an article, indicating position embeddings are crucial for training the BERT-*imp* model.

2.2 DPP Training

DPP training focuses on estimating the weights of features used in $q_i = \exp(\boldsymbol{\theta}^\top \mathbf{f}(i))$, which is a log-linear model used for computing sentence quality. The sentence similarity scores S_{ij} are produced by BERT-*sim*; they do not change during DPP training. We obtain contextualized representations for the i-th sentence, i.e., $\mathbf{f}(i) \in \mathbb{R}^d$, from the penultimate layer ($\mathbf{u}_i$) of BERT-*imp*.

In addition, a number of surface indicators[1], denoted by $\mathbf{v}_i \in \mathbb{R}^{d'}$, are extracted for sentence i. To combine surface indicators and contextualized

System	DUC-04		
	R-1	**R-2**	**R-SU4**
Opinosis (Ganesan et al., 2010)	27.07	5.03	8.63
Extract+Rewrite (Song et al., 2018)	28.90	5.33	8.76
Pointer-Gen (See et al., 2017)	31.43	6.03	10.01
SumBasic (Vanderwende et al., 2007)	29.48	4.25	8.64
KLSumm(Haghighi et al., 2009)	31.04	6.03	10.23
LexRank (Erkan and Radev, 2004)	34.44	7.11	11.19
ICSISumm (Gillick and Favre, 2009)	37.31	9.36	13.12
DPP (Kulesza and Taskar, 2012)†	38.10	9.14	13.40
DPP-Caps (Cho et al., 2019)	38.25	9.22	13.40
DPP-Caps-Comb (Cho et al., 2019)	39.35	10.14	14.15
DPP-BERT (ours)	38.14	9.30	13.47
DPP-BERT-Comb 64 (ours)	38.78	9.78	14.04
DPP-BERT-Comb 128 (ours)	**39.05**	**10.23**	**14.35**

Table 2: Results on the DUC-04 dataset evaluated by ROUGE. † indicates our reimplementation of Kulesza and Taskar (2012) system.

representations, we concatenate $\mathbf{u}_i$ and $\mathbf{v}_i$ as sentence features. We also take a weighted average[2] of S_{ij} and C_{ij} as an estimate of pairwise sentence similarity, where C_{ij} is the cosine similarity of sentence TF-IDF vectors. DPP training learns feature weights $\boldsymbol{\theta} \in \mathbb{R}^D$, where $D = d + d'$ if the sentence features are concatenated, otherwise $D = d$. DPP is trained on multi-document summarization data with gradient descent (Eq. (4)).

3 Experiments

In this section we describe the dataset used to train the BERT-*sim* and BERT-*imp* models, benchmark datasets for multi-document summarization, and experimental settings. Our system shows competitive results comparing to state-of-the-art methods. Example summaries are provided to demonstrate the effectiveness of the proposed method.

3.1 Dataset

CNN / DailyMail This dataset (Hermann et al., 2015) is utilized to train the BERT-*sim* and BERT-*imp* models. For BERT-*sim*, we pair each human summary sentence with its most similar document sentence to create a positive instance; negative instances are randomly sampled sentence pairs. For BERT-*imp*, the most similar document sentence receives a label of 1; randomly sampled sentences are labelled as 0. In total, our training / dev / test sets contain 2,084,798 / 105,936 / 86,144 sentence pairs and the instances are balanced.

---

[1] The sentence features include the length and position of a sentence, the cosine similarity between sentence and document TF-IDF vectors (Kulesza and Taskar, 2011). We abstain from using sophisticated features to avoid model overfitting.

[2] The coefficient is set to be 0.9 for both datasets.

DUC/TAC We evaluate our DPP approach (§2) on multi-document summarization datasets including DUC and TAC (Over and Yen, 2004; Dang and Owczarzak, 2008). The task is to generate a summary of 100 words from a collection of news articles. We report ROUGE F-scores (Lin, 2004)[3] on DUC-04 (trained on DUC-03) and TAC-11 (trained on TAC-08/09/10) following standard settings (Hong et al., 2014). Ground-truth extractive summaries used in DPP training are obtained from Cho et al. (2019).

3.2 Experiment Settings

We implement our system using TensorFlow on an NVIDIA 1080Ti GPU. We consider the maximum length of a sentence to be 64 or 128 words. The batch size is 64 for the 64 max sentence length and 32 for 128. We use Adam optimizer (Kingma and Ba, 2015) with the default setting and set learning rate to be 2e-5. We train BERT-*imp* and BERT-*sim* on CNN/DM. The prediction accuracy of BERT-*sim* and BERT-*imp* (with length-128) are respectively 96.11% and 69.05%. Similar results are observed with length-64: 95.79% and 69.63%.

3.3 Summarization Results

We compare our system with strong summarization baselines (Table 2 and 3). *SumBasic* (Vanderwende et al., 2007), *KL-Sum* (Haghighi and Vanderwende, 2009), and *LexRank* (Erkan and Radev, 2004) are extractive approaches; *Opinosis* (Ganesan et al., 2010), *Extract+Rewrite* (Song et al., 2018), and *Pointer-Gen* (See et al., 2017) are abstractive methods; *ICSISumm* (Gillick et al., 2009) is an ILP-based summarization method; and *DPP-Caps-Comb*, *DPP-Caps* are results combining DPP and capsule networks reported by Cho et al. (2019) w/ and w/o using sentence TF-IDF similarity ($C_{i,j}$).

We experiment with variants of our DPP model: *DPP-BERT, DPP-BERT-Combined*. The former utilizes the outputs from BERT-*sim* and BERT-*imp* to compute S_{ij} and q_i, whereas the latter combines BERT-*sim* output with sentence TF-IDF similarity ($C_{i,j}$), and concatenates BERT-*imp* features with linguistically informed features.

Our DPP methods outperform both extractive and abstractive baselines, indicating the effectiveness of optimization-based methods for extractive multi-document summarization. Furthermore, we

	TAC-11		
System	**R-1**	**R-2**	**R-SU4**
Opinosis (Ganesan et al., 2010)	25.15	5.12	8.12
Extract+Rewrite (Song et al., 2018)	29.07	6.11	9.20
Pointer-Gen (See et al., 2017)	31.44	6.40	10.20
SumBasic (Vanderwende et al., 2007)	31.58	6.06	10.06
KLSumm (Haghighi et al., 2009)	31.23	7.07	10.56
LexRank (Erkan and Radev, 2004)	33.10	7.50	11.13
DPP (Kulesza and Taskar, 2012)†	36.95	9.83	13.57
DPP-Caps (Cho et al., 2019)	36.61	9.30	13.09
DPP-Caps-Comb (Cho et al., 2019)	37.30	10.13	13.78
DPP-BERT (ours)	37.04	10.18	13.79
DPP-BERT-Comb 64 (ours)	38.46	10.79	14.45
DPP-BERT-Comb 128 (ours)	**38.59**	**11.06**	**14.65**

Table 3: ROUGE results on the TAC-11 dataset.

observe that *DPP-BERT-Combined* yields the best performance, achieving 10.23% and 11.06% F-scores respectively on DUC-04 and TAC-11. This finding suggests that sentence similarity scores and importance features from the *DPP-BERT* system and TF-IDF based features can complement each other to boost system performance. We conjecture that TF-IDF sentence vectors are effective at representing topical terms (e.g., *3 million*), thus helping DPP better select representative sentences. Another observation is that *DPP-BERT* and *DPP-BERT-Combined* consistently outperform *DPP-Caps* and *DPP-Caps-Comb*, indicating its excellence for DPP-based summarization.

In Table 4 we show example system summaries and a human-written reference summary. *DPP-BERT* and *DPP-BERT-Combined* both are capable of selecting a balanced set of representative and diverse summary sentence from multi-documents. *DPP-BERT-Combined* selects more relevant sentences than *DPP-BERT* comparing to the human summary, leading to better ROUGE scores.

4 Conclusion

In this paper we describe a novel approach using determinantal point processes for extractive multi-document summarization. Our DPP+BERT models harness the power of deep contextualized representations and optimization to achieve outstanding performance on multi-document summarization benchmarks. Our analysis further reveals that, despite the success of deep contextualized representations, it remains necessary to combine them with surface indicators for effective identification of summary-worthy sentences.

---

[3]with options -n 2 -m -w 1.2 -c 95 -r 1000 -l 100

<table>
<tr><td>

Human Reference Summary

- On March 1, 2007, the Food/Drug Administration (FDA) started a broad safety review of children's cough/cold remedies.
- They are particularly concerned about use of these drugs by infants.
- By September 28th, the 356-page FDA review urged an outright ban on all such medicines for children under six.
- Dr. Charles Ganley, a top FDA official said "We have no data on these agents of what's a safe and effective dose in Children." The review also stated that between 1969 and 2006, 123 children died from taking decongestants and antihistimines.
- On October 11th, all such infant products were pulled from the markets.

DPP-BERT Summary

- The petition is far from the first warning about children using the medicines.
- The FDA will formally consider revising labeling at a meeting scheduled for Oct. 18-19.
- Federal drug regulators have started a broad review of the safety of popular cough and cold remedies meant for children, a top official said Thursday.
- Similarly, hydrocodone has never been shown to be safe and effective in children, and its dangers as a powerful and potentially addictive narcotic are clear.

DPP-BERT-Combined Summary

- The U.S. government is warning parents not to give cough and cold medicines to children under 2 without a doctor's order, part of an overall review of the products' safety and effectiveness for youngsters.
- Drug makers on Thursday voluntarily pulled kids' cold medicines off the market less than two weeks after the U.S. government warned of potential health risks to infants.
- Safety experts for the Food and Drug Administration urged the agency on Friday to consider an outright ban on over-the-counter, multi-symptom cough and cold medicines for children under 6.
- In high doses, cold medicines can affect the heart's electrical system, leading to arrhythmias.

</td></tr>
</table>

Table 4: Example system summaries and their human reference summary. Sentences selected by DPP-BERT-Combined are more similar to the human summary than those of DPP-BERT; both include diverse sentences.

Acknowledgments

We are grateful to the anonymous reviewers for their helpful suggestions. This research was supported in part by the National Science Foundation grant IIS-1909603.

References

Sangwoo Cho, Logan Lebanoff, Hassan Foroosh, and Fei Liu. 2019. Improving the similarity measure of determinantal point processes for extractive multi-document summarization. In *Proceedings of the Annual Meeting of the Association for Computational Linguistics (ACL)*.

Zihang Dai, Zhilin Yang, Yiming Yang, Jaime Carbonell, Quoc Le, and Ruslan Salakhutdinov. 2019. Transformer-XL: Attentive language models beyond a fixed-length context. In *Proceedings of the Annual Meeting of the Association for Computational Linguistics (ACL)*.

Hoa Trang Dang and Karolina Owczarzak. 2008. Overview of the TAC 2008 update summarization task. In *Proceedings of Text Analysis Conference (TAC)*.

Jacob Devlin, Ming-Wei Chang, Kenton Lee, and Kristina Toutanova. 2018. BERT: pre-training of deep bidirectional transformers for language understanding. *arXiv:1810.04805*.

Günes Erkan and Dragomir R. Radev. 2004. LexRank: Graph-based lexical centrality as salience in text summarization. *Journal of Artificial Intelligence Research*.

Kavita Ganesan, ChengXiang Zhai, and Jiawei Han. 2010. Opinosis: A graph-based approach to abstractive summarization of highly redundant opinions. In *Proceedings of the International Conference on Computational Linguistics (COLING)*.

Mike Gartrell, Elvis Dohmatob, and Jon Alberdi. 2018. Deep determinantal point processes. *https://arxiv.org/abs/1811.07245*.

Dan Gillick and Benoit Favre. 2009. A scalable global model for summarization. In *Proceedings of the NAACL Workshop on Integer Linear Programming for Natural Langauge Processing*.

Dan Gillick, Benoit Favre, Dilek Hakkani-Tur, Berndt Bohnet, Yang Liu, and Shasha Xie. 2009. The ICSI/UTD summarization system at TAC 2009. In *Proceedings of TAC*.

Boqing Gong, Wei-Lun Chao, Kristen Grauman, and Fei Sha. 2014. Diverse sequential subset selection for supervised video summarization. In *Proceedings of Neural Information Processing Systems (NIPS)*.

Aria Haghighi and Lucy Vanderwende. 2009. Exploring content models for multi-document summarization. In *Proceedings of the North American Chapter of the Association for Computational Linguistics (NAACL)*.

Karl Moritz Hermann, Tomas Kocisky, Edward Grefenstette, Lasse Espeholt, Will Kay, Mustafa Suleyman, and Phil Blunsom. 2015. Teaching machines to read and comprehend. In *Proceedings of Neural Information Processing Systems (NIPS)*.

Kai Hong, John M Conroy, Benoit Favre, Alex Kulesza, Hui Lin, and Ani Nenkova. 2014. A repository of state of the art and competitive baseline summaries for generic news summarization. In *Proceedings of the Ninth International Conference on Language Resources and Evaluation (LREC)*.

Diederik P. Kingma and Jimmy Ba. 2015. Adam: A method for stochastic optimization. In *Proceedings of the International Conference on Learning Representations (ICLR)*.

Alex Kulesza and Ben Taskar. 2011. Learning determinantal point processes. In *Proceedings of the Conference on Uncertainty in Artificial Intelligence (UAI)*.

Alex Kulesza and Ben Taskar. 2012. *Determinantal Point Processes for Machine Learning*. Now Publishers Inc.

Logan Lebanoff, Kaiqiang Song, Franck Dernoncourt, Doo Soon Kim, Seokhwan Kim, Walter Chang, and Fei Liu. 2019. Scoring sentence singletons and pairs for abstractive summarization. In *Proceedings of the Annual Meeting of the Association for Computational Linguistics (ACL)*.

Chin-Yew Lin. 2004. ROUGE: a package for automatic evaluation of summaries. In *Proceedings of ACL Workshop on Text Summarization Branches Out*.

Hui Lin and Jeff Bilmes. 2010. Multi-document summarization via budgeted maximization of submodular functions. In *Proceedings of NAACL*.

Yinhan Liu, Myle Ott, Naman Goyal, Jingfei Du, Mandar Joshi, Danqi Chen, Omer Levy, Mike Lewis, Luke Zettlemoyer, and Veselin Stoyanov. 2019. RoBERTa: A robustly optimized BERT pretraining approach. *https://arxiv.org/pdf/1907.11692.pdf*.

Paul Over and James Yen. 2004. An introduction to DUC-2004. *National Institute of Standards and Technology*.

Matthew E. Peters, Mark Neumann, Mohit Iyyer, Matt Gardner, Christopher Clark, Kenton Lee, and Luke Zettlemoyer. 2018. Deep contextualized word representations. In *Proceedings of the North American Chapter of the Association for Computational Linguistics (NAACL)*.

Abigail See, Peter J. Liu, and Christopher D. Manning. 2017. Get to the point: Summarization with pointer-generator networks. In *Proceedings of the Annual Meeting of the Association for Computational Linguistics (ACL)*.

Aidean Sharghi, Ali Borji, Chengtao Li, Tianbao Yang, and Boqing Gong. 2018. Improving sequential determinantal point processes for supervised video summarization. In *Proceedings of the European Conference on Computer Vision (ECCV)*.

Chao Shen and Tao Li. 2010. Multi-document summarization via the minimum dominating set. In *Proceedings of the International Conference on Computational Linguistics (COLING)*.

Kaiqiang Song, Lin Zhao, and Fei Liu. 2018. Structure-infused copy mechanisms for abstractive summarization. In *Proceedings of the International Conference on Computational Linguistics (COLING)*.

Lucy Vanderwende, Hisami Suzuki, Chris Brockett, and Ani Nenkova. 2007. Beyond SumBasic: Task-focused summarization with sentence simplification and lexical expansion. *Information Processing and Management*, 43(6):1606–1618.

Zhilin Yang, Zihang Dai, Yiming Yang, Jaime Carbonell, Ruslan Salakhutdinov, and Quoc V. Le. 2019. XLNet: Generalized autoregressive pretraining for language understanding. *https://arxiv.org/abs/1906.08237*.

Dani Yogatama, Fei Liu, and Noah A. Smith. 2015. Extractive summarization by maximizing semantic volume. In *Proceedings of the Conference on Empirical Methods on Natural Language Processing (EMNLP)*.

Ke Zhang, Wei-Lun Chao, Fei Sha, and Kristen Grauman. 2016. Video summarization with long short-term memory. In *Proceedings of the European Conference on Computer Vision (ECCV)*.

Analyzing Sentence Fusion in Abstractive Summarization

Logan Lebanoff[♠][*]   John Muchovej[♠][*]   Franck Dernoncourt[♣]
Doo Soon Kim[♣]   Seokhwan Kim[♡]   Walter Chang[♣]   Fei Liu[♠]

[♠]University of Central Florida   [♣]Adobe Research   [♡]Amazon Alexa AI

{loganlebanoff, john.muchovej}@knights.ucf.edu   feiliu@cs.ucf.edu
{dernonco, dkim, wachang}@adobe.com   seokhwk@amazon.com

Abstract

While recent work in abstractive summarization has resulted in higher scores in automatic metrics, there is little understanding on how these systems combine information taken from multiple document sentences. In this paper, we analyze the outputs of five state-of-the-art abstractive summarizers, focusing on summary sentences that are formed by sentence fusion. We ask assessors to judge the grammaticality, faithfulness, and method of fusion for summary sentences. Our analysis reveals that system sentences are mostly grammatical, but often fail to remain faithful to the original article.

1 Introduction

Modern abstractive summarizers excel at finding and extracting salient content (See et al., 2017; Chen and Bansal, 2018; Celikyilmaz et al., 2018; Liu and Lapata, 2019). However, one of the key tenets of summarization is consolidation of information, and these systems can struggle to combine content from multiple source texts, yielding output summaries that contain poor grammar and even incorrect facts. Truthfulness of summaries is a vitally important feature in order for summarization to be widely accepted in real-world applications (Reiter, 2018; Cao et al., 2018b). In this work, we perform an extensive analysis of summary outputs generated by state-of-the-art systems, examining features such as truthfulness to the original document, grammaticality, and method of how sentences are merged together. This work presents the first in-depth human evaluation of multiple diverse summarization models.

We differentiate between two methods of shortening text: sentence compression and sentence fusion. Sentence compression reduces the length of a *single* sentence by removing words or rephrasing parts of the sentence (Cohn and Lapata, 2008;

Wang et al., 2013; Li et al., 2013, 2014; Filippova et al., 2015). Sentence fusion reduces *two or more* sentences to one by taking content from each sentence and merging them together (Barzilay and McKeown, 2005; McKeown et al., 2010; Thadani and McKeown, 2013). Compression is considered an easier task because unimportant clauses within the sentence can be removed while retaining the grammaticality and truth of the sentence (McDonald, 2006). In contrast, fusion requires selection of important content and stitching of that content in a grammatical and meaningful way. We focus on sentence fusion in this work.

We examine the outputs of five abstractive summarization systems on CNN/DailyMail (Hermann et al., 2015) using human judgments. Particularly, we focus on summary sentences that involve sentence fusion, since fusion is the task that requires the most improvement. We analyze several dimensions of the outputs, including faithfulness to the original article, grammaticality, and method of fusion. We present three main findings:

- 38.3% of the system outputs introduce incorrect facts, while 21.6% are ungrammatical;

- systems often simply concatenate chunks of text when performing sentence fusion, while largely avoiding other methods of fusion like entity replacement;

- systems struggle to reliably perform complex fusion, as entity replacement and other methods result in incorrect facts 47–75% of the time.

2 Evaluation Setup

Evaluation of summarization systems relies heavily on automatic metrics. However, ROUGE (Lin, 2004) and other n-gram based metrics are limited in evaluation power and do not tell the whole story (Novikova et al., 2017). They often focus on informativeness, which misses out on important facets

---

*These authors contributed equally to this work.

System	ROUGE			Created By				Avg Summ
	R-1	R-2	R-L	Compress	Fuse	Copy	Fail	Sent Len
PG (See et al., 2017)	39.53	17.28	36.38	63.14	6.44	**30.24**	0.18	15.7
Novel (Kryciski et al., 2018)	40.19	17.38	37.52	71.25	19.77	5.39	3.59	11.8
Fast-Abs-RL (Chen and Bansal, 2018)	40.88	17.80	**38.54**	**96.65**	0.83	2.21	0.31	15.6
Bottom-Up (Gehrmann et al., 2018)	41.22	18.68	38.34	71.15	16.35	11.76	0.74	10.7
DCA (Celikyilmaz et al., 2018)	**41.69**	**19.47**	37.92	64.11	23.96	7.07	4.86	14.5
Reference Summaries	-	-	-	60.65	**31.93**	1.36	**6.06**	**19.3**

Table 1: Comparison of state-of-the-art summarization systems. Middle column describes how summary sentences are generated. *Compress*: single sentence is shortened. *Fuse*: multiple sentences are merged. *Copy*: sentence is copied word-for-word. *Fail*: did not find matching source sentences.

of summaries such as faithfulness and grammaticality. In this paper we present a thorough investigation of several abstractive summarization systems using human evaluation on CNN/DailyMail. The task was accomplished via the crowdsourcing platform Amazon Mechanical Turk. We particularly focus on summary sentences formed by sentence fusion, as it is arguably a harder task and is a vital aspect of abstractive summarization.

2.1 Summarization Systems

We narrowed our evaluation to five state-of-the-art summarization models[1], as they represent some of the most competitive abstractive summarizers developed in recent years. The models show diversity across several dimensions, including ROUGE scores, abstractiveness, and training paradigm. We briefly describe each system, along with a comparison in Table 1.

- **PG** (See et al., 2017) The pointer-generator networks use an encoder-decoder architecture with attention and copy mechanisms that allow it to either generate a new word from the vocabulary or copy a word directly from the document. It tends strongly towards extraction and copies entire summary sentences about 30% of the time.

- **Novel** (Kryciski et al., 2018) This model uses an encoder-decoder architecture but adds a novelty metric which is optimized using reinforcement learning. It improves summary novelty by promoting the use of unseen words.

- **Fast-Abs-RL** (Chen and Bansal, 2018) Document sentences are selected using reinforcement learning and then compressed/paraphrased using an encoder-decoder model to generate summary sentences.

- **Bottom-Up** (Gehrmann et al., 2018) An external content selection model identifies which words from the document should be copied to the summary; such info is incorporated into the copy mechanism of an encoder-decoder model.

- **DCA** (Celikyilmaz et al., 2018) The source text is divided among several encoders, which are all connected to a single decoder using hierarchical attention. It achieves one of the highest ROUGE scores among state-of-the-art.

2.2 Task Design

Our goal is to assess the quality of summary sentences according to their grammaticality, faithfulness and method of fusion. We design a crowd task consisting of a single article with six summary sentences: one sentence is guaranteed to be from the reference summary, the other five are taken from system summaries. An annotator is instructed to read the article, then rate the following characteristics for each summary sentence:

Faithfulness For a summary to be useful, it must remain true to the original text. This is particularly challenging for abstractive systems since they require a deep understanding of the document in order to rephrase sentences with the same meaning.

Grammaticality System summaries should follow grammatical rules in order to read well. Maintaining grammaticality can be relatively straightforward for sentence compression, as systems generally succeed at removing unnecessary clauses and interjections (See et al., 2017). However, sentence fusion requires greater understanding in order to stitch together clauses in a grammatical way.

Method of Merging Each summary sentence in our experiments is created by fusing content from two document sentences. We would like to understand how this fusion is performed. The following possibilities are given:

---

[1] The summary outputs from PG, Bottom-Up, and Fast-Abs-RL are obtained from their corresponding Github repos. Those from Novel and DCA are graciously provided to us by the authors. We thank the authors for sharing their work.

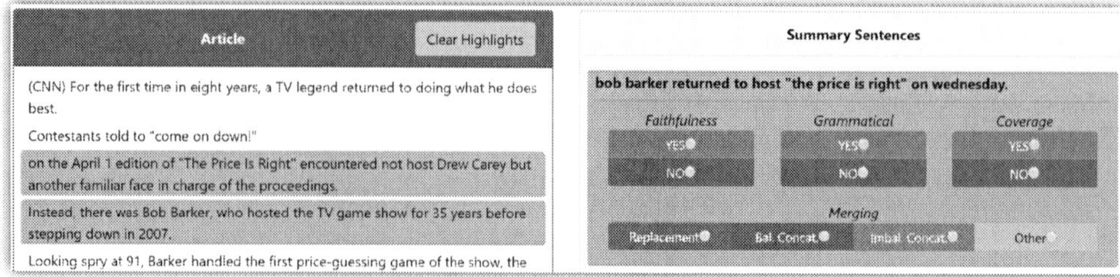

Figure 1: Annotation interface. A sentence from a random summarization system is shown along with four questions.

- *Replacement:* a pronoun or description of an entity in one sentence is replaced by a different description of that entity in the other sentence.

- *Balanced concatenation:* a consecutive part of one sentence is concatenated with a consecutive part of the other sentence. The parts taken from each sentence are of similar length.

- *Imbalanced concatenation:* similar to the case of "balanced concatenation," but the part taken from one sentence is larger than the part taken from the other sentence.

- *Other:* all remaining cases.

Coverage An annotator is asked to rate how well highlighted article sentences "covered" the information contained in the summary sentence. Two article sentences that best match a summary sentence are selected according to a heuristic developed by Lebanoff et al. (2019). The same heuristic is also used to determine whether a summary sentence is created by compression or fusion (more details later in this section). Given the importance of this heuristic for our task, we would like to measure its effectiveness on selecting article sentences that best match a given summary sentence.

We provide detailed instructions, including examples and explanations. We randomly select 100 articles from the CNN/DailyMail test set. This results in 100 tasks for annotators, where each task includes an article and six summary sentences to be evaluated—one of which originates from the reference summary and the other five are from any of the system summaries. Each task is completed by an average of 4 workers. All workers are required to have the "Master" qualification, a designation for high-quality annotations. Of the 600 summary sentences evaluated, each state-of-the-art system contributes as follows—*Bottom-Up*: 146, *DCA*: 130, *PG*: 37, *Novel*: 171, *Fast-Abs-RL*:

16, and *Reference*: 100. The number of sentences we evaluate for each system is proportional to the number of observed fusion cases.

In order to answer the *Method of Merging* and *Coverage* questions, the annotator must be provided with which two article sentences were fused together to create the summary sentence in question. We use the heuristic proposed by Lebanoff et al. (2019) to estimate which pair of sentences should be chosen. They use averaged ROUGE-1, -2, -L scores (Lin, 2004) to represent sentence similarity. The heuristic calculates the ROUGE similarity between the summary sentence and each article sentence. The article sentence with the highest similarity is chosen as the first sentence, then overlapping words are removed from the summary sentence. It continues to find the article sentence most similar to the remaining summary sentence, which is chosen as the second sentence. Our interface automatically highlights this pair of sentences (Figure 1).

The same heuristic is also employed in deciding whether a summary sentence was generated by sentence compression or fusion. The algorithm halts if no article sentence is found that shares two or more content words with the summary sentence. If it halts after only one sentence is found, then it is classified as *compression*. If it finds a second sentence, then it is classified as *fusion*.

3 Results

We present experimental results in Table 2. Our findings suggest that system summary sentences formed by fusion have low faithfulness (61.7% on average) as compared to the reference summaries. This demonstrates the need for current summarization models to put more emphasis on improving the faithfulness of generated summaries. Surprisingly, the highest performing systems, DCA and Bottom-Up, according to ROUGE result in

System	Faithful	Grammatical	Coverage
DCA	47.0	72.4	62.6
Bottom-Up	56.9	78.9	78.5
Novel	58.5	78.5	75.3
Fast-Abs-RL	69.0	77.6	82.8
PG	76.9	84.6	89.5
Reference	88.4	91.6	74.9

Table 2: Percentage of summary sentences that are faithful, grammatical, etc. according to human evaluation of several state-of-the-art summarization systems (see §2 for details).

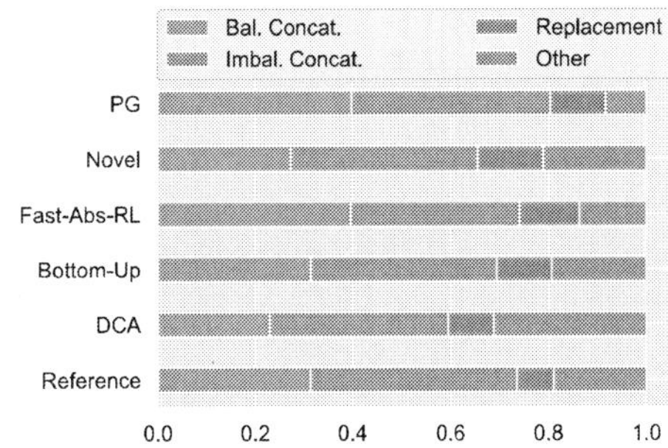

Figure 2: Frequency of each merging method. Concatenation is the most common method of merging.

System	Faithful	Grammatical	Coverage
Bal Concat	82.55	86.91	94.43
Imbal Concat	69.40	80.25	84.58
Replacement	53.06	82.04	77.55
Other	25.20	68.23	27.04

Table 3: Results for each merging method. Concatenation has high faithfulness, grammaticality, and coverage, while Replacement and Other have much lower scores.

the lowest scores for being faithful to the article. While we cannot attribute the drop in faithfulness to an over-emphasis on optimizing automatic metrics, we can state that higher ROUGE scores does not necessarily lead to more faithful summaries, as other works have shown (Falke et al., 2019). Bottom-Up, interestingly, is 20 points lower than PG, which it is closely based on. It uses an external content selector to choose what words to copy from the article. While identifying summary-worthy content improved ROUGE, we believe that Bottom-Up stitches together sections of content that do not necessarily belong together. Thus, it is important to identify not just summary-worthy content, but also *mergeable* content.

System summary sentences created by fusion are generally grammatical (78.4% on average), though it is still not up to par with reference summaries (91.6%). The chosen state-of-the-art systems use the encoder-decoder architecture, which employs a neural language model as the decoder, and language models generally succeed at encoding grammar rules and staying fluent (Clark et al., 2019). The coverage for reference summaries is moderately high (74.9%), demonstrating the effectiveness of the heuristic of identifying where summary content is pulled from. Especially for most of the systems, the heuristic successfully finds the correct source sentences. As it is based mostly on word overlap, the heuristic works better on summaries that are more extractive, hence the higher coverage scores among the systems compared to reference summaries, which are more abstractive.

Figure 2 illustrates the frequency of each merging method over the summarization systems. Most summary sentences are formed by concatenation. PG in particular most often fuses two sentences using concatenation. Surprisingly, very few reference summaries use entity replacement when performing fusion. We believe this is due to the extractiveness of the CNN/DailyMail dataset, and

would likely have higher occurrences in more abstractive datasets.

Does the way sentences are fused affect their faithfulness and grammaticality? Table 3 provides insights regarding this question. Grammaticality is relatively high for all merging categories. Coverage is also high for balanced/imbalanced concatenation and replacement, meaning the heuristic works succesfully for these forms of sentence merging. It does not perform as well on the Other category. This is understandable, since sentences formed in a more complex manner will be harder to identify using simple word overlap. Faithfulness has a similar trend, with summaries generated using concatenation being more likely to be faithful to the original article. This may explain why PG is the most faithful of the systems, while being the simplest—it uses concatenation more than any of the other systems. We believe more effort can be directed towards improving the more complex merging paradigms, such as entity replacement.

There are a few potential limitations associated with the experimental design. Judging whether a sentence is faithful to the original article can be a difficult task to perform reliably, even for humans. We observe that the reference summaries achieve lower than the expected faithfulness and grammaticality of 100%. This can have two reasons. First, the inter-annotator agreement for this task is relatively low and we counteract this by employing an average of four annotators to complete each task. Second, we make use of an automatic heuristic to highlight sentence pairs from the article. While it generally finds the correct sentences—average Coverage score of 77.3%—the incorrect pairs may have biased the annotators away from sentences that humans would have found more appropriate. This further exemplifies the difficulty of the task.

4 Related Work

Sentence fusion aims to produce a single summary sentence by fusing multiple source sentences. Dependency graphs and discourse structure have proven useful for aligning and combining multiple sentences into a single sentence (Barzilay and McKeown, 2005; Marsi and Krahmer, 2005; Filippova and Strube, 2008; Cheung and Penn, 2014; Gerani et al., 2014). Mehdad et al. (2013) construct an entailment graph over sentences for sentence selection, then fuse sentences together using a word graph. Abstract meaning representation and other graph-based representations have also shown success in sentence fusion (Liu et al., 2015; Nayeem et al., 2018). Geva et al. (2019) fuse pairs of sentences together using Transformer, focusing on discourse connectives between sentences.

Recent summarization research has put special emphasis on faithfulness to the original text. Cao et al. (2018a) use seq-to-seq models to rewrite templates that are prone to including irrelevant entities. Incorporating additional information into a seq-to-seq model, such as entailment and dependency structure, has proven successful (Li et al., 2018; Song et al., 2018). The closest work to our human evaluation seems to be from Falke et al. (2019). Similar to our work, they find that the PG model is more faithful than Fast-Abs-RL and Bottom-Up, even though it has lower ROUGE. They show that 25% of outputs from these state-of-the-art summarization models are unfaithful to the original article. Cao et al. (2018b) reveal a similar finding that 27% of the summaries generated by a neural sequence-to-sequence model have errors. Our study, by contrast, finds 38% to be unfaithful, but we limit our study to only summary sentences created by *fusion*. Our work examines a wide variety of state-of-the-art summarization systems, and perform in-depth analysis over other measures including grammaticality, coverage, and method of merging.

5 Conclusion

In this paper we present an investigation into sentence fusion for abstractive summarization. Several state-of-the-art systems are evaluated, and we find that many of the summary outputs generate false information. Most of the false outputs were generated by entity replacement and other complex merging methods. These results demonstrate the need for more attention to be focused on improving sentence fusion and entity replacement.

Acknowledgments

We are grateful to the anonymous reviewers for their helpful comments and suggestions. This research was supported in part by the National Science Foundation grant IIS-1909603.

References

Regina Barzilay and Kathleen R. McKeown. 2005. Sentence Fusion for Multidocument News Summarization. *Computational Linguistics*, 31(3):297–328.

Ziqiang Cao, Wenjie Li, Sujian Li, and Furu Wei. 2018a. Retrieve, Rerank and Rewrite: Soft Template Based Neural Summarization. In *Proceedings of the 56th Annual Meeting of the Association for Computational Linguistics (Volume 1: Long Papers)*, pages 152–161, Melbourne, Australia. Association for Computational Linguistics.

Ziqiang Cao, Furu Wei, Wenjie Li, and Sujian Li. 2018b. Faithful to the original: Fact aware neural abstractive summarization. In *Thirty-Second AAAI Conference on Artificial Intelligence*.

Asli Celikyilmaz, Antoine Bosselut, Xiaodong He, and Yejin Choi. 2018. Deep Communicating Agents for Abstractive Summarization. In *Proceedings of the 2018 Conference of the North American Chapter of the Association for Computational Linguistics: Human Language Technologies, Volume 1 (Long Papers)*, pages 1662–1675, New Orleans, Louisiana. Association for Computational Linguistics.

Yen-Chun Chen and Mohit Bansal. 2018. Fast Abstractive Summarization with Reinforce-Selected Sentence Rewriting. In *Proceedings of the 56th Annual Meeting of the Association for Computational Linguistics (Volume 1: Long Papers)*, pages 675–686, Melbourne, Australia. Association for Computational Linguistics.

Jackie Chi Kit Cheung and Gerald Penn. 2014. Unsupervised Sentence Enhancement for Automatic Summarization. In *Proceedings of the 2014 Conference on Empirical Methods in Natural Language Processing (EMNLP)*, pages 775–786, Doha, Qatar. Association for Computational Linguistics.

Kevin Clark, Urvashi Khandelwal, Omer Levy, and Christopher D. Manning. 2019. What does BERT look at? an analysis of BERT's attention. In *Proceedings of the 2019 ACL Workshop BlackboxNLP: Analyzing and Interpreting Neural Networks for NLP*, pages 276–286, Florence, Italy. Association for Computational Linguistics.

Trevor Cohn and Mirella Lapata. 2008. Sentence compression beyond word deletion. In *Proceedings of the 22nd International Conference on Computational Linguistics (Coling 2008)*, pages 137–144, Manchester, UK. Coling 2008 Organizing Committee.

Tobias Falke, Leonardo F. R. Ribeiro, Prasetya Ajie Utama, Ido Dagan, and Iryna Gurevych. 2019. Ranking Generated Summaries by Correctness: An Interesting but Challenging Application for Natural Language Inference. In *Proceedings of the 57th Annual Meeting of the Association for Computational Linguistics*, pages 2214–2220, Florence, Italy. Association for Computational Linguistics.

Katja Filippova, Enrique Alfonseca, Carlos A. Colmenares, Lukasz Kaiser, and Oriol Vinyals. 2015. Sentence Compression by Deletion with LSTMs. In *Proceedings of the 2015 Conference on Empirical Methods in Natural Language Processing*, pages 360–368, Lisbon, Portugal. Association for Computational Linguistics.

Katja Filippova and Michael Strube. 2008. Sentence fusion via dependency graph compression. In *Proceedings of the Conference on Empirical Methods in Natural Language Processing - EMNLP '08*, page 177, Honolulu, Hawaii. Association for Computational Linguistics.

Sebastian Gehrmann, Yuntian Deng, and Alexander Rush. 2018. Bottom-Up Abstractive Summarization. In *Proceedings of the 2018 Conference on Empirical Methods in Natural Language Processing*, pages 4098–4109, Brussels, Belgium. Association for Computational Linguistics.

Shima Gerani, Yashar Mehdad, Giuseppe Carenini, Raymond T. Ng, and Bita Nejat. 2014. Abstractive summarization of product reviews using discourse structure. In *Proceedings of the 2014 Conference on Empirical Methods in Natural Language Processing (EMNLP)*, pages 1602–1613, Doha, Qatar. Association for Computational Linguistics.

Mor Geva, Eric Malmi, Idan Szpektor, and Jonathan Berant. 2019. DiscoFuse: A Large-Scale Dataset for Discourse-Based Sentence Fusion. *arXiv:1902.10526 [cs]*. ArXiv: 1902.10526.

Karl Moritz Hermann, Tomas Kocisky, Edward Grefenstette, Lasse Espeholt, Will Kay, Mustafa Suleyman, and Phil Blunsom. 2015. Teaching Machines to Read and Comprehend. In *Proceedings of Neural Information Processing Systems (NIPS)*.

Wojciech Kryciski, Romain Paulus, Caiming Xiong, and Richard Socher. 2018. Improving Abstraction in Text Summarization. In *Proceedings of the 2018 Conference on Empirical Methods in Natural Language Processing*, pages 1808–1817, Brussels, Belgium. Association for Computational Linguistics.

Logan Lebanoff, Kaiqiang Song, Franck Dernoncourt, Doo Soon Kim, Seokhwan Kim, Walter Chang, and Fei Liu. 2019. Scoring Sentence Singletons and Pairs for Abstractive Summarization. In *Proceedings of the 57th Annual Meeting of the Association for Computational Linguistics*, pages 2175–2189, Florence, Italy. Association for Computational Linguistics.

Chen Li, Fei Liu, Fuliang Weng, and Yang Liu. 2013. Document summarization via guided sentence compression. In *Proceedings of the 2013 Conference on Empirical Methods in Natural Language Processing*, pages 490–500, Seattle, Washington, USA. Association for Computational Linguistics.

Chen Li, Yang Liu, Fei Liu, Lin Zhao, and Fuliang Weng. 2014. Improving multi-documents summarization by sentence compression based on expanded constituent parse trees. In *Proceedings of the 2014 Conference on Empirical Methods in Natural Language Processing (EMNLP)*, pages 691–701, Doha, Qatar. Association for Computational Linguistics.

Haoran Li, Junnan Zhu, Jiajun Zhang, and Chengqing Zong. 2018. Ensure the Correctness of the Summary: Incorporate Entailment Knowledge into Abstractive Sentence Summarization. In *Proceedings of the 27th International Conference on Computational Linguistics*, pages 1430–1441, Santa Fe, New Mexico, USA. Association for Computational Linguistics.

Chin-Yew Lin. 2004. ROUGE: A package for automatic evaluation of summaries. In *Text Summarization Branches Out*, pages 74–81, Barcelona, Spain. Association for Computational Linguistics.

Fei Liu, Jeffrey Flanigan, Sam Thomson, Norman Sadeh, and Noah A. Smith. 2015. Toward abstractive summarization using semantic representations. In *Proceedings of the 2015 Conference of the North American Chapter of the Association for Computational Linguistics: Human Language Technologies*, pages 1077–1086, Denver, Colorado. Association for Computational Linguistics.

Yang Liu and Mirella Lapata. 2019. Hierarchical transformers for multi-document summarization. In *Proceedings of the 57th Annual Meeting of the Association for Computational Linguistics*, pages 5070–5081, Florence, Italy. Association for Computational Linguistics.

Erwin Marsi and Emiel Krahmer. 2005. Explorations in Sentence Fusion. In *Proceedings of the Tenth European Workshop on Natural Language Generation (ENLG-05)*.

Ryan McDonald. 2006. Discriminative sentence compression with soft syntactic evidence. In *11th Conference of the European Chapter of the Association for Computational Linguistics*, Trento, Italy. Association for Computational Linguistics.

Kathleen McKeown, Sara Rosenthal, Kapil Thadani, and Coleman Moore. 2010. Time-efficient creation of an accurate sentence fusion corpus. In *Human Language Technologies: The 2010 Annual Conference of the North American Chapter of the Association for Computational Linguistics*, pages 317–320, Los Angeles, California. Association for Computational Linguistics.

Yashar Mehdad, Giuseppe Carenini, Frank Wm Tompa, and Raymond T. Ng. 2013. Abstractive Meeting Summarization with Entailment and Fusion. In *ENLG*.

Mir Tafseer Nayeem, Tanvir Ahmed Fuad, and Yllias Chali. 2018. Abstractive Unsupervised Multi-Document Summarization using Paraphrastic Sentence Fusion. In *Proceedings of the 27th International Conference on Computational Linguistics*, pages 1191–1204, Santa Fe, New Mexico, USA. Association for Computational Linguistics.

Jekaterina Novikova, Ondřej Dušek, Amanda Cercas Curry, and Verena Rieser. 2017. Why we need new evaluation metrics for NLG. In *Proceedings of the 2017 Conference on Empirical Methods in Natural Language Processing*, pages 2241–2252, Copenhagen, Denmark. Association for Computational Linguistics.

Ehud Reiter. 2018. A structured review of the validity of BLEU. *Computational Linguistics*, 44(3):393–401.

Abigail See, Peter J. Liu, and Christopher D. Manning. 2017. Get To The Point: Summarization with Pointer-Generator Networks. In *Proceedings of the 55th Annual Meeting of the Association for Computational Linguistics (Volume 1: Long Papers)*, pages 1073–1083, Vancouver, Canada. Association for Computational Linguistics.

Kaiqiang Song, Lin Zhao, and Fei Liu. 2018. Structure-Infused Copy Mechanisms for Abstractive Summarization. In *Proceedings of the 27th International Conference on Computational Linguistics*, pages 1717–1729, Santa Fe, New Mexico, USA. Association for Computational Linguistics.

Kapil Thadani and Kathleen McKeown. 2013. Supervised Sentence Fusion with Single-Stage Inference. In *Proceedings of the Sixth International Joint Conference on Natural Language Processing*, pages 1410–1418, Nagoya, Japan. Asian Federation of Natural Language Processing.

Lu Wang, Hema Raghavan, Vittorio Castelli, Radu Florian, and Claire Cardie. 2013. A sentence compression based framework to query-focused multi-document summarization. In *Proceedings of the 51st Annual Meeting of the Association for Computational Linguistics (Volume 1: Long Papers)*, pages 1384–1394, Sofia, Bulgaria. Association for Computational Linguistics.

Summarizing Relationships for Interactive Concept Map Browsers

Abram Handler,[*] Prem Ganeshkumar,[†] Brendan O'Connor[*] and Mohamed AlTantawy[†]

Agolo[†]
New York, NY

College of Information and Computer Sciences[*]
University of Massachusetts, Amherst
ahandler@cs.umass.edu

Abstract

Concept maps are visual summaries, structured as directed graphs: important concepts from a dataset are displayed as vertexes, and edges between vertexes show natural language descriptions of the relationships between the concepts on the map. Thus far, preliminary attempts at automatically creating concept maps have focused on building static summaries. However, in interactive settings, users will need to dynamically investigate particular relationships between pairs of concepts. For instance, a historian using a concept map browser might decide to investigate the relationship between two politicians in a news archive. We present a model which responds to such queries by returning one or more short, importance-ranked, natural language descriptions of the relationship between two requested concepts, for display in a visual interface. Our model is trained on a new public dataset, collected for this task.

Code and data are available at:
https://github.com/slanglab/
concept_maps_newsum19

1 Introduction

Concept maps are visual summaries, structured as directed graphs (Figure 1). Important concepts from a corpus are shown as vertexes. Natural language descriptions of the relationships between concepts are shown as textual labels, along the edges on the map. Initial attempts to generate English-language concept maps within natural language processing (Falke and Gurevych, 2017) have focused on creating static diagrams which summarize collections of documents.

However, in interactive settings, users will want to query relationships with a concept map interface, rather than simply read over fixed output from a summarization system. For instance, in the concept map browser shown in Figure 1, a user

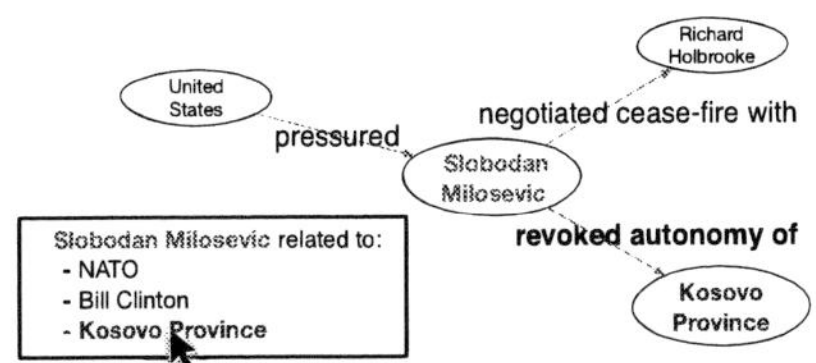

Figure 1: An example concept map browser. The system indicates that (t_1)="Slobodan Milosevic" is related to (t_2)="Kosovo Province." The user clicks to investigate the relationship, and the system must generate a summary explaining how Milosevic is related to Kosovo.

has queried for the relationship between Milosevic and Kosovo. An interactive system should include both concepts in a visual network, along with a labeled edge that summarizes their relationship (e.g. "Slobodan Milosevic revoked autonomy of Kosovo Province").

This study is concerned with how to add such labeled summary edges to a map. Given a pair of input query concepts, denoted (t_1) and (t_2), we attempt to select the best extractive, natural language *summary statement* which summarizes their relationship. Because there is no existing supervision to guide such a selection, we collect a new dataset of annotated summary statements, which we use to supervise a new model for this task.

Our study thus presents a full system for summarizing the relationship between an arbitrary pair of query concepts, extending prior work on relational summarization and concept maps (Falke and Gurevych, 2017; Handler and O'Connor, 2018).

2 Related work: relationship extraction

This study builds on prior efforts from Handler and O'Connor (2018), who propose extractively summarizing relationships via a two-stage process that first (1) identifies wellformed spans from a

Proceedings of the 2nd Workshop on New Frontiers in Summarization, pages 111–115
Hong Kong, China, November 4, 2019. ©2019 Association for Computational Linguistics

corpus that start with (t_1) and end with (t_2) and then (2) chooses the best summary statement from among these wellformed candidates. Handler and O'Connor (2018) show that extracting wellformed spans can find many more readable candidates than traditional relation extraction techniques. But they do not offer a method for the second step of picking a summary statement, which is the focus of this study.

We approach this new task of choosing the best summary statement from available candidates by collecting new supervision, tailored to the particular problem of summarizing relationships on concept maps. This form of supervision has a different focus from the existing Falke and Gurevych (2017) concept map dataset. Where Falke and Gurevych (2017) seek to create the best overall concept map for a given *topic*, this work seeks to find the best summary relationship for a given *relationship*. Therefore, unlike Falke and Gurevych (2017), our dataset includes labels for the most readable and informative statement describing the relationship between a $(t_1) - (t_2)$ query pair.

3 Overall technical approach

Like Handler and O'Connor (2018), we approach the problem of finding a short relationship *summary statement* with a two-stage approach.

Stage 1: We identify candidate summary statements using Handler and O'Connor (2018)'s method, which returns the probability that a span of tokens beginning with (t_1) and ending with (t_2) reads as a fluid and coherent sentence when extracted from naturally-occurring text.[1] (For brevity, we refer the reader to prior work for details, including discussion of why span extraction is preferred to relation extraction techniques). Table 1 provides examples of spans that do and do not make sense when extracted in this manner. We define all spans between (t_1) and (t_2) with a probability of well-formedness greater than .5 to be the **candidate set** for the pair $(t_1) - (t_2)$. A sample candidate set is shown in Table 2.

Stage 2: In stage two, we choose the best summary statement from the candidate set. We collect new annotation to supervise this decision. Our annotation procedure assigns a score $\alpha(s) \in \{-3, -2, ...+3\}$ to each s in a candidate set,

Milosevic withdrew from Kosovo ~~in 1999~~.
~~Clinton spoke with~~ Milosevic about Kosovo.

Table 1: Some spans (top) are plausible summary statements, because they make sense when removed from context sentences. Others spans (bottom) are not plausible summary statements because they don't make sense when extracted from sentences. We use an approach from Handler and O'Connor (2018) to identify such spans.

which is intended to reflect how well s summarizes a particular relationship. We use this supervision to train a model to predict $\alpha(s)$. We propose that the statement with the highest predicted $\alpha(s)$ score should be displayed on a concept map.

4 Candidate extraction

We approach the problem of summarizing relationships for concept maps by collecting a new dataset of annotated summary statements, drawn from news stories focusing on the Balkan Peninsula in the 1990s. Political scientists use rich news archives from this complex period to better understand conflict (Schrodt et al., 2001).

We create our dataset from *New York Times* articles (Sandhaus, 2008) published from 1990–1999, which mention at least one country from the Balkans. Following prior work on relational summarization, for each country, we use the package `phrasemachine` (Handler et al., 2016) to identify the 100 highest-frequency noun phrases within articles which mention that country.[2] The `phrasemachine` package uses a regular expression over part of speech tags to efficiently extract noun phrases, a useful syntactic category which includes both named entity spans (e.g. Boris Yeltsin) as well as other concepts (e.g. peace treaty). From all non-empty pairs of highest-frequency concepts, we sample a total of 689 pairs with more than two extracted candidates. In total there are 5,214 candidate statements across 689 sampled sets.[3] On average there are 7.56 state-

---

[1]We also allow statements which begin with (t_2) and end with (t_1); the order of query concepts is important in interfaces which display concept maps, but beyond the scope of this work. We limit statements to a max. of 75 characters.

[2]`https://github.com/slanglab/phrasemachine`

[3]**Additional notes.** The countries are: Kosovo, Albania, Serbia, Croatia, Montenegro, Macedonia, Bulgaria, Romania, Moldova and Bosnia. (We exclude the former Yugoslavia; its landmass included other countries on our corpus). `phrasemachine` sometimes returns overlapping phrases, leading to duplicate sets. We merge duplicates with a heuristic which uses hand-written rules based on (i) token overlap between concepts and (ii) overlapping sentences be-

	A1	A2	A3
s_1 General Grachev's favor is his loyalty to Mr. Yeltsin	-	W	-
s_2 Mr. Yeltsin openly accused General Grachev	-	-	-
s_3 General Grachev, Defense Minister by dint of his loyalty to Mr. Yeltsin	W	-	W
s_4 General Grachev's plea today will do nothing to help Mr. Yeltsin	-	-	-
s_5 Mr. Yeltsin might also appear weak if he had to replace General Grachev	B	B	B

Table 2: A candidate set for (t_1) = "Mr. Yeltsin" and (t_2) = "General Grachev," along with decisions from three annotators (A1, A2 and A3) selecting the best (B) and worse (W) summary statement in the set. All annotators agree that s_5 is the best, so $\alpha(s_5)$ =3. (During annotation, the order of all sets was randomized).

ments per set ($\sigma = 10.6$).

5 Candidate annotation

5.1 Method

Some candidate sets in our dataset are easy for a person to judge and rank. For instance, it is possible to quickly read over the small set shown in Table 2 and identify statements which are clearly better and clearly worse synopses of the relationship between "General Grachev" and "Mr. Yeltsin".

However, other candidate sets in our dataset are too large and too complex to read and analyze quickly. (The largest candidate set in our dataset contains 143 statements in total). We accommodate both large and small sets with a "low-context" (Falke and Gurevych, 2017) annotation technique. We split candidate sets into one or more subsets, and ask annotators to rank the best and worst summary statements in each subset. Then we aggregate these local judgements about the best and worst candidates within each subset to create a global score. This global score, $\alpha(s)$, attempts to capture the overall quality of a given summary statement s.

This method of soliciting local judgements about subsets and then aggregating into an overall score is known as Best-Worst Scaling (Louviere, 1991). Best-Worst Scaling has been shown to make more efficient use of human judgements for a natural language task than traditional techniques (Kiritchenko and Mohammad, 2017).

5.2 Details of Best–Worst annotation

We present all candidate sets to three different non-native English speakers, hired via a professional annotation firm. All annotators completed graduate work in either linguistics or the humanities, and were based in the Middle East. For each annotator, we divide each candidate set into J random tuples (a tuple consists of up to eight candidate statements), and ask the annotator to choose the best and worst from each tuple. Annotators are instructed that the best statement should be the one that both sounds the most natural and that most helps them understand the history and politics of the Balkan region. They are instructed that the most unnatural sounding and least informative statement should be chosen as worst. In total, each candidate statement is shown to each annotator exactly once.[4] After annotators have judged each individual set, we aggregate with Orme (2009)'s counting formula: we set the score $\alpha(s) \in \{-3, -2, \ldots, +3\}$ of each summary statement s to be the number of times s was chosen as the best, minus the number of times it was chosen as the worst.

Following prior work (Kiritchenko and Mohammad, 2017), we evaluate inter-annotator agreement via split-half reliability. For each candidate set, we randomly split annotators into two groups, and compute the score for each s using each group of annotators. Then we compute the Spearman correlation (ρ) between the two sets of scores, yielding an average of $\rho = 0.495$ across 1000 random splits.

6 Modeling

The previous section describes a procedure for assigning a score, $\alpha(s)$ for each s in our dataset. We use these scores to train a model, $p(\alpha(s)|s)$. During modeling, we divide the dataset into training and test sets at the entity level, ensuring that there

---

tween sets. We exclude pairs which are very obviously unrelated to the Balkans (e.g. *Chinatown* and *Little Italy*). Our annotation budget determined the number of annotated sets.

[4]Unlike in traditional Best-Worst annotation, the number of candidates in each tuple may vary depending on the size of the candidate set. If a candidate set has a cardinality of less than eight, the size of the tuple is set to the size of the candidate set; otherwise the size of a tuple is capped at eight. We make this choice because many candidate sets have a small cardinality, and it does not make sense to break up small sets (e.g. 5 or 6 candidates) into very small tuples.

are no relationships between concepts in the training and test set. Ensuring that there are no relationships shared across sets is important because a model might use knowledge about relationships gleaned from training data (e.g. Milosevic led Serbia) to make inferences about relationships in the test data (e.g. Milosevic led the Serbian Socialist party). 627 candidates are used for training; the remaining 62 are for testing.[5]

We model $p(\alpha(s)|s)$ using ordinal regression, implemented with the MORD package (Pedregosa-Izquierdo, 2015). We use unigram features, morphological features, part-of-speech-tag features and binary features (e.g. s includes punctuation mark) to represent the candidate statement. Handler and O'Connor (2018)'s method (§4) returns a probability that a summary statement is grammatically wellformed. We include this probability as a feature in our model. We also include the token length of a summary statement as a feature. We tune MORD's regularization penalty parameter to maximize 5-fold, cross-validated Spearman's ρ using the training set.[6]

6.1 Evaluation and analysis

We use the test set to measure the extent to which our model's predictions correlate with gold scores, achieving a Spearman's $\rho = 0.443$ between our model's predictions and the gold scores. This is close to the $\rho = 0.495$ computed to measure inter-annotator agreement (§5.2).

We instructed annotators to select summary statements that were both informative and grammatically wellformed. We use the probability of grammatical well-formedness from the candidate detection method (§4) as a feature in our model. This measure appears to partially reflect annotator judgements: there is a Spearman's $\rho = 0.154$ between the two metrics across the dataset. Research into human perceptions of grammatical well-formedness (Sprouse and Schütze, 2014; Warstadt et al., 2018) could be applied to make

---

[5]To implement the train–test split, we form an initial provisional division of concepts into two sets. For all relationships between concepts that cross the two sets, we move the entity from the test set to the training set. All scored summary statements between concepts in the training set are used for training; the remainder are for test. We manually tune the size of the initial split so that 10% of concepts are in the final test set.

[6]We examine 10^i for $i = -3, -2..2, 3$ and use 10^1. Additionally, the MORD API implements several variants of ordinal regression. We use the LogisticSE variant because it achieves the highest cross-validated ρ on the training set.

better predictions in the future.

Model	Spearman's ρ
$p(\alpha(s)|s)$ (Ordinal regression)	**0.443**
Logistic regression	0.304
Inter-annotator agreement	0.495

Table 3: Spearman's ρ for our ordinal regression model $p(\alpha(s)|s)$, compared both to the inter-annotator agreement and a simpler logistic regression model.

Predicting annotator perceptions of informativeness is more challenging. For instance, annotators preferred "Mr. Milosevic has been formally charged with war crimes" ($\alpha(s) = 3$) to "President Slobodan Milosevic may be indicted for war crimes" ($\alpha(s) = 1$). The former expresses a completed action which arguably entails the latter, hypothetical action. How to best model (Bowman et al., 2015), formalize (MacCartney and Manning, 2009) and even study (Gururangan et al., 2018) such complex semantic relationships is an unsolved problem in NLP.

We use the number of tokens in a summary statement (subtracting out the length of query concepts) as a feature. We observe a Spearman's $\rho = .337$ between $\alpha(s)$ and the token length of s. We hypothesize that this feature might serve as a very coarse proxy for informativeness: although not instructed to do so, annotators might choose longer statements ahead of shorter statements because they express more about the Balkans.

7 Conclusion

We extend prior work focused on finding candidate summary statements (Handler and O'Connor, 2018) and constructing concept maps for an overall topic (Falke and Gurevych, 2017), by presenting a complete system for summarizing the relationship between an arbitrary pair of query concepts. Our method learns a model for selecting statements that best summarize relationships, which is supervised with a new, annotated resource for the task. We find that shallow cues like statement length and grammatical wellformedness are helpful for identifying good summary statements, but also that representing deeper semantic relationships (e.g. entailment) remains an ongoing challenge for automatically building concept maps.

Our study adopts the standard supervised paradigm underlying much current work on summarization (Hermann et al., 2015; Grusky et al., 2018). We gather human judgements of salience and well-formedness (in our case, judgements are expressed via Best-Worst Scaling), and then train a model to best replicate such judgements. Because such supervision is costly and difficult to collect, carries risks of annotation artifacts (Gururangan et al., 2018) and might transfer poorly to new domains, in the future, we plan to explore if other forms of task-based supervision and task-based evaluation (Jing et al., 1998) may be better suited to the specialized task of automatic concept map summarization. For instance, instead of asking a human to identify better and worse summary statements, we might examine how well a user (or model) presented with summary statement s can answer if other summary statements s' are true or false. If some s helps identify many other true s', then s is (potentially) a good summary. We look forward to examining this idea in future work, following recent studies of question-based evaluation for the summarization task (Eyal et al., 2019).

8 Acknowledgement

Thanks to Haw-Shiuan Chang, Tu Vu and Kalpesh Krishna for helpful comments on earlier drafts of this work. Thanks to the anonymous reviewers for their helpful suggestions, in particular for pointing out possible connections between relationship summarization and joint extraction of relations and entities.

References

Samuel R. Bowman, Gabor Angeli, Christopher Potts, and Christopher D. Manning. 2015. A large annotated corpus for learning natural language inference. In *EMNLP*.

Matan Eyal, Tal Baumel, and Michael Elhadad. 2019. Question answering as an automatic evaluation metric for news article summarization. In *NAACL*.

Tobias Falke and Iryna Gurevych. 2017. Bringing structure into summaries: Crowdsourcing a benchmark corpus of concept maps. In *EMNLP*.

Max Grusky, Mor Naaman, and Yoav Artzi. 2018. Newsroom: A dataset of 1.3 million summaries with diverse extractive strategies. In *NAACL*.

Suchin Gururangan, Swabha Swayamdipta, Omer Levy, Roy Schwartz, Samuel Bowman, and Noah A. Smith. 2018. Annotation artifacts in natural language inference data. In *NAACL*.

Abram Handler, Matthew Denny, Hanna Wallach, and Brendan O'Connor. 2016. Bag of what? simple noun phrase extraction for text analysis. In *Proceedings of the First Workshop on NLP and Computational Social Science*.

Abram Handler and Brendan O'Connor. 2018. Relational summarization for corpus analysis. In *NAACL*.

Karl Moritz Hermann, Tomás Kociský, Edward Grefenstette, Lasse Espeholt, Will Kay, Mustafa Suleyman, and Phil Blunsom. 2015. Teaching machines to read and comprehend. In *NIPS*.

Hongyan Jing, Regina Barzilay, Kathleen McKeown, and Michael Elhadad. 1998. Summarization evaluation methods : Experiments and analysis. In *AAAI Spring Symposium*.

Svetlana Kiritchenko and Saif Mohammad. 2017. Best-worst scaling more reliable than rating scales: A case study on sentiment intensity annotation. In *ACL*.

J.J. Louviere. 1991. Best-worst scaling: A model for the largest difference judgments. Technical report, University of Alberta.

Bill MacCartney and Christopher D Manning. 2009. An extended model of natural logic. In *Proceedings of the eighth international conference on computational semantics*.

Bryan Orme. 2009. Maxdiff analysis: Simple counting, individual-level logit, and hb. Technical report, Sawtooth Software.

Fabian Pedregosa-Izquierdo. 2015. *Feature extraction and supervised learning on fMRI : from practice to theory*. Theses, Université Pierre et Marie Curie - Paris VI.

Evan Sandhaus. 2008. The New York Times Annotated Corpus. *Linguistic Data Consortium*, LDC2008T19.

Philip A Schrodt, Deborah J Gerner, Rajaa Abu-Jabr, Oemeur Yilmaz, and Erin M Simpson. 2001. Analyzing the dynamics of international mediation processes in the middle east and balkans. In *Annual Meeting of the American Political Science Association*.

John Sprouse and Carson Schütze. 2014. *Research Methods in Linguistics*, chapter Judgment Data. Cambridge University Press, Cambridge, UK.

Alex Warstadt, Amanpreet Singh, and Samuel R. Bowman. 2018. Neural network acceptability judgments. *CoRR*, abs/1805.12471v1.

Exploiting Discourse-Level Segmentation for Extractive Summarization

Zhengyuan Liu, Nancy F. Chen
Institute for Infocomm Research, A*STAR
{liu_zhengyuan, nfychen}@i2r.a-star.edu.sg

Abstract

Extractive summarization selects and concatenates the most essential text spans in a document. Most, if not all, neural approaches use sentences as the elementary unit to select content for summarization. However, semantic segments containing supplementary information or descriptive details are often nonessential in the generated summaries. In this work, we propose to exploit discourse-level segmentation as a finer-grained means to more precisely pinpoint the core content in a document. We investigate how the sub-sentential segmentation improves extractive summarization performance when content selection is modeled through two basic neural network architectures and a deep bi-directional transformer. Experiment results on the CNN/Daily Mail dataset show that discourse-level segmentation is effective in both cases. In particular, we achieve state-of-the-art performance when discourse-level segmentation is combined with our adapted contextual representation model.

1 Introduction

Document summarization is a core task in natural language processing, targeting to automatically generate a shorter version of one or multiple documents while retaining the most important information. As a straightforward and effective method, extractive summarization creates a summary by selecting and subsequently concatenating the most salient semantic units in a document; much effort has been devoted to this area. While traditional approaches rely heavily on human-engineered features, which is time-consuming and difficult to expand to massive data, neural networks can be trained in an end-to-end manner with fewer linguistic annotation, achieving favorable improvements on large-scale benchmarks (Hermann et al., 2015; Cheng and Lapata, 2016; Zhou et al., 2018).

However, the selected content in current neural approaches is often not succinct enough. As

Document (Truncated): Sky watchers in western north america are in for a treat : a nearly five-minute total lunar eclipse this morning . Here's how it's unfolding : it started at 3:16 a.m. pacific daylight time , when the moon began moving into earth's shadow . For the next hour and 45 minutes , that shadow will move across the moon and engulf it at 4:58 a.m. pacific time . The total eclipse will only last four minutes and 43 seconds , and nasa says that makes it the shortest one of the century . Watch it live on nasa tv . While people west of the mississippi river will have the best view , at least apartial eclipse will be visible across the nation . But sunrise will interrupt the show on the east coast . Parts of south america , india , china and russiaalso will be able to see the eclipse , but it won't be visible in greenland , iceland , europe , africa or the middle east . A lunar eclipse happens when the sun , earth and moon form a straight line in space , with the earth smack in the middle . The sunshines on the earth and creates a shadow . As the moon moves deeper into that shadow , it appears to turn dark and may even appear to be a reddish color . Why red ? Because earth's atmosphere is filtering out most of the blue light ... ...

Reference Summary: The total eclipse will only last 4 minutes and 43 seconds . People west of the mississippi river will have the best view . Parts of south america , india , china and russia also will see the eclipse .

Figure 1: An example of news summarization. Colored spans are salient segments selected to form a summary, and their corresponding sentences are underlined.

shown in Figure 1, human editors tend to further distill the selected sentences by removing nonessential phrases or clauses to compose more concise summaries. While the extracted sentences often contain the main points of the document, such sentences are usually embellished with more clauses or segments of background knowledge to give the readers more context, descriptive details to paint a more colorful picture, supplementary information to make the content more comprehensive, or subtle nuances to give a more polished touch. Therefore, sentence-level extraction might dilute the density of the key information in the summary.

To tackle this problem, we postulate that content selection can benefit from finer-grained text segmentation. Inspired by the rhetorical structure theory (RST) (Mann and Thompson, 1988), we propose to split documents to sub-sentential segments following its discourse structure, as RST provides a coherent and well-organized representation of documents and suggests discourse-level

Proceedings of the 2nd Workshop on New Frontiers in Summarization, pages 116–121
Hong Kong, China, November 4, 2019.

segmentation can help model semantic information with more refined granularity. This can help us more precisely pinpoint the key information when we subsequently use neural models to select content for summarization. We empirically compare two different selector architectures: a multi-layer recurrent neural network (RNN) and a Transformer network, as they each have their own model assumptions and knowledge representations (Liu et al., 2019), and we further fine-tune a contextualized language model based on the deep bi-directional Transformer. Our experiments on the CNN/Daily Mail dataset demonstrate that discourse-level segmentation is effective, achieving state-of-the-art performance when combined with an adapted large-scale pre-trained model of contextualized language representation.

2 In Relation to Other Work

Content selection plays a key role for both extractive and abstractive paradigms of text summarization (Nallapati et al., 2017; Zhou et al., 2018; Gehrmann et al., 2018; Hsu et al., 2018). While traditional approaches utilize human-engineered linguistic features (Jones, 2007; Shen et al., 2007), neural network approaches learn the features in a data-driven manner, with components such as semantic vector representation of words (Pennington et al., 2014), contextual representation with various neural structures (Schuster and Paliwal, 1997; Kalchbrenner et al., 2014), attention mechanism and hierarchical document modeling (Cheng and Lapata, 2016). Despite the achievement of sophisticated neural extractive models (Kedzie et al., 2018), sentences are the default elementary semantic unit, potentially leading to low density of key information in the summary. Thus, we target to introduce a finer-grained segmentation scheme.

Discourse structure has proved effective for analyzing and extracting important spans in a document (Louis et al., 2010; Hirao et al., 2015). Utilizing the elementary unit segmentation for extractive summarization has been studied via traditional feature-based approaches (Li et al., 2016). However, to the best of our knowledge, it has not been adopted in the recent neural approaches for summarization. While discourse analysis contains unit segmentation, nucleus-satellite recognition and relation classification (Carlson et al., 2001), segmentation has the highest accuracy (Joty et al., 2013; Heilman and Sagae, 2015), thus making it a more

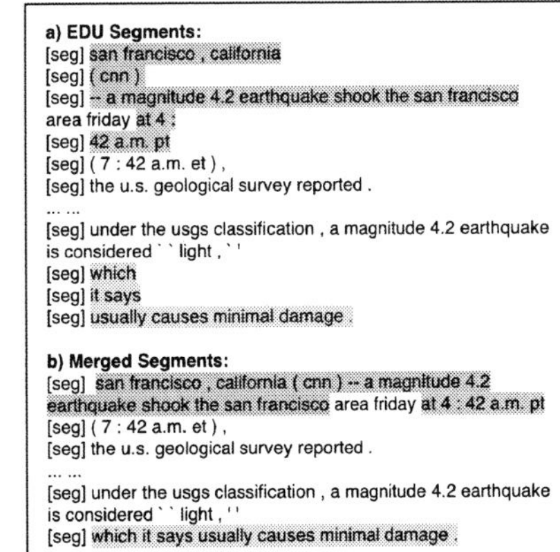

Figure 2: Examples of discourse-level segmentation. a) spans in blue and yellow are the EDUs with semantically fragmented information and spans in red are the inaccurate EDU splits; b) the sub-sentential segments after merging.

mature pre-processing task to be integrated with downstream tasks such as summarization.

3 Discourse-Level Segmentation

For discourse-level segmentation for content selection, our target is to split a document into sub-sentential segments that preserve congruently semantic information.

In the RST discourse framework, a document is split into elementary discourse units (EDUs) that are contiguous token spans similar to independent clauses, and re-organized in a binary tree structure. EDU pairs are assigned to specific discourse relations like elaboration, condition, and contrast, ensuring the semantic coherence and integrity of the entire structure. Therefore, we followed the conventions annotated in the RST Discourse Treebank[1] (Carlson et al., 2001), which contains discourse tree annotations for 385 WSJ articles from the Penn Treebank corpus (Marcus et al., 1993). We trained a fast and robust model[2] (Heilman and Sagae, 2015) on the treebank, obtaining over 0.84 accuracy on its validation set. Next, we applied the model to segment the documents, and here we firstly conducted sentence splitting as it improved the accuracy of subsequent EDU segmentation. Then, we specified $[edu\_seg]$ tags between two EDUs and $[sen\_seg]$ tags between two sentences.

---

[1] https://catalog.ldc.upenn.edu/LDC2002T07
[2] https://github.com/EducationalTestingService/discourse-parsing

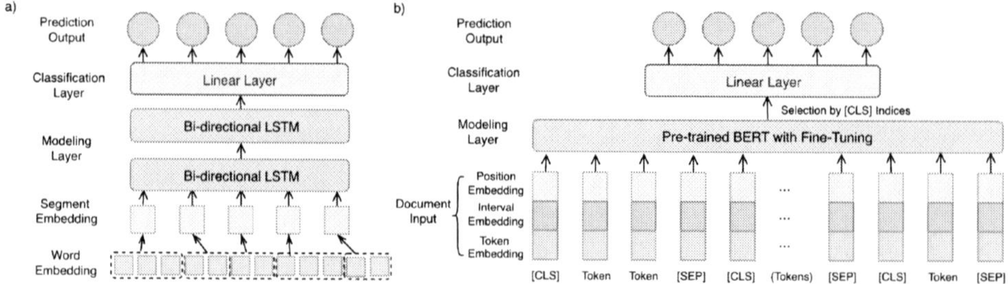

Figure 3: Content selector designs: a) RNN architecture; b) BERT architecture.

As shown in Figure 2a, some EDUs are too semantically fragmented to form an informative segment. In addition, there are inevitable errors in the segmentations, which is not unexpected due to the limited size of the training corpus. In order to balance the segment length and informativeness in addition to mitigating the side-effects from inaccurate EDU segmentation, we therefore defined a set of criteria such as word length, the existence of verbs, and symmetry of quotation marks, to merge short EDUs into longer sub-sentential segments, which are typically at the clause-level. A discourse segment is on average 14 tokens after merging compared to average 7.5 tokens before merging (see Figure 2b).

4   Neural Content Selection

Given a document d containing a number of text spans $[span_1, span_2, ..., span_n]$, the content selector assigns a score $y_i \in [0, 1]$ to each span i, indicating its probability of being included in the summary. We implemented and compared three neural architectures, which we elaborate below.

4.1   RNN Selector

Recurrent neural network, with its capability of sequential information modeling, is widely applied in extractive summarization.

Here we introduce a multi-layer RNN architecture as the selector, which is simple but competitive as in (Kedzie et al., 2018). As shown in Figure 3a, the input is a sequence of discourse-level segment embeddings, which is calculated by averaging word embeddings. The sentence boundary tags $[sen\_seg]$ are converted to a randomly initialized embedding vector. In the modeling layer, a multi-layer Bi-directional LSTM (Schuster and Paliwal, 1997) is used, in which the forward and backward hidden states are concatenated. Then the hidden representation is fed to a linear layer

with a sigmoid function, to predict the probability of extracting each segment.

In our setting, word embeddings were initialized with pre-trained 300-dimension GloVe (Pennington et al., 2014) and fixed during training. Vocabulary size was set to 200k. Out-of-vocabulary words were mapped to a zero embedding. For the modeling layer, it was empirically shown that a two-layer Bi-LSTM worked best. Adam optimizer with $3e-4$ learning rate was used (Kingma and Ba, 2015). Drop-out with $rate = 0.2$ was applied in the modeling and classification layers (Srivastava et al., 2014).

4.2   Transformer Selector

The Transformer (Vaswani et al., 2017) is another effective and efficient neural architecture for language modeling. To compare it with the recurrent encoding scheme, we changed the modeling layer of the design in Section 4.1, by replacing the Bidirectional LSTM with a multi-head attention encoding component. In our setting, we empirically set the layer number of Transformer encoder to 3, and the self-attention head number to 5. The hidden and feed-forward dimension size were set to 400 and 1024 respectively. To better utilize the sequential information, we pre-calculated the position embedding with 100 dimension size and concatenated it with the segment embedding as input. The other hyperparameters of training were set as the same as the RNN selector.

4.3   BERT Selector

Deep contextual representation models with the sophisticated architecture for capturing complex features and unsupervised pre-training on large-scale corpora (e.g. ELMo (Peters et al., 2018) and BERT (Devlin et al., 2018)), have boosted the performance of various NLP tasks. It has been shown that the pre-trained models have implicitly learned linguistic properties such as syntax (Hewitt and

Model	ROUGE-1 F1	ROUGE-2 F1
Lead-3	40.43	17.64
SummaRuNNer*	39.60	16.20
NeuSUM*	41.59	19.01
S-Level Oracle	53.29	32.14
S-Level Bi-LSTM	38.86	17.31
S-Level Transformer	38.57	17.26
S-Level BERT	41.02	19.39
D-Level Oracle	57.74	35.16
D-Level Bi-LSTM	40.36	18.42
D-Level Transformer	40.03	17.83
D-Level BERT	**42.78**	**20.23**

Table 1: Experimental results of baselines, oracles and models on Sentence-Level (S-Level) and Discourse-Level (D-Level) segmentation. * denotes results from the papers.

Manning, 2019) and semantic dependency (Conneau et al., 2018).

Since BERT is originally trained as a contextualized language representation model, we adapted and fine-tuned it for discourse-level content selection, as illustrated in Figure 3b. While BERT can be applied to encode sequences separately or jointly, the latter works better for document tasks (Qiao et al., 2019). Therefore, we decided to take the adapted embedding list as our document input. For each segment, we inserted a [CLS] token before and a [SEP] token after it, then converted it to token embeddings with word-piece tokenization (Wu et al., 2016). To distinguish multiple segments, we assigned $0/1$ to adjacent segment pairs respectively as interval label. Combined with position embedding, the document input was fed to BERT for contextualized encoding. After that, we collected all the hidden states of [CLS] tokens in the last layer of BERT, which captured the contextual information of segments, then fed them to a linear layer with sigmoid function to get the predicted salient scores.

In our setting, we used the PyTorch version of 'bert-base-uncased' BERT[3], and fine-tuned all the layers during training. We truncated the lengthy documents to the size of 512 due to the limitation of position index and the significant increase of computational cost by the sliding-window strategy. Adam algorithm (Kingma and Ba, 2015) with warm-up learning was used for optimization. Drop-out rate was set to 0.2 was applied after the modeling layer (Srivastava et al., 2014).

For all models, we obtained the normalized predicted score y_i of each segment i. The loss is calculated as the binary cross entropy of y_i against

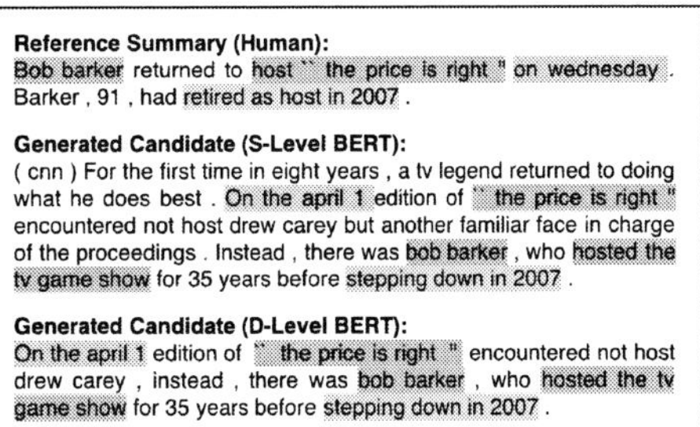

Figure 4: Examples of generated summaries. Colored spans contain key information from the gold reference.

ground-truth $\hat{y}_i$. Each epoch constitutes a full pass through the data with shuffling. During training, the best models were selected with early stopping strategy on the validation set.

5 Experiment & Results

Experiments were conducted on the CNN/Daily Mail dataset (Hermann et al., 2015). We applied discourse-level segmentation in Section 3 on the training, validation, and test set. Since there is no oracle extractive summary set for generating gold labels $\hat{y}_i$, we constructed them with a greedy algorithm similar to (Kedzie et al., 2018), and obtained the discourse-level oracle summaries by concatenating segments with gold label indices.

Having gotten the prediction outputs, we selected 4 discourse-level segments with the highest scores for each document sample, and then evaluated the candidates against reference summaries with the F1 scores of ROUGE-1 and ROUGE-2 (Lin, 2004). We compared our method with several strong extractive baselines: SummaRuNNer (Nallapati et al., 2017), NeuSUM (Zhou et al., 2018), and Lead-3, a simple but competitive baseline, which takes the first 3 sentences of the document as a summary. Moreover, as control, we split documents into sentences, built a sentence-level oracle set, and trained the selector models in which the most 3 salient sentences were selected.

Results are listed in Table 1, all models with discourse-level segmentation outperform those with sentence-level segmentation, demonstrating the effectiveness of our finer-grained means. Even the vanilla multi-layer Bi-LSTM is competitive when compared to the previous state-of-the-art models, and it slightly outperformed the Transformer architecture. Moreover, the fine-tuned BERT model achieves further improvement, suggesting its contextual modeling which is implicitly

---

[3]https://github.com/huggingface/pytorch-transformers

conducted at the sentence-level can be transferred to sub-sentential levels. Additionally, we observed that merging initial EDUs in Section 3 significantly contributed to obtaining better performance, suggesting that preserving semantic congruence is crucial in sub-sentential segmentation.

An example from our results demonstrates that discourse-level extractive summarization retains most of the key information in the reference, and it is more concise than the sentence-level counterpart (see Figure 4). It is able to trim the trivial details that are nonessential to the core meaning of the source text, achieving 19% decrease of the average word length when compared to the sentence-level baseline (from 71 tokens to 57 tokens).

6 Conclusion

In this paper, we proposed using sub-sentential segmentation for single-document extractive summarization. We exploited a discourse-level segmentation scheme and verified its effectiveness by obtaining improvements over sentence-level schemes. We adapted and fine-tuned a deep contextual model for our task and achieved state-of-the-art performance. Incorporating discourse tree structures implicitly or explicitly in the neural network approaches for summarization is an area of interest for future work.

Acknowledgments

The authors would like to thank insightful discussions with Bonnie Webber, Wenqiang Lei, and Ai Ti Aw. This research is supported by the Agency for Science, Technology and Research (A*STAR) under its AME Programmatic Funding Scheme (Project No. A18A2b0046).

References

Lynn Carlson, Daniel Marcu, and Mary Ellen Okurovsky. 2001. Building a discourse-tagged corpus in the framework of rhetorical structure theory. In *Proceedings of the Second SIGdial Workshop on Discourse and Dialogue*.

Jianpeng Cheng and Mirella Lapata. 2016. Neural summarization by extracting sentences and words. In *Proceedings of the 54th Annual Meeting of the Association for Computational Linguistics (Volume 1: Long Papers)*, pages 484–494, Berlin, Germany. Association for Computational Linguistics.

Alexis Conneau, Germán Kruszewski, Guillaume Lample, Loïc Barrault, and Marco Baroni. 2018. What you can cram into a single $&!#* vector: Probing sentence embeddings for linguistic properties. In *Proceedings of the 56th Annual Meeting of the Association for Computational Linguistics (Volume 1: Long Papers)*, pages 2126–2136, Melbourne, Australia. Association for Computational Linguistics.

Jacob Devlin, Ming-Wei Chang, Kenton Lee, and Kristina Toutanova. 2018. BERT: pre-training of deep bidirectional transformers for language understanding. *CoRR*, abs/1810.04805.

Sebastian Gehrmann, Yuntian Deng, and Alexander Rush. 2018. Bottom-up abstractive summarization. In *Proceedings of the 2018 Conference on Empirical Methods in Natural Language Processing*, pages 4098–4109, Brussels, Belgium. Association for Computational Linguistics.

Michael Heilman and Kenji Sagae. 2015. Fast rhetorical structure theory discourse parsing. *CoRR*, abs/1505.02425.

Karl Moritz Hermann, Tomas Kocisky, Edward Grefenstette, Lasse Espeholt, Will Kay, Mustafa Suleyman, and Phil Blunsom. 2015. Teaching machines to read and comprehend. In *Advances in neural information processing systems*, pages 1693–1701.

John Hewitt and Christopher D Manning. 2019. A structural probe for finding syntax in word representations. In *Proceedings of the 2019 Conference of the North American Chapter of the Association for Computational Linguistics: Human Language Technologies*. Association for Computational Linguistics.

Tsutomu Hirao, Masaaki Nishino, Yasuhisa Yoshida, Jun Suzuki, Norihito Yasuda, and Masaaki Nagata. 2015. Summarizing a document by trimming the discourse tree. *IEEE/ACM Transactions on Audio, Speech and Language Processing (TASLP)*, 23(11):2081–2092.

Wan-Ting Hsu, Chieh-Kai Lin, Ming-Ying Lee, Kerui Min, Jing Tang, and Min Sun. 2018. A unified model for extractive and abstractive summarization using inconsistency loss. In *Proceedings of the 56th Annual Meeting of the Association for Computational Linguistics (Volume 1: Long Papers)*, pages 132–141. Association for Computational Linguistics.

Karen Spärck Jones. 2007. Automatic summarising: The state of the art. *Information Processing & Management*, 43(6):1449–1481.

Shafiq Joty, Giuseppe Carenini, Raymond Ng, and Yashar Mehdad. 2013. Combining intra- and multi-sentential rhetorical parsing for document-level discourse analysis. In *Proceedings of the 51st Annual Meeting of the Association for Computational Linguistics (Volume 1: Long Papers)*, pages 486–496,

Sofia, Bulgaria. Association for Computational Linguistics.

Nal Kalchbrenner, Edward Grefenstette, and Phil Blunsom. 2014. A convolutional neural network for modelling sentences. In *Proceedings of the 52nd Annual Meeting of the Association for Computational Linguistics (Volume 1: Long Papers)*, pages 655–665, Baltimore, Maryland. Association for Computational Linguistics.

Chris Kedzie, Kathleen McKeown, and Hal Daume III. 2018. Content selection in deep learning models of summarization. In *Proceedings of the 2018 Conference on Empirical Methods in Natural Language Processing*, pages 1818–1828, Brussels, Belgium. Association for Computational Linguistics.

Diederik P Kingma and Jimmy Ba. 2015. Adam: A method for stochastic optimization. In *Proceedings of the 3rd International Conference for Learning Representations*.

Junyi Jessy Li, Kapil Thadani, and Amanda Stent. 2016. The role of discourse units in near-extractive summarization. In *Proceedings of the 17th Annual Meeting of the Special Interest Group on Discourse and Dialogue*, pages 137–147, Los Angeles. Association for Computational Linguistics.

Chin-Yew Lin. 2004. ROUGE: A package for automatic evaluation of summaries. In *Text Summarization Branches Out: Proceedings of the ACL-04 Workshop*, pages 74–81, Barcelona, Spain. Association for Computational Linguistics.

Nelson F Liu, Matt Gardner, Yonatan Belinkov, Matthew Peters, and Noah A Smith. 2019. Linguistic knowledge and transferability of contextual representations. In *Proceedings of the 2019 Conference of the North American Chapter of the Association for Computational Linguistics: Human Language Technologies*. Association for Computational Linguistics.

Annie Louis, Aravind Joshi, and Ani Nenkova. 2010. Discourse indicators for content selection in summarization. In *Proceedings of the 11th Annual Meeting of the Special Interest Group on Discourse and Dialogue*, pages 147–156. Association for Computational Linguistics.

William C Mann and Sandra A Thompson. 1988. Rhetorical structure theory: Toward a functional theory of text organization. *Text-Interdisciplinary Journal for the Study of Discourse*, 8(3):243–281.

Mitchell P. Marcus, Beatrice Santorini, and Mary Ann Marcinkiewicz. 1993. Building a large annotated corpus of English: The Penn Treebank. *Computational Linguistics*, 19(2):313–330.

Ramesh Nallapati, Feifei Zhai, and Bowen Zhou. 2017. Summarunner: A recurrent neural network based sequence model for extractive summarization of documents. In *Thirty-First AAAI Conference on Artificial Intelligence*.

Jeffrey Pennington, Richard Socher, and Christopher Manning. 2014. Glove: Global vectors for word representation. In *Proceedings of the 2014 Conference on Empirical Methods in Natural Language Processing (EMNLP)*, pages 1532–1543. Association for Computational Linguistics.

Matthew Peters, Mark Neumann, Mohit Iyyer, Matt Gardner, Christopher Clark, Kenton Lee, and Luke Zettlemoyer. 2018. Deep contextualized word representations. In *Proceedings of the 2018 Conference of the North American Chapter of the Association for Computational Linguistics: Human Language Technologies, Volume 1 (Long Papers)*, pages 2227–2237, New Orleans, Louisiana. Association for Computational Linguistics.

Yifan Qiao, Chenyan Xiong, Zhenghao Liu, and Zhiyuan Liu. 2019. Understanding the behaviors of bert in ranking. *arXiv preprint arXiv:1904.07531*.

Mike Schuster and Kuldip K Paliwal. 1997. Bidirectional recurrent neural networks. *IEEE Transactions on Signal Processing*, 45(11):2673–2681.

Dou Shen, Jian-Tao Sun, Hua Li, Qiang Yang, and Zheng Chen. 2007. Document summarization using conditional random fields. In *Proceedings of the 20th International Joint Conferences on Artificial Intelligence.*, pages 2862–2867.

Nitish Srivastava, Geoffrey Hinton, Alex Krizhevsky, Ilya Sutskever, and Ruslan Salakhutdinov. 2014. Dropout: a simple way to prevent neural networks from overfitting. *The Journal of Machine Learning Research*, 15(1):1929–1958.

Ashish Vaswani, Noam Shazeer, Niki Parmar, Jakob Uszkoreit, Llion Jones, Aidan N Gomez, Łukasz Kaiser, and Illia Polosukhin. 2017. Attention is all you need. In *Advances in neural information processing systems*, pages 5998–6008.

Yonghui Wu, Mike Schuster, Zhifeng Chen, Quoc V Le, Mohammad Norouzi, Wolfgang Macherey, Maxim Krikun, Yuan Cao, Qin Gao, Klaus Macherey, et al. 2016. Google's neural machine translation system: Bridging the gap between human and machine translation. *arXiv preprint arXiv:1609.08144*.

Qingyu Zhou, Nan Yang, Furu Wei, Shaohan Huang, Ming Zhou, and Tiejun Zhao. 2018. Neural document summarization by jointly learning to score and select sentences. In *Proceedings of the 56th Annual Meeting of the Association for Computational Linguistics (Volume 1: Long Papers)*, pages 654–663, Melbourne, Australia. Association for Computational Linguistics.

Author Index